Common & uncommon uses of HERBS for HEALTHFUL LIVING

RICHARD LUCAS

ARCO

New York

An ARC Book
published by Arco Publishing Company, Inc.
219 Park Avenue South, New York, N. Y. 10003
by arrangement with Parker Publishing Co.

Second ARC Printing, 1972

Library of Congress Catalog Number 74-128898

ISBN 0-668-02396-1

Printed in U.S.A.

A SPECIAL NOTICE FOR THE READER

It is not the purpose of this book to replace the professional services of your physician. By all means see a doctor for any condition which requires his services.

Remedies from various plants and flora have been used for thousands of years and modern science is now re-evaluating many of the old-time herbal "folk remedies." Improved technical methods and modern laboratory equipment are demonstrating that various plants contain an abundance of valuable remedial properties. These findings have resulted in the revival of a vast new interest in this field of herbal remedies, including other uses of herbs for modern living.

The botanical materia medica and scientific information set out in this book are taken from the writings of doctors, scientific laboratory reports, documents, treatises, and other accredited sources. No attempt should be made on the part of the reader to use any of this information as a form of treatment without first consulting his doctor.

FOREWORD BY A DOCTOR OF MEDICINE

Whenever I step into a fruit juice stand and order a glass of healthful juice, I think of Richard Lucas' book *NATURE'S MEDICINES*, in which an entire chapter is devoted to the fruit from the "medicine tree." This was Mr. Lucas' first book.

Now it has been followed by his second book which is to be heartily welcomed because it provides information on some of those herbal pharmaceuticals or substances that were not included in his first book.

Again, Mr. Lucas has made this study a careful and interesting one, supplying valuable information on products like seaweeds, kelp, olive oil, and many others. I would dare a reader to look through the index and not be tempted to read immediately this or that chapter. He will do so with profit.

Professors of Pharmacology and Botany may quarrel with this or that technical detail of the author's statements, but since Mr. Lucas has written a popular, educational and not an erudite, strictly scientific treatise, an evaluation, perhaps too critical, of some of the quoted sources would be of no practical significance. What is important is the fact that Mr. Lucas has again enriched our knowledge in a readable and often enchanting manner.

Like its precursor, this new book should find its place in the home, and also on the bookshelves of medical practitioners, students and pharmacists, as a useful reference work, well-supplementing a pharmacopoeia, or a drug encyclopedia.

Harry Benjamin, M.D.

INTRODUCTION

Some of the world's greatest healing agents were derived from the plant kingdom. Over 5,000 years ago a Chinese emperor, Shen-ung, wrote a book in which he described thousands of botanicals employed by the Chinese as medicine. Among these was *Ma-huang*, a plant highly esteemed as a remedy for bronchial spasms, asthmatic attacks, colds, and similar disorders. Modern scientists examined the plant and found that it contained a substance which is called *ephedrine*, and physicians soon began prescribing it for pulmonary complaints just as the Chinese have done for centuries. It is also contained in many "patient" or proprietary medicines as a de-congestant.

The aborigines of South America used bark of a Peruvian tree for the treatment of malaria. This tree was named *Chincona* after the wife of a Spanish viceroy (Count de Chincon) who was cured of fever by the use of this tree bark around the year 1638. In Europe its reputation as a remedy for malaria became so great that the powdered bark was often sold for its weight in gold. However, it was not until almost two centuries later that scientists isolated *quinine* from the bark, a substance which has proved invaluable as a treatment for malaria ever since.

The natives of southeast Asia treated leprosy and skin diseases with the oil and seeds of the *Chaulmoogra* tree. Modern researchers have succeeded in producing an effective treatment for the same disorders from the properties supplied by this tree. *Cascara Sagrada*, known to the Inca Indians as "sacred bark," was found to be a valuable aid in chronic constipation.

Present-day pharmacologists are finding that the great number of plants which have supplied such valuable medicines in the past offer but a fraction of the remarkable properties that botanicals are able to provide. For example, according to a medical report, 18 heart patients were treated with mulberries, and all but two showed marked improvement. Pain and shortness of breath were reduced, and in some cases swelling of the ankles vanished. *Pipsissewa*, commonly called Prince's Pine, has been found to contain bacteria-destroying properties. Substances discovered in the juice of the buttercup arrest the growth of streptococci, pneumococci, staphylococci, anthrax, and tuberculosis germs.

The common beet and garlic are being investigated as cancer fighting agents. From an Australian vine comes a substance which produces an alkaloid that shrinks tumors in laboratory tests on animals. Anti-fertility drugs which control ovulation (birth control pills) are obtained from the steroids of the Mexican wild yam. These and other plants are undergoing exhaustive studies by scientists.

It is the purpose of this book to present recorded herbal folk remedies which have been employed for centuries by the American Indians, the gypsies, the ancient and early herbalists, the countryfolk, and the old-time country doctors or family physicians. Scientific evaluation and modern employment of the various herbs is also cited for your information. In addition, one chapter contains information on a number of botanicals which are being scientifically investigated for anti-cancer activity. Another chapter deals with the employment of herbs for coping with emotional stress. The very fact that many of these simple remedies are undergoing such a rapid revival is sufficient evidence of the sound judgment of the men and women of the past who kept insisting that medicine derived from plants or herbs was effective in dealing with certain health situations.

It is from the writings of the ancient and early herbalists that our modern scientists often obtain leads for plants to test for possible healing properties.

Since repeated reference to these early writings is given in this book, a brief background concerning the individual herbalists of former times is in order.

The most prominent of the ancient herbal practitioners were Hippocrates, Theophrastus, Pliny, Dioscorides, and Galen. The writings of Hippocrates were numerous and even to this day his doctrines are universally recognized. He lived from 460 to 377 B.C. and till this day is called the Father of Medicine. Between three and four hundred plants are mentioned in what are known as the Hippocratic writings and about one-third of that list is still in use today. His Hippocratic oath can be seen exhibited on the office walls of many Doctors of Medicine.

Immediately following Hippocrates was the Greek philosopher Theophrastus, 372 to 287 B.C., who succeeded Aristotle and wrote a *History of Plants*. He assigned various properties to each botanical and in this way influenced the later development of herbal therapies.

Pliny, the well-known author of *Natural History* lived from 23 to 79 A.D. His work consisted of 37 volumes of which seven were devoted to medical botany. His love for the good earth is expressed beautifully in the following words:

> It is the Earth, like a kind mother, receives us at our birth, and sustains us when born. It is this alone, of all the elements around us, that is never found an enemy to man. The body of waters deluge him with rains; oppress him with hail, and drown him with inundations; the air rushes in storms, prepares the tempest, or lights up the volcano; but the Earth, gentle and indulgent, ever subservient to the wants of man, spreads his walks with flowers, and his table with plenty; returns with interest every good committed to her care; and though she produces the poison, she still supplies the antidote; though constantly teased the more to furnish the luxuries of man than his necessities, yet even to the last, she continues her kind indulgence, and when life is over, she piously hides his remains in her bosom.

The next man to make a lasting contribution concerning medical botany was Dioscorides. He lived during the first century A. D. and became a physician to the Roman army in Asia. Dioscorides contributed a number of studies on herbal remedies, and much of his writings have survived for modern usage. Among the plants he listed were garlic, aloes, myrrh, mallows, lilies, and roses. A translation of at least one of his books from Greek to English has been published in recent years. The *Dioscordian Herbal* became the main source of information from which later works along the same lines were derived.

Galen, 131 to 200 A.D. was a native of Pergamus, in Asia Minor. It was in a medical school in his own city that he studied first, and later at Alexandria. Before settling in Rome, Galen wrote largely on subjects directly or indirectly connected with medicine. He was extremely independent in his opinions and ideas, had little regard for authority, and so great was his wisdom and skill in the healing arts that he came to be regarded as an "oracle." His popularity grew to such an extent that other physicians became jealous of him and he fled Rome fearing for his life. He returned later to assume the post of physician to the emperor Marcus Aurelius. Galen is believed to have been the author of nearly 400 works, and among these was a herbal so complete that for years no entirely new herbal made its appearance.

With the advent of the Dark Ages, herbology as an art was almost obliterated, and it was only due to the monks who had studied the herbal works of others that this form of healing survived. They cultivated herb gardens, and through experimentation and practice, combined their own knowledge of the medicinal herbs with what they had read.

The most prominent of the early modern herbalists were Gerard, Parkinson, and Culpeper. Gerard was born in Nantwich, Cheshire, and educated at Williston where he studied medicine. One of his best known works, first published in 1597, was called *The Herball or General Historie of Plants*.

John Parkinson, 1567-1629, became director of the Royal Gardens at Hampton Court, Apothecary of London, and King's Herbalist. He followed the Persian method of dividing a garden into four parts: the Garden of Flowers for garlands and fragrances; the Kitchen Garden, for vegetables and herbs; the Simples, for healing herbs; and the Orchard. The garden was arranged in the shape of the Christian Cross with a long, large center path adjoined on each side by a smaller path. The first of Parkinson's well-known published works was *Paradisus Terrestris*, which appeared in 1629 and *Theatrum Botanicum* in 1640.

The last and one of the greatest and most popular of the early modern herbalists was Nicholas Culpeper who was born in London in the year 1616. He is frequently referred to as the Father of English Herbology, and one of his books, *The Complete Herbal* is still in demand after having passed through countless editions since its first publication over 300 years ago.

Culpeper studied at Cambridge and later became apprenticed to a London apothecary. His absorbing interest in medicines from plants led him to set up his own herbal practice in Spitalfields where patients thronged to consult him for health remedies. He was regarded as the "poor man's physician" because of dedication to the needs of others, especially the poor. Culpeper translated the *Pharmocopoeia Londinensis* from Latin to English, and added "*A Catalog of the Simples* [herbs] *Conducing to the Dispensatory.*"

Many of the plants mentioned in Culpeper's writings are still in medicinal use today, and in some instances, his clinical indications have proved correct. In reference to this remarkable herbalist of former times, Dr. Johnson wrote: "Culpeper, the man that first ranged the woods and climbed the mountains in search of medicinal and salutary herbs, has undoubtedly merited the gratitude of posterity."

This book has been faithfully structured to present the wisdom of the dedicated herbalists of ancient and modern times to help you understand the marvels contained in nature's healing herbs.

CONTENTS

1. **ELDER: FAVORITE ALL-TIME REMEDY . . .**   1
   Elder—A Favorite Gypsy Folk Remedy   2
   Comments on the Gypsy Remedies. Elderberry Ointment. Gypsy Beauty Cream. Two Varieties of Elder. A Reported Supernatural Background of Elder. Elder as Known to the Early Herbalists.
   Elder Remedies of a Famous German Herbalist   5
   Father Kneipp's Philosophy. Healthful Properties Contained in Elder.
   Modern Uses of Elder   6
   Reported Benefits of Elder Flowers and Peppermint Herb Tea. Elder for Neuralgia. Coping with Sciatica. How to Counteract Dryness of Skin. Coping with Inflammation of the Bladder. Nature's Herbal Way Is Usually Best.

2. **DANDELION:**
   THE WAYSIDE HEALING WONDER   10
   The Determined Dandelion. The Dandelion as Nature's Barometer. Health Properties in Dandelion. Dandelion — A Nutritious Herbal Dish. Synede.
   Dandelion Remedies   12
   A Medicinal Doctor's Opinion of Dandelion as a Health Builder. Use in Urinary Disorders.
   A Selection of Dandelion Herbal Formulas   14
   For Nettle Rash or Hives. A Soothing Stomach Powder. Ovarian Cysts. Skin Diseases.
   Additional Reported Remedies
       Using Dandelion   15
   Dandelion Has Wide Range for Healthful Action. Reported Uses of Dandelion for Diabetics. Dandelion's Golden Glory.

3. **GOLDEN HEALING OIL**
   FROM THE OLIVE TREE   18
   Tree of Ages. Emblem of Peace.
   The Health Value of Olive Oil   19
   Using Olive Oil for Ulcers. Benefits of Olive Oil for Heart and Arteries. Olive Oil in Coping with

3. **GOLDEN HEALING OIL**
     FROM THE OLIVE TREE *(Cont.)*

Cholesterol Conditions. Use of Olive Oil as Protection Against X-Rays and Irradiation. Olive Oil as a Laxative. Olive Oil as a Gall Bladder Tonic and Gallstone Reliever. Olive Oil and the Hair and Gums.

Miscellaneous Healthful Uses of Olive Oil   24

Dry Skin. Wounds, Sores, Abrasions. Sunburn Lotion. First Aid for the Eyes. Deafness. Eyelashes — Fingernails. Neuralgia of the Breasts. Olive Oil Cited in the U.S. Dispensatory. Nervous Disorders.

4. **NETTLE:**
     THE VERSATILE HEALING PLANT **27**

Remedial Uses of Nettle   27
Health Qualities Found in Nettle   29

As a Bleeding Arrester. Uses in Dysentery and Gout Cases. A Remarkable Recovery from Tuberculosis. How Nettles Have Been Prescribed. As Constipation and Migraine Relief. High Blood Pressure, Anemia, and Other Blood Disorders. Relieving Hives. Nettle Therapy in India and Pakistan. The Inherent Power of Herbs to Heal.

5. **SAGE: THE HERITAGE HERB**
     FOR GOOD HEALTH **34**

Former Uses.
An Explorer's Experience With
     Sage as His Life Saver   35
What Sage Generally Contains.
The Findings of Scientific Studies of Sage   36
Modern Uses.
Reported Miscellaneous Uses of Sage   38
As a Gargle. As a Hair Tonic.
Health Value of Chia Seeds from Sage   39
Use of Chia Seeds Persisted for Centuries. Chia's Power-Packed Nutritional Values.
Many Ways of Preparing Chia Seeds   41
Make the Test Yourself.

6: THE ONION: BULB OF
VALUABLE NATURAL MEDICINALS 42

Folk Customs Associated With Onion   42
Folk Customs Still Followed Today in Some Locations. One Doctor's View.
THE Medicine Bulb   43
Various Folk Remedies Using Onions   44
Onion Remedies of the "Family Physician."
Modern Health Use of Onions   46
Properties Contained in Onions. Medical Use of Onions. Onion Therapy by an English Doctor. Onion Therapies in India. Onion Therapies Used by a French Doctor.
Mysterious M-Rays Found in Onions   49
A Warning About Overeating Onions   49

7. HEALING PLANTS FROM THE SEA 51
Sea Algae   52
Seaweed as Food and Medicine   52
Uses of Kelp   53
Iodine Source. "Goitre Belts."
A Nutritionalist's Views
on Health Value of Iodine   54
Using Iodine for Obesity Control   55
Various Ways of Using Kelp in the Diet   56
Beneficial Effects Noted on the Body.
Carrageen   57
Reported Uses of Carrageen. Using Carrageen for Peptic Ulcers. Carrageen in the Diet. Carrageen Recipes. A Cosmetic Cream for a Glowing Complexion.
Further Value of Algae   61
Algae — A Source of Zinc. Intestinal Worms. Search for Anti-Cancer Properties in Seaweeds.

8. HERBAL HEALTH SECRETS
OF THE AMERICAN INDIANS 63
Observations on American Indian Herbal Lore   63
White Captive Learns Indian Materia Medica   64
Hunter's Observations. Indian Herbal Remedies Cited. Modern Usages.
Aniseed   69

8. HERBAL HEALTH SECRETS
        OF THE AMERICAN INDIANS *(Cont.)*

Pipsissewa 70
Slippery Elm 70
Indian Remedies Recorded by Lighthall 72
*Poplar. Blue Flag. Elecampane. Butternut. Red
Clover. Sarsaparilla.*
Modern Uses of Plants Cited by Lighthall 77
Blue Flag. Butternut. Elecampane.
Science Continues the Study of Indian Herbs 79
Scientific Research on
    Indian Birth Control Plant 79
*Indian Herbal Remedy Found Effective in Diar-
rhea. Records of Eye Cataracts Successfully
Treated with Herbs. Indian Poison Oak Remedy.*

9. MISTLETOE:
        MYSTIC HERB OF THE DRUIDS   83
*Distinguishing between Two Varieties of Mistletoe.
Mistletoe — A Remedy Based in Antiquity. Con-
stituents in Mistletoe.*
Modern Uses of Mistletoe 85
*Additional Recorded Uses of Mistletoe. Neuritis
Symptoms.*
Tranquility Without Drugs 88
Cancer 89

10. THE HUMBLE PARSLEY:
        A TREASURY OF NATURAL REMEDIES . .   91
As a Popular Garnish.
Health Value of Parsley 92
*Parsley Generally Neglected as a National Source
of Good Health. Reported Usage in Kidney and
Bladder Trouble. Reported Usage for Diabetes,
Prostate, and Rheumatism. Gentleman in His
Sixties. Controlling Weakness of the Kidneys and
Bladder.*
Parsley as It Acts on the Brain 95
Parsley Piert 96
*Urinary Disorders. Cystitis. A Case History of
Cystitis Healed.*
Parsley as a Necessary Food
    and Nature's Medicine 98

11. SASSAFRAS—"CHIEF MEDICINE" PLANT . . 100
Use of Sassafras by the Indians   100
Early Description.
Sassafras as the Early "Wonder Drug"   102
Research Findings in Sassafras.
Modern Use of Sassafras   103
*Skin Diseases. Arthritis and Rheumatism. Practical
Tips on Sassafras. Sassafras Enters the Space Age.*

12. THE "GREEN HOPE"
IN THE FIGHT AGAINST CANCER 107
Some of the Causes. Cancer Research Accelerated.
The Search for
Curative Possibilities in Herbs   109
Additional Plants Under Study   111
*Australian Scrub Ash. Bamboo Grass. Beets.
Brewers' Yeast. Calaguala. Calvatia Giganteum.
Camptotheca Acuminata. Garlic. Ipecac. Juniper.
American Mandrake. Periwinkle. Vine of the
Genus Tylophora. Violet. Russian Research.*
Hope Springs Eternal   119

13. VARIETY OF USES OF ROSEMARY 120
Traditional Background   120
Christian Traditions Associated with Rosemary.
Reported Health Uses of Rosemary   121
*Father Kneipps Heart and Stomach Remedy.
What Rosemary Contains. The Memory. Reported
Uses for Bone and Joint Pains. Ear Disease. Mi-
graine Headache. Strength for the Heart Muscles.
The Liver. Headache. Hair Health and Beauty.*
Rosemary—A Valuable and
Delicious Culinary Herb   126

14. HOW TO USE HERBS
FOR BATHING AND BEAUTY BENEFITS . . 128
Function and Duties of the Skin   129
*Temperature, Absorption and Respiration. Excre-
tion of Body Waste Products.*
Importance of Correct Bathing for Health   130
*The Ancient Art of Bathing. Ancient Bathing
Establishments.*

14. HOW TO USE HERBS FOR BATHING AND BEAUTY BENEFITS *(Cont.)*

Addition of Beneficial Herbs to the Bath for Health   131
The Health Value of Herbal Baths.

How Herbs May be Used in Bathing for Health   132
Temperature of the Bath.

Fragrant Baths   133
Recipes for Fragrant Baths. Other Herbs for Fragrant Baths.

Miscellaneous Herbal Baths   134
Relieving Muscular Aches and Pains. Herb Oils for Sore or Strained Muscles. Relieving Nervousness or Tension. Helping to Stimulate Circulation. Relieving Dry, Itchy Skin.

Herbal Foot Baths   136
Hay-Flower and Oat Straw Foot Baths. Special Directions for Hot and Cold Foot Baths. Alleviating Corns, Calluses, Bunions. Coping with Athlete's Foot.

Miscellaneous Herbal Aids for External Use   138
Chapped Hands, Chilblains. Warts. Poison Oak, Poison Ivy. Gnat Bites, Insect Repellents.

Herbal Beauty Aids   140
The Beauty Recipe of a Queen. Magic Water. Skin Blemishes and Freckles.

15. HERBS AND THEIR EFFECT ON THE EMOTIONS 144

Is There a Mind-Cancer Link?   145
Other Studies. Scientific Breakthrough. Brief Summary of Findings.

How Herbs Help Emotions for Better Health   147

The Dr. Bach Flower Remedies   148
Mental States Classified.

Dr. Bach's Discovery of Herbal Remedies for Coping With Mentally-Induced Illnesses   149
Specific Properties of Herbs Extracted by the Sun Method.

Some Case Histories Under Dr. Bach's Treatment   150

15. HERBS AND THEIR EFFECT ON THE EMOTIONS (Cont.)

Clematis Remedy. Centaury Remedy. Combinations of Remedies Used by Dr. Bach. Dr. Bach's Rescue Remedy.

Dr. Bach's Desire to Share His Discoveries   155
The Bach Foundation's Work in England. A Medical Doctor's Opinion of the Bach Remedies.

16. HERBAL SMOKING SUBSTITUTES FOR TOBACCO 157

Herbal Smoking Mixtures   157
Angelica. Bearberry. Beech. Buckbean. Coltsfoot. Corn Silk. Cubeb Berries. Deer's Tongue. Dittany-American. Eucalyptus. Ginseng. Licorice. Life Everlasting. Marjoram. Mullein. Red Raspberry. Rosemary. Sage. Sassafras. Sumach. Sweet Clover. Sweet Gale. Sweet Woodruff. Yerba Santa.
Herbs to Discourage the Tobacco Habit   167

17. ROUNDUP OF MISCELLANEOUS HERBS . . 168

Burdock   168
Camomile   169
Camomile. As a "Plant Physician." Constituents and Modern Uses. Reported Uses in Retention of Urine. Chamomile. Constituents and Uses.
Celery   172
Rheumatism. Variety of Uses.
Corn Silk   174
Pharmaceutical Constituents of Corn Silk.
Damiana   176
Reported Modern Uses.
Fig   177
Figs as Food and Medicine. Boils. Miscellaneous Fig Remedies Reported. Properties Contained in Figs. Anti-Cancer Factor in Figs? As a Constipation Remedy.
Fringe Tree   181
Remedial Use of Fringe Tree. Gallstone Conditions.
Gentian   184
Gentian Bitters. Gentian Bitters as a Remedy.

17. ROUNDUP OF MISCELLANEOUS HERBS *(Cont.)*

High Cranberry   186
Pharmaceutical Constituents of High Cranberry.
Hops   187
*Use of Hop Pillows in Nervous Ailments. Reported
Medicinal Uses of Hops. Findings of Scientific
Studies of Hops. Herbal Tonics in General.*
Hydrangea   190
*Case of Terminal Illness Reported Healed with
Hydrangea. Cherokee Seven-Barks Remedy.*
Lady's Slipper   191
Marshmallow   193
*Pharmaceutical Constituents and Uses. Colitis. Re-
lieving Duodenal Ulcers.*
Motherwort   196
*Motherwort Known as the "Herb of Life." Re-
ported Remedial Use.*
Plantain   199
*Remedial Background of Plantain. Plantain as
Used by the Indians. Constituents of Plantain. As
Used by Many Nations. Reported Relief of Neu-
ralgia. Reported Uses for Ear Trouble. Ribwort.*
Shepherd's Purse   202
Constituents and Uses.
Twin Leaf   204
Valerian   205
Constituents.
Wood Betony   206
*Recorded Uses of Wood Betony. Nervous Tension
—Head Pains. Alleviating Hay Fever.*
Wormwood   208
*Properties and Uses. As Used for Fallen Arches.
Reported Uses for Liver Complaint and Indiges-
tion. A Serious Battle Wound Healed.*

EPILOGUE **212**

GLOSSARY OF TERMS **213**

**HERB DEALERS
          AND HOMEOPATHIC PHARMACIES** **218**

INDEX **221**

1

ELDER: FAVORITE
ALL-TIME REMEDY

The Gypsies left Persia nearly 500 years ago, and India Long before that time. Originally of vagabond and nomadic habits, some Gypsies have settled in various countries such as Turkey, Spain, England and Russia, while others still maintain their itinerant life and tribal organization. These bands of self-contained and ruggedly independent people always remain a separate race in whatever land they settle. As most are unable to read or write, they have forgotten the reasons for many of their customs and traditions; nevertheless, they still practice them faithfully. For example, they make their umbrellas out of whalebone. An old-fashioned idea perhaps, but this type of umbrella affords a non-metallic protection against lightning.

Of special interest to us however, is the remarkable knowledge of herbal remedies that the Gypsies possess. Their caravans can be seen loaded with mysterious boxes of freshly gathered herbs as the roaming Gypsies travel from village to village, selling their aromatic merchandise, and relating to the villagers the herbal folklore that dates from the misty regions of the past.

Among the list of remedies that have survived the experience of generations are marigold flowers for wounds, mistletoe for nervous debility, gentian as a tonic, and coltsfoot and yarrow for bronchitis. Far removed from Gypsy encampments are the offices of the modern medical herbalists where the same herbs are prescribed for the same disorders. The Gypsies used foxglove as a remedy for heart trouble long before science discovered digitalis, a drug obtained from the foxglove plant which the modern physician now prescribes for certain heart conditions. The Gypsies have always claimed that nettles were good for the skin. Nettles have been found rich in iron which aids and improves the complexion. The violet plant is an old Romany (Gypsy) remedy for tumors and surface cancer. This is one of the plants now under study by the National Cancer Institute. Laboratory experiments showed that when the remedy was tried on a cancerous mouse it did damage to the cancer.

ELDER—A FAVORITE GYPSY FOLK REMEDY

The Gypsies regard the elder as one of the "healingest trees on earth." In her book, *Herbs for Daily Use*,[1] Mary Thorne Quelch writes of a Gypsy friend who related the following folk remedies in which the elder is used: For coughs and colds equal parts of elderberry, crab apple and blackberry juice are boiled together with a little sugar to form a syrup, and a teaspoonful is taken as needed. To alleviate thirst in conditions of fever, boiling water is poured over dried elder flowers with a lump or two of sugar and drank cold. The same infusion taken hot is used as a remedy for head colds. Elder water is employed as a wash for sore eyes and other eye complaints. The Gypsies prepare a healing ointment by placing the fresh flowers on home cured lard (salt-free) and cooking the mixture slowly until all the elder juice is fully extracted.

Comments on the Gypsy Remedies

Mrs. Quelch comments on the elder remedies given by the Gypsy, and cites the additional value and use of the plant. Of the healing ointment described by her friend she says, "For cuts, burns, scalds and similar accidents, this ointment cannot be praised too highly, while its virtues as a cosmetic are great. It will smooth away lines and wrinkles and do much towards closing enlarged pores." Of the infusion (tea), Mrs. Quelch tells us that it is also soothing to the nerves, induces sleep and has been advised for hysterical and epileptic patients. She draws attention to its diuretic (kidney stimulating)

[1] Mary Thorne Quelch, *Herbs for Daily Use* (London: Faber and Faber Limited, 1959).

action, and says that the infusion made in the usual propor-
ions and taken in wineglassful doses four times a day has
been used in cases of dropsy or urinary complications with
good effect.

Elderberry Ointment

According to Mrs. Quelch, the *green* berries stewed in
camphorated oil also make an excellent soothing and healing
ointment. To prepare the recipe the green berries are thoroughly washed and put into a suitable container with enough
camphorated oil added to cover them. The container itself is
then covered with a saucer or lid and placed in a pan of
boiling water or in a very slow oven for four or five hours,
keeping the water in the container boiling if that method is
used. The decoction is then strained through muslin (squeezing well), and put into bottles or jars for use when required.
To soothe coughs or ease difficulties in breathing, for example, bronchitis, relief is given if the back and chest are
rubbed with the oil. We are also told that it is a good dressing
for sprains, burns, or strains. The ripe berries made into a
conserve are used to ease soreness of the throat.

Gypsy Beauty Cream

The following recipe appeared in *The Medical Herbalist:*[2]

> one oz. red dock root
> two oz. cold cream
> two oz. pure pork lard
> two oz. elder-tree flowers

Place the lard in an earthen jar, cut up the dock root
and add the elder-tree flowers to the lard. Heat for an
hour; strain, add the cold cream and mix well together
until cold. This is a fine remedy for blackheads.

Two Varieties of Elder

The American elder *Sambucus canadensis* is a shrub reaching from six to twelve feet in height with small white flowers

[2] John R. Yemm, F.N.A., D.O., N.D., *The Medical Herbalist*
(Vol. XI), p. 232.

and purple-black or red berries and is found growing in all parts of the country in low damp ground and thickets. The common elder of Europe, *Sambucus nigra*, is larger in size, approaching that of a tree. The word "elder" is from the Anglo-Saxon *aeld* meaning "fire," due to the practice in olden times of removing the pith from the young branches and using them as blowing tubes to kindle fire. Because the tubes were also made into shepherds' pipes the elder is still frequently called the Pipe Tree. The shoots with the pith removed were used by youngsters for making popguns. Elder water sprinkled on roses and honeysuckles is said to protect the flowers from the infestations of insects.

A Reported Supernatural Background of Elder

Those who have made an intensive study of occult phenomena claim that the elder is surrounded by a wide healing "aura," or radiation around it. In former times it was a common practice to plant the tree near the home as a protection against disease and evil spirits, and an ancient elder was often pointed out as having a mysterious and supernatural history. An elder twig carried close to the flesh was said to be a priceless charm for good luck and good health. With the modern knowledge of radionic phenomena it may be possible that in some instances a part of the tree worn close to the body may prove beneficial in certain physical disorders. A parallel may be seen here in the practice among some people of wearing a copper bracelet for the relief of rheumatism.

According to legend, the tree supplied the wood from which the Cross upon which Christ was crucified was made, and therefore cannot be struck by lightning. Today science has noted the strange properties the elder possesses with regard to static electricity. As recently as the last century the superstition still prevailed that it was bad luck to completely destroy or uproot an elder tree.

Elder as Known to the Early Herbalists

Apart from its legendary and superstitious aspects the elder has had a solid reputation for its medicinal virtues since earliest times. Hippocrates listed it among the prominent plants of his *materia medica* and it was also mentioned by

Pliny and other ancient writers. Culpeper cited its use in a wide variety of ailments, including dropsy. John Evelyn was equally impressed with the virtues of the elder and said that if its medicinal properties were fully known, "I cannot tell why our countrymen should ail; for him there is a remedy [elder] for his sickness in every field and hedgerow." Boorhave wrote that whenever he passed an elder tree he always tipped his hat in deepest respect and thankfulness to the Creator for giving such a profound blessing to mankind!

ELDER REMEDIES OF A FAMOUS GERMAN HERBALIST

Father Sebastian Kneipp was a parish priest and renowned herbalist of Worishofen (Bavaria), Germany, during the last century. Attracted by the success of his herbal remedies, numerous invalids gathered round him daily, eager for his help. The rich, the poor, the prince or the beggar were all welcomed. For over 40 years he conducted his health clinic in Bavaria, and his work is still carried on to this day. His fame as a healer steadily grew and during the later years of his life became so great that he was consulted by royalty. Among Father Kneipp's patients were Empress Fredericka of Germany, Empress Elizabeth of Austria, the Prince of Wales (later King Edward VIII), Pope Leo XIII, Baron Rothschild, and many other notables. His book, *My Water Cure*,[3] is considered a health classic.

In his writings, Father Kneipp gives an impressive account of the value and use of the elder. He says that it is excellent for purifying the blood and for this purpose recommends a cup of tea made from its flowers or blossoms. The tea is allowed to boil for ten minutes and should be taken daily one hour before breakfast. He refers to this as a "spring course of medicine" but adds that it may also be taken at any other time of the year. He also relates the following:

> If the berries are boiled down with sugar, or better still with honey, they will prove especially good in wintertime for people who have but little exercise and and are condemned to a sedentary life. A spoonful of the above preserve stirred in a glass of water, makes the most splendidly cooling and refreshing drink, operates on the healthful secretion of the urine, and has a generally good effect on the kidneys.

[3] Reprinted by Health Research, Mokelumne Hill, Calif.

Many people in country areas dry the berries. But whether these dried berries are boiled as porridge, or stewed to eat, or eaten dry, in all forms they are considered an excellent remedy against violent diarrhea.

Father Kneipp's Philosophy

Father Kneipp summarized his philosophy of good health in the following words: "It is not enough for man to beg his Creator for health and long life. He should also use his intelligence to discover and bring to light the treasures graciously hidden by God in Nature as a means of healing the ills of this human life."

Healthful Properties Contained in Elder

Elderberry tea has been employed for generations as a folk remedy for such conditions as colds, coughs, and influenza. Yet it was only in recent years that science discovered that elderberries contain viburnic acid, a substance which induces perspiration, and is useful in cases of bronchitis and similar ailments. The berries also provide vitamins A, B, and C. A glucoside, *eldrin*, which is identical with rutin was found in the flowers. In addition they contain a fragrant volatile oil and malates of potash and lime. Other constituents of the plant are fat, gum, wax, starch, pectin, albumen, resin, grape sugar and various alkaline and earthy salts. The bark and leaves of the European species *Sambucus nigra* contain the glucoside *sambunigrin*.

MODERN USES OF ELDER

During the past several years, elder bark has been employed by European physicians as a diuretic in cases of cardiac (heart) and renal dropsies and in some instances even in epilepsy with good effect. The homeopaths prepare a special tincture made from the green inner bark of the young elderberry branches and employ it for the relief of asthma.

As a domestic remedy, a tea made with one ounce of elder flowers to one pint of water is considered almost as a specific in the alleviation of influenza. This simple infusion or tea is very popular in England where the sale of dried elder flowers has increased by 50 percent during the past several years. Elderberry wine taken hot with sugar or honey just before retiring at night is another well-known and popular remedy for colds.

Reported Benefits of Elder Flowers and Peppermint Herb Tea

The origin of this herbal combination goes a long way back in folk medicine and has maintained its healing reputation according to reports right up to modern times. The following excerpts relating to its use are taken from *Grace*[4] magazine:

If the truth were more fully known, many deep-seated chest diseases could possibly have been avoided in their early stages through the fruit of the popgun tree [elder]. Healing virtues of the elder are proverbial . . . it is best known for the combination of its flowers with peppermint herb.

But you know, today we don't want to be bothered with steaming hot infusions at bedtime to sweat out our hearts under the bed clothes! As we drift into the "tablet" age it is so convenient to take something out of a bottle instead of two teaspoonfuls of this old countryman's cordial in a teacup of hot water.

Tried it? It warms you gloriously, sustains the heart, soothes inflamed mucous membranes, and imparts the notion that maybe it is time for you to be getting off to bed . . . a sound sleep and sweet dreams . . . the morning should see you back at your usual temperature and with all the tap-washers securely fastened. Mrs. A. always keeps it in the house for influenza. She says she takes it "cold" for her recurrent cystitis. Today, quite a lot of people take it in the cold infusion as an external wash for a nasty smarting pruritis. More and more is being sold. Glad news.

A medical herbalist suggests this method of using the elderflower-peppermint combination:[5]

A good all-round combination for influenza of all kinds. Place one ounce of the mixture in one pint cold water and bring to boil. Remove vessel on boiling. Dose: One wineglassful every two hours until symptoms abate.

[4] Winter 1960, p. 126.
[5] Bartram, *Health From Herbs,* December 1957, p. 465.

Elder for Neuralgia

Two Prague doctors, Epstein and Jokel,[6] have experimented with elderberry juice in cases of trigeminal neuralgia. Dr. Epstein treated 48 patients suffering from this painful disorder by administering 20 grams of pure elderberry juice daily for five days. He claims that the results were remarkable. In acute cases the condition often cleared up after only one dose. In chronic cases several days were required before the ailment yielded to the elderberry treatment. Later, he found that some alcohol (20 percent) added to the juice was more effective and shortened the period of time required for a complete healing. So convinced was he of the value of his unique treatment that if beneficial results did not occur he considered the disorder to be other than trigeminal neuralgia. Dr. Jokel's findings confirmed those of Dr. Epstein.

Coping with Sciatica

Dr. Vetlesen,[7] a Norwegian, experimented with other forms of neuritis. He combined ten grams of port wine with 30 grams of elderberry juice and prescribed this as a daily dose to patients suffering from sciatica. In acute cases the ailment yielded in from one to 11 days, while in chronic cases it required from eight to 17 days. In relapsing cases, 23 days' treatment was necessary to establish a complete healing with lasting results. Other European doctors have confirmed these experiences.

How to Counteract Dryness of Skin[8]

One oz. elder flowers; one oz. yarrow; one oz. violet leaves. Mix. Place one-third of mixture in one pint of water and bring to boil. Remove vessel as soon as boiling is reached. Allow to cool. Strain. Drink one wineglassful, *cold* three times daily.

Coping with Inflammation of the Bladder

A noted scientist, Dr. Von Czarnowski recommended the following herbal formula for inflammation of the bladder

[6] *Prager Med. Wschr.*, 1914.
[7] *Norske Magfa Laege Videnskaben*, 1916.
[8] J. L. Dring, *Health From Herbs*, June 1954, p. 167.

and mucous lining of the urinary passages: Equal parts of elder flowers, St. John's wort, German chamomile flowers, blackberry leaves, and Linden flowers are thoroughly mixed together. From two to four heaping teaspoonfuls of the herbal mixture is placed in a cup and boiling water added. This is allowed to stand until cold. It is then strained. One cupful is taken three times daily, one-half hour before meals.

Nature's Herbal Way Is Usually Best

According to written records some of the herbs prescribed thousands of years ago by the Egyptian priest-physicians are still in use today. Among these herbs is the elder. In spite of the lack of modern equipment, without the knowledge of microbiology, former generations were successfully treating their ills with plant substances which have now been scientifically proven to contain therapeutic properties. Up until recent years, however, orthodox practitioners still regarded herbal folk medicine as nothing more than backwoods superstition and old wives' tales.

We should be very grateful for the perseverance and integrity of the men and women of the past who fought so valiantly against ridicule and persecution to preserve the empirical knowledge of plant remedies. Hippocrates stated that, "Nature is the healer of all disease," and pointed out that the physician is only her servant, while Aristotle said, "If there is one way better than another, it is the way of nature." These statements are as true today as they were when first uttered over two thousand years ago.

2

DANDELION: THE WAYSIDE HEALING WONDER

Around the turn of the century, Dr. Sparks wrote:

> Fifteen years ago I was afflicted with the liver complaint. I used all my skill trying to cure it, but failed. I then tried two physicians in Philadelphia, Doctors Wilson and Jordan, but without success.

Dr. Sparks goes on to say that an old nurse told him that dandelion root was an effective folk remedy for this disorder, so he decided to give it a try. He claims that its use promptly restored his health. From then on he employed the herb in his practice, regarding it as his favorite prescription for liver complaint. According to Dr. Sparks, his patients obtained favorable results "either by the simple extract of the herb and root, or by taking a teacupful of a strong decoction of it twice a day." He adds, "In almost every instance I have succeeded in restoring those who have used this plant."

Are there any facts which support the claims made by this "horse and buggy" doctor of yesteryear with reference to the healing power of the common dandelion? Or were such claims based on wrong diagnosis or overenthusiasm and exaggeration, which in either case renders them unworthy of further consideration? Before passing judgment on this forerunner of the modern physician let us acquaint ourselves with the humble plant of the wayside to which he refers.

The Determined Dandelion

The common dandelion (*Leontodon taraxacum*) is a native of Greece. It thrives under almost any condition and has spread to nearly every part of the world. Those who have tried to banish it from even one small lawn have become convinced that its motto is "Never say die!" The first part of the botanical name, *Leontodon*, was derived from two Greek words meaning "lion" and "tooth." The word dandelion has a similiar meaning and is a corruption of the French *dent de lion* or lion's tooth. Some believe the name was given to the plant because the jagged leaf looks like the teeth of a lion. Others disagree and say that it was because of the yellow flower which bears a resemblance to the golden teeth of the heraldic lion. The name *taraxacum* was taken from an Arabian alteration of a Greek word meaning "edible." The herb was first mentioned as a medicine in the writings of the Arabian physicians around the tenth century, under the name *Tarakhshagun*.

The Dandelion as Nature's Barometer

The dandelion possesses the unusual ability of protecting itself from the heat of the sun by closing its petals completely if the warmth becomes excessive. The downy puffball which appears after the flower has gone to seed is reputed to serve as a barometer to predict fair or stormy weather. In his *Knowledge of Plants*, Coles tells us that if the down flies off the dandelion when there is no wind it is a sure sign of rain.

In olden times the feathery seed balls were used as oracles by young lovers. A maiden would blow three times on the dandelion down to determine if her sweetheart was thinking of her. If a lone feather remained it meant that she was not forgotten. Similar superstitions connected with the use of the plant were quite common.

Health Properties in Dandelion

Dandelion greens contain 7,000 units of vitamin A per ounce. They also provide an abundance of vitamins B₁ and C. Two alkaloids, the most valuable of which is *taraxacin*, have been isolated from dandelion root. In Europe many scientific experiments have been conducted with the plant which have confirmed the traditional belief that its use is beneficial to the health of the liver. Dr. Le Clerc and others found it to be a true hepatic stimulant. The root is said to contain more of its active principles during the autumn than at any other season of the year, however, the composition of the soil in different areas is also taken into account.

The dandelion is a wonderful purifying agent as it contains a good assortment of alkaline salts, such as calcium, sodium and potassium. We are told that it stimulates the flow of bile as well as producing a mild action on the liver. Due to its content of potash, it is considered an effective diuretic. Dandelion also contains cholin, a factor of the vitamin B complex which science has found to be essential to liver function.

Dandelion—A Nutritious Herbal Dish

Dandelion greens are very nutritious and may be boiled and served like spinach, or the fresh leaves can be mixed with salads. In France they are eaten in sandwiches. The greens were so highly prized by the Apache Indians that they would spend many days searching the countryside for them. The amount of fresh dandelion leaves that one Indian would consume was astonishing. Many Indian tribes cooked the greens with vinegar or water, or with meat, and included the roots in salads. Tribes of the Eastern states, as well as those of Wisconsin, Minnesota, Utah, Nevada, Arizona and California, all relished the dandelion as a nutritious treat.

In country households dandelion roots were roasted slowly in the oven then pulverized and used as a substitute for coffee. This is a healthful beverage and does not contain caffeine. "Dandelion coffee" has become a commercial product which is now sold by health food stores and herb companies.

Synede

This is a popular health food dish. Approximately one cup of chopped dandelion leaves is placed on one side of a soup plate. A teaspoonful of honey is dripped over the leaves, then a teaspoon of olive oil and lemon juice is poured over them. Four heaping tablespoonfuls of powdered or ground nuts are placed on the empty side of the soup dish. The nuts are mixed with the salad little by little as it is eaten. This has been used as a general tonic and blood builder.

DANDELION REMEDIES

In olden times, herbalists who peddled their botanicals

among the European villages were known as Green Men and a number of the country inns of England still bear this name today. Plant remedies of the Green Men were handed down from one generation to the next and many formulas have survived to the present time.

The following herbal combination was recommended as a daily health beverage to sharpen the senses, maintain resilience of the arteries and to strengthen the liver:

> Simple infusion (tea): Nettles, two oz.; dandelion, one oz.; coltsfoot, one oz. Mix. Place two or three teaspoonfuls in a teapot and infuse as ordinary tea. Add sugar and milk to taste. Drink a teacupful as a beverage instead of coffee or soda.

A Medical Doctor's Opinion of Dandelion as a Health Builder[1]

Swinburne Clymer, M.D., gives his medical opinion regarding the medicinal value of the dandelion. He says that it is a tonic and stomachic and possesses slightly aperient and diuretic action. In his practice he has found that:

> Dandelion has a beneficial influence upon the biliary [bile] organs, removing torpor and engorgement of the liver as well as of the spleen. It is beneficial in dropsy when due to inertia of the abdominal organs, and in uterine obstruction and in chronic skin diseases it is always indicated.
>
> Only the green herb, whether for tincture or infusion, should be used. When buying tincture be certain it is from the fresh plants. Dandelion greens eaten as foods have the same influence on the blood and organs though in a lesser degree. Dose of the tincture, five to 40 drops.

Use in Urinary Disorders

Dr. Clymer refers to a combination of dandelion, corn silk and golden seal when he writes the following:[2]

Whenever a sediment resembling brick dust is found

[1] *Nature's Healing Agents* (Quakertown, Pa.: The Humanitarian Society, Reg.), 1960, p. 129.

[2] *Nature's Healing Agents*, p. 158.

in the urine, corn silk (*Stigmata maidis*) is the indicated agent and is one of the decidedly few agents that will accomplish its removal successfully. Like couch grass, corn silk is a demulcent to the kidneys, bladder and urinary organs, and is indicated whenever there is irritation of these organs. When there is neuralgic trouble due to irritation of the female organs, corn silk is indicated. A syrup made of corn silk, dandelion and *Hydrastis* [golden seal] is a valuable combination to be given in hot water. Collect the dandelion root (one-half pound) and corn silk (four ounces) and boil in (one quart) water, strain and add sugar, then add the Tincture of *Hydrastis* (two ounces). Dose: one teaspoonful in half a cup of water.

Corn silk, with the addition of agrimony, has long been a favorite remedy in bedwetting.

A SELECTION OF DANDELION HERBAL FORMULAS

Following is a list of herbal formulas in which dandelion is one of the ingredients. These remedies are reported from medical writings that are generally considered standard in their field.

For Nettle Rash or Hives

Treatment: Stinging nettle .... one oz.
            Yarrow .... one oz.
            Golden Seal .... one-quarter oz.
            Dandelion root .... two oz.

Simmer for 20 minutes in two pints of water and take a tablesponful every four hours. A tepid bath is very soothing to the irritable skin.—John Yemm, F.N.A., D.O., N.D.[3]

A Soothing Stomach Powder

Gentian .... one oz.
Valerian .... one oz.
Black root (Culver's physic) ...... one-half oz.
Dandelion (roasted powder) .... two oz.
Cayenne .... one drachm

Mix until the whole is well incorporated. Infuse one ounce in a pint of boiling water, and when cool strain

[3] *The Medical Herbalist*, p. 124.

and bottle for use. Dose: A wineglassful three times a day.

This is a most excellent medicine, and may be used with advantage in all cases of dyspepsia, more particularly when complicated with diseases of the liver, spleen, or pancreas.

—John Skelton, M.D.[4]

Ovarian Cysts

Formula: Take an ounce each of raspberry leaves, black-currant leaves, witch-hazel leaves and powdered myrrh. Boil in a quart of water in a covered vessel for ten minutes, simmer for half an hour and strain. Mix a quarter of a pint of this mixture with a pint of cooled boiled water, and use as a douche nightly. Regulate the bowels with senna and take the following medicine, a tablespoonful three times daily:

Dandelion, one oz.; comfrey, one oz.; yellow dock, one oz.; yarrow, one oz.; licorice root, two oz.

Divide into three parts. To one part add a pint of boiling water, simmer for 20 minutes, cool, and strain.[5]

Skin Diseases

It may be desirable to treat your skin diseases internally and thus help eliminate the cause, with one of the many herbal combinations available for this purpose. A reportedly effective internal remedy is as follows:

Sarsaparilla root	one oz.
Yellow dock root	one oz.
Blue flag root	one oz.
Dandelion root	one oz.

Mix. Place one-quarter of the mixture in one and a half pints water and simmer for 20 minutes. Strain. Dose: One wineglassful three times daily.[6]

ADDITIONAL REPORTED REMEDIES USING DANDELION

T. H. Bartram, M.N.I.M.H., M.R.S.H., has a lot to say

[4] *Science and Practice of Herbal Medicine*, p. 712.
[5] Winifred Blyth, M.N.I.M.H., "Women's Health Queries," *Health From Herbs*, July 1955, p. 204.
[6] *Health From Herbs*, January 1954, p. 21.
[7] *Health From Herbs*, June 1953, p. 165.

about the health value of the common dandelion.[7] He tells us that the use of *dandelion coffee* has been excellent for *preventing* the formation of *gall stones* in patients who are unduly susceptible to them. In addition he says: "Hepatitis, or inflammation of the liver, and jaundice, when uncomplicated, readily yield to the *taraxacin* of dandelion. Its *inulin* is nutritive, especially in the wasting of the anemias when liver malfunction is often a causative factor."

Bartram cites the method of preparation as a simple decoction—one-half ounce of the dried roots to one pint of water which is brought to a boil and allowed to simmer for ten minutes. He cautions that excessive boiling impairs the strength of the dandelion roots. The decoction, he says, is to be "taken in wineglassful doses three times daily after meals."

He lists other methods of preparation as follows:

Fluid extract. Dose—half teaspoonful to a wineglassful of water, after meals, three times daily.

Dandelion coffee. Roots should be slowly roasted in an oven and pulverized by pounding in a pestle and mortar, or by grinding. Addition of a little salt improves. The result can be used with hot milk and sweetening.

One advantage over ordinary coffee is the absence of wakefulness following its use as a night cap. It is wonderfully relaxing and affords sound sleep.

Green leaves. Every vegetarian is aware of the health-giving properties of dandelion leaves in salads. During the month of May they are succulent and readily digested by sensitive stomachs. The leaves may also be boiled as a vegetable and served like spinach.

Dandelion Has Wide Range for Healthful Action

Bartram tells us that dandelion is used for *dyspepsia,* and *kidney trouble,* and as a *mild laxative* in conditions of chronic constipation. He says that *warts* can be eliminated by local application of the expressed juice from the green stalks; that the use of dandelion promotes a *healthy circulation, strengthens* weak *arteries,* cleanses the skin of *blemishes,* and restores *gastric balance* in patients who have suffered from severe vomiting.

Reported Uses of Dandelion for Diabetics

Bartram assures us that although dandelion is not the first herbal remedy that comes to the mind of the medical herbalist as a treatment for rheumatism, good results have been obtained by taking a teacupful of the decoction daily over a long period of time. He also gives the following information on the remedial use of the plant:

> In combination with periwinkle, it has in a large number of patients, considerably reduced the sugar content of the urine. With shepherd's purse it has grappled with many a case of almost hopeless uremia. For blood in the urine we would employ shepherd's purse because of its higher degree of astringency; but for excessive phosphates and sulphates we would use dandelion.
>
> For the greenish hue of urine, indicating the presence of bile pigments, dandelion is the remedy, par excellence. It is appropriate in all diseases involving an enlarged spleen.

With regard to Bartram's dandelion-periwinkle combination, it may be pointed out that the natives of South Africa have used periwinkle as a remedy for diabetes for a very long time. A number of years ago considerable attention was drawn to the periwinkle plant when a news item appeared in the South African and London press stating that a registration officer at Durban was declared completely healed of diabetes after two months' treatment with periwinkle.

Dandelion's Golden Glory

Bartram concludes with the following comments:

> Mentioned in Arabian medicine, dandelion has yet to rise to the zenith of its power in the world of therapeutics. Its action is evasive, subtle, passing unnoticed amid the clamor of twentieth century medicine. The day is sure to dawn when its virtues shall shine as the noon-day sun, putting to shame the dangerous drugs of our day, whose questionable cures have cursed the earth with a volume of chronic disease hitherto unknown to man.
>
> With this brilliant compositae the meadows of May glow with greater glory, providing luscious field fare for the flock, and golden medicine for those appreciative of its power.

3

GOLDEN HEALING OIL FROM
THE OLIVE TREE

Olive trees are native to the warm regions of Europe and Asia, and were grown by the Egyptians over four thousands years ago. They were introduced in America around the year 1769 when Franciscan Fathers brought some olive seeds or cuttings with them to the New World and planted them near the site of present day San Diego, California.

Tree of Ages

The olive is a tree of great antiquity, attaining the age of over two thousand years. It is said that eight of the original olive trees in the Garden of Gethsemane are still in existence. With reference to this, Dean Stanley wrote:

> In spite of all the doubts that can be raised against their antiquity, or the genuineness of their site, the eight aged olive trees, if only by their manifest difference from all others on the mountain, have always struck even the most indifferent observers. They are now indeed less striking in the modern garden enclosure built around them by the Franciscans, than when they stood free and unprotected on the rough hillside, but they will remain so long as their already protracted life is spared, the most memorable of their race on the surface of the earth. Their gnarled trunks and scanty foliage will always be regarded as the most affecting of the sacred memorials in or about Jerusalem.

Emblem of Peace

Since time immemorial the olive tree has been regarded as a symbol of peace in almost every land in the world. Early navigators found that green olive branches carried in the hands or placed in the ground were universally employed and understood as emblems of peace among all the islanders, even of the South Seas. The Greeks prayed for prosperity and peace with green olive boughs held in their hands, garlands around their necks and crowns upon their heads. It was also the custom of the Greeks, especially of the Athenians, to carry an olive branch to the homes of their neighbors on the day of the New Year as a symbol of peaceful intentions. Among the Chinese, disputes or quarrels were settled by sending the offended person an olive wrapped in red paper.

In Parkhurst's *Lexicon* we read:

> The olive tree, from the effect of the oil in relaxing and preventing or mitigating pain, seems to have been from the beginning an emblem of the benignity of the Divine nature; and particularly, after the Fall, to have represented the goodness and placability of God through Christ, and the blessed influences of the Holy Spirit in mollifying and healing our disordered nature, and in destroying or expelling from it the poison of the old (spiritual) serpent, even as olive oil does that of the natural serpent or viper. Hence we see a peculiar propriety in the olive leaf or branch being chosen by Divine Providence as a sign to Noah of the abatement of the deluge (Gen. 8:11); we may also account for olive branches being ordered as one of the materials of the booths at the feast of tabernacles (Neh. 8:15); and whence they became emblems of peace to various and distant nations.

THE HEALTH VALUE OF OLIVE OIL

The olive is one of our most valuable sources of food oil. It contains 60 percent fat and is considered a good cleansing and healing agent due to its high content of *potassium*. It is also rich in *sodium* and *calcium*. Olive oil is easily digested and imparts a generally soothing and healing influence to the digestive tract. Unfortunately, it is often diluted or adulterated with cottonseed oil for commercial sale. The pure or virgin oil is more expensive and can be easily recognized by the taste if compared with that of a preserved olive.

Olive oil is used for culinary purposes, salad dressings, the manufacture of cosmetics, soaps, and cleansing solutions. In medicine it enters into the composition of liniments, pills, sunburn lotions, plasters, and ointments. The pure oil is used both internally and externally for the treatment of a variety of disorders.

Using Olive Oil for Ulcers

In a medical-health publication, *Hamdard Digest* (India), Dr. J. Dewitt Fox writes that he treats his ulcer patients with olive oil. He relates an incident of a young friend of his, a Mexican doctor, who took him to dinner at a restaurant in Mexico. Dr. Fox was astonished at the amount of hot sauces his friend consumed without the slightest indication of stomach distress. When questioned about this, his friend replied, "First I take a little olive oil. It protects my stomach."

Dr. Fox suggests that olive oil be substituted for the cream generally advised as a part of the ulcer diet: "Two tablespoons of olive oil with, or followed by, six ounces of milk will do the same or even a better job of healing than the cream. It will also reduce stomach acids, and because the oil is unsaturated, will not raise the blood cholesterol."

Mr. J. I. Rodale of *Prevention* magazine has recognized the value of olive oil where conditions of ulcers exist. He says, "A young relative has for several years been troubled with a rather severe ulcer condition. Recently the young man discovered the use of olive oil before meals lessens the discomfort he suffers after eating. Since then he has made it a habit to start every meal with a teaspoonful of olive oil and the results have been marvelous for him."

Some medical men speculate that olive oil may contain vitamin U, a substance which is believed to have a healing influence on ulcers.

Benefits of Olive Oil for Heart and Arteries

Results of a scientific study indicate that olive oil may be an important factor in the very low rate of heart and artery incidence found among the middle-aged men of Greece. Dr. Christo Arvanis of Athens University and Dr.

Ancel Keys of the University of Minnesota examined 1,215 men on the islands of Corfu and Crete. The patients were between the ages of 40 and 59. Only four cases of heart and artery diseases were found during a six year study! Reporting on their findings, the famous cardiologists told an international meeting of heart specialists in Athens that olive oil plays an important part in the diet of Greeks and appears related to their low-mortality from heart disorders.

Olive Oil in Coping with Cholesterol Conditions

Studies in France subsidized by the Institut d'Hygiene and indicating that the use of olive oil can effectively reduce blood cholesterol were reported in the *American Journal of Clinical Nutrition* (Feb. 1964). For approximately four months a number of hospital patients suffering from high blood cholesterol were given as much olive oil to drink as they wanted, *but no other oil or fat was allowed*. At the end of that time the cholesterol level of seven patients dropped 26 percent. In ten others, it dropped 14.2 percent. The article also points out that: "It is a well-known fact that the Mediterranean peoples, who are great consumers of olive oil, are generally less affected with atheromatoses (arteriosclerosis or hardening of the arteries) than the Anglo-Saxon."

The article also refers to experiments and research of other scientific investigators. In Zagreb, Yugoslavia, two groups of people were experimentally observed. One group was given olive oil while the other consumed animal fats. The group using animal fats had about 20 percent more cholesterol than the group using the olive oil.

Use of Olive Oil as Protection Against X-Rays and Irradiation

In the February 1962 issue of *La Vie Claire*, we find the following:

Professors Julian Sanz Ibanez and Adolfo Castellanos of the Cajal Institute in Madrid, in the course of a study on X-Rays on rats, concluded that olive oil protected the latter with full efficacy against progressive doses ranging from 300 to 2,400 roentgens [measures of X-Ray intensity].

An experiment was reported in the *Clinical Review Es-*

pagnol (April 15, 1963) in which various proportions of olive oil were added to the diets of six groups of mice (15 males and 15 females). These six groups as well as one group that did not receive the olive oil were subjected to doses of irradiation for 14 weeks. At the completion of the experiment it was found that the six groups of mice receiving the olive oil were protected against any damage known to be caused by such irradiation. Best results were obtained when the diet was fortified by a 15 percent content of olive oil. The mice that were given no olive oil suffered from damage to the liver, kidneys, and lungs as well as adverse effects on the skin and hair.

Olive Oil as a Laxative

The laxative effect of olive oil has been known for ages. Remedies calling for the use of the oil for constipation were cited in many of the early herbal books. It was also a favorite laxative prescribed by a number of the old-time family physicians. A medical book written early in this century gives the following information which bears this out:

> This oil [olive] taken internally is useful in inflammation of the stomach and bowels. Dose as a laxative, one tablespoonful; and with some patients it may require even more. Olive oil is one of the mildest laxatives we have, and should always be used with little children where castor oil is now used. In consequence of the injurious and destructive effect castor oil has on their tender digestive organs, it should never be given if it can be avoided.[1]

Both Dr. Fox and Dr. Granata found that olive oil was valuable in preventing constipation. Dr. Fox advises taking two tablespoonfuls before bedtime.

Olive Oil as a Gall Bladder Tonic and Gallstone Reliever

Bile is a yellow fluid secreted by the liver into the intestinal tract. It helps to produce an alkaline reaction in the intestines, to absorb and emulsify fats, and to prevent putrefaction. The gall bladder is a hollow pear-shaped organ

[1] *Encyclopedia of Health and Home,* Vitalogy Assoc., Chicago, 1921.

which stores and concentrates bile. It is situated beneath the liver. If the bile duct does not contract enough to completely empty itself the inadequacy causes accumulations of bile to back up which can eventually result in gallstones.

In the October-December 1962 issue of *Minerva Dietologica*, Dr. E. Granata writes that olive oil is a valuable preventative against gallstones. The oil causes strong healthy contractions of the gall bladder, greatly favoring complete emptying, and can be regarded as a very good gall bladder tonic. Dr. Granata's findings were confirmed by an International News Service release in which it was reported that olive oil is an essential factor in stimulating bile secretion and absorbing fatty acids.

It may be pointed out that in 1893 an experiment was reported by a Dr. E. M. Brockbank, in which a gallstone lost 68 percent of its weight in two days when immersed in pure olive oil.

Olive Oil and the Hair and Gums

Mr. J. I. Rodale became aware of the value of olive oil several years ago and has been highly enthusiastic about its use as a disease preventative. He says:

> One of my hunches: Go all out on olive oil. Take a teaspoonful of it before each meal, as I am now doing. I find it protective to the gums. Even for external use it is good. A friend swears by Conti's hair shampoo (it has an olive oil base). He claims it is wonderful for dandruff. Italians consume a lot of olive oil, and look at the wonderful hair of Italian women!

Mr. Rodale also tells us that a wigmaker from Williamsburg, Virginia, appeared on a television program and said that most of the hair used in his work comes from Europe. He prefers Italian hair because it has such fine quality and believes that it is the olive oil in the Italian diet that gives this marvelous texture and health to the hair. On another program it was remarked that an American woman tried to sell her beautiful-looking head of hair but found that nobody wanted it! Mr. Rodale asks this thought provoking question: "Is it possible that using olive oil in the diet would be a means of counteracting baldness?" He adds, "I have been to Italy many times and would say that one could see with the naked eye fewer naked heads than in the U.S."

MISCELLANEOUS HEALTHFUL USES OF OLIVE OIL

Dry Skin

Olive oil is one of the ingredients of a time-tested herbal aid for dry or scaly skin. It is prepared by mixing two teaspoonfuls of fine oatmeal with enough olive oil to form a soft paste. One-half cup of hot water is added and the mixture allowed to cool. It is then strained through muslin, squeezing thoroughly to fully extract the liquid. The strained solution is dabbed or patted on the skin two or three times a day and allowed to soak in. This preparation must be made fresh at least every other day as it will not keep.

Wounds, Sores, Abrasions

A popular herbal application for wounds, swellings, ulcers, sores and abrasions is called Oil of St. John's Wort. This remedy is recommended by medical herbalists and is made by infusing the fresh flowers of St. John's Wort (*Hypericum perforatum*) in olive oil.

Sunburn Lotion

Olive Oil .... one-half oz.
Glycerine .... one-half oz.
Distilled Witch Hazel .... one-half oz.

Mix together and apply as required for the relief of painful sunburn.

First Aid for the Eyes

Occasionally foreign particles such as grit, ashes, or dirt accidentally get into the eyes. An old-time family doctor book states that two drops of warm olive oil may be dropped directly on the eyeball as a first-aid measure until the services of a physician can be obtained.

Deafness[2]

Deafness may be produced by a cold. When this is

[2] *Encyclopedia of Health and Home.*

the case, drink freely of smartweed tea or pleurisy root tea, for a few days. Stew garlic in olive oil, strongly pressed and strained. A few drops each day should be put into the ear from a warm teaspoon, and plug the ear with cotton or wool. You will find this remedy unsurpassed in this form of deafness originating from a cold.

Eyelashes—Fingernails

In some countries women apply olive oil to the eyelashes daily, claiming that it makes the lashes grow longer.

Olive oil is applied to the fingernails in cases of *onychorrhexis* (reeded nails), a condition which is common among the aged.

Neuralgia of the Breasts[3]

Take one part of witch hazel and ten of olive oil. Mix, and apply to the breast frequently. It is said that it will afford speedy relief and comfort.

Olive Oil Cited in the U.S. Dispensatory

The 25th edition of the *Dispensatory of the United States of America*[4] gives this information on the value and use of olive oil:

Uses. Olive oil is nutritious and mildly laxative and may be used in milder cases of chronic constipation, especially when associated with malnutrition (J.A.M.A., 1919, 73, 1441). Like other fats it delays gastric emptying. It causes contraction of the gall bladder and is used for diagnostic purposes. In atonic conditions of the gall bladder it is used therapeutically, although, at first, it may cause discomfort. In the form of an enema (150 to 500 ml. warmed to almost body temperature) it is often a useful remedy in fecal impaction. . . .

As an emollient, olive oil is applied topically to the skin or mucous membranes. Internally, the usual dose, as a laxative or cholagogue, is from 15 to 60 ml. (approximately one-half to two fluid ounces).

[3] *Encyclopedia of Health and Home.*

[4] Osol-Farrar-Pratt (Philadelphia: J. B. Lippincott Company, 1960).

Nervous Disorders[5]

William G. Orr, a herbalist, was decorated by the French government for his method of emulsifying olive oil. This form was used to treat soldiers in World War I who were suffering from shell-shock or nervous conditions. Orr's method was to add malted milk and water to the olive oil. The mixture was placed in a suitable container and shaken thoroughly.

In reference to this method, Dr. Eric Powell points out that today we have electric mixers (blenders) which will do the job much better and with less trouble. He says: "Simply add a dessertspoonful of oil to a tablespoonful of . . . (malted milk) with half a pint or more of hot water or milk, or half and half, and thoroughly mix with a kitchen mixer." Dr. Powell recommends the use of the emulsified oil for those who suffer from malnutrition, nervous debility, and stomach or bowel trouble.

(*Additional reference: Prevention* (Magazine), Rodale Press, Inc., Emmaus, Pa.)

[5] *Fitness And Health From Herbs* (Magazine), December 1963.

4

NETTLE: THE VERSATILE
HEALING PLANT

In former times nettle was cultivated as a garden crop and had so many uses that it was tithed. In one of his letters, the poet Campbell wrote: "In Scotland I have eaten nettles, I have slept in nettle sheets, and dined off a nettle tablecloth. The young and tender nettle is an excellent pot herb. The stalks of the old nettle are as good as flax for making cloth. I have heard my mother say she thought nettle cloth more durable than any other species of linen."

The preparation of nettle fibre and the retting of stalks is an age-old industry which has been carried on for centuries. The finest linen can be made from some of the species and it is only the larger production of flax that prevents nettle from becoming an important economic product. Thread as well as linen was made from nettle and several dyes were obtained from the plant. The herb has also been employed in the manufacture of paper.

REMEDIAL USES OF NETTLE

The botanical name of nettle (*Urtica dioica*) is from *uro*, "to burn," in reference to the stinging properties of most species of the plant. People in country regions often treat nettle stings by following the age-old recommendation to "Look for a large Dock leaf, and having found it, rub some spittle over the part affected, and apply the leaf." However, the juice of the nettle itself is said to be the best antidote for its own sting.

As a folk remedy for the relief of asthma the leaves were dried and burned, and the smoke inhaled. Gerard referred to the value of the plant for this disorder when he said, "The nettle is a good medicine for them that cannot breathe unless they hold their heads upright. . . ." The Romans prepared a healing ointment by steeping the leaves in oil. In Russia the plant is used for the relief of toothache and sciatica, while in Jamaica the fresh juice is dropped into open wounds. The Indians used it for urinary disorders and to arrest bleeding.

In Germany and Russia, country people treat rheumatism by "urtication," that is by rubbing or striking the affected part with a bundle of fresh nettles. This is done for one or two minutes daily and sometimes more often. Father Kneipp recommended the same method and use of the plant for rheumatism with the assurance that, "The fear of the un-accustomed rod will soon give way to joy at its remarkable healing efficacy." He also said that nettle prepared as a tea is a good remedy for phlegm in the lungs, and to cleanse the stomach.

A case was reported where a woman who had been suffer-ing for years with rheumatism went blackberry picking, and much to her consternation repeatedly brushed her legs against nettle. To her astonishment about three days later her rheu-matic limbs were practically free of pain and she has been better ever since.

Dr. Fernie strongly recommended the use of nettle to arrest bleeding. The 17th edition of the U.S. Dispensatory stated that the plant had been used in medicine as a local irritant and diuretic, and particularly for the purpose of arresting uterine hemorrhages: "The fluid extract may be given in doses of half a fluid drachm, or a decoction of an ounce [of the leaves] to a pint in a teacupful dose."

Drs. Wood and Ruddock[1] considered nettle an excellent remedy for hives, recommending the use of the tincture in five-drop doses four or five times a day. They also covered the following disorders for which they found the plant effective:

It has been employed successfully in diarrhea and dysentery. It should be drunk freely in the form of a decoction. For hemorrhages, the expressed juice of the fresh leaves is regarded as more effective than the

[1] *Encyclopedia of Health and Home*, p. 555.

decoction, given in teaspoonful doses every hour or so as often as the nature of the case demands. It is a favorite remedy among the Germans for neuralgia to be taken in doses of four tablespoonfuls of the decoction three times a day, and at the same time bruise the leaves and apply as a poultice to the affected parts.

HEALTH QUALITIES FOUND IN NETTLE

Nettle is one of the few *plants* that contain vitamin D. This vitamin is necessary for the assimilation of calcium and for development of the bones. The herb also contains vitamin C and carotin. A considerable amount of iron, phosphorus, potassium, calcium, silica, and other valuable minerals are present in nettle.

As a Bleeding Arrester

Further examination of the plant's constituents makes it apparent that its employment by the old-time family physician *as a remedy to arrest bleeding* was a valid one as nettle contains nitrate of potash, tannin, and formic and gallic acid which are astringent components. Many modern authorities are cited by Dr. Leclerc regarding the use of nettle for nose bleeding and bleeding from the lungs and uterus. He reports that he used the plant with good effect in one case of hemophilia. For this, as well as in general conditions of bleeding or hemorrhages he administered three ounces of the expressed juice as a dose or a prepared syrup which was previously made by infusing one-half lb. of nettles in two and a half pints of water for 12 hours. This was filtered and double its weight in sugar added. Six ounces were given as a dose and repeated if necessary.

Uses in Dysentery and Gout Cases

Both chronic and acute cases of enteritis and dysentery were successfully treated with nettle by Dr. Oudar of Paris. A tincture of the plant administered in ten drop doses, or as a tea, was shown by Dr. Burnett to be highly effective in treating attacks of gout.

The action of nettle is classified as astringent, diuretic and tonic.

A Remarkable Recovery from Tuberculosis

Dr. Vogel[2] says that nettle can bring health to many people and that it has even saved the lives of some when they know of the herb and how to use it. He tells us that many years ago he gave a lecture in Winterthur and mentioned that nettle was a valuable aid for anyone suffering from tuberculosis. A year later he gave another lecture at the same hall and a gentleman in the audience told the assembly that he had heard Dr. Vogel's previous lecture regarding the healing properties of nettle. He explained that his wife had been seriously ill with tuberculosis of the lung and, as her doctor could not give any real hope of a cure, he decided to give his wife food rich in calcium. Every day he gave her fresh nettle juice or fresh green nettles chopped fine and added to her soup. To the doctor's great astonishment, in a year's time the patient was considered a healthy woman. Dr. Vogel was delighted to hear of this experience. He says he realizes that searching for fresh nettles daily and putting them through a mincer to extract the juice is troublesome. But he points out that, "it is surely worth all this to give someone back his health."

How Nettles Have been Prescribed

In Dr. Vogel's opinion, "No other plant can equal the nettle in cases of anemia, chlorosis, rachitis (rickets), scrofula, respiratory diseases, and especially lymphatic troubles." In addition, he suggests a number of ways in which nettles may be used. The young leaves can be chopped fine and sprinkled as a garnish on soup. As the juice is not too palatable it may be mixed with potatoes or other vegetables, or with oatmeal soup. As a medicine, he advises a dessertspoonful (of the juice) per day for an adult, and half to one teaspoonful for a child. To benefit from at least part of this healing remedy and in addition to enjoy a pleasant meal, young nettles are stewed in oil with a little onion. He says this is a healthful dish which has an excellent taste when eaten with baked or mashed potatoes. In accordance with his experience and views he adds:

[2] Dr. h. c. A. Vogel, *The Nature Doctor* (Teufen AR Switzerland: Bioforce-Verlag, 1960), p. 177.

Let us therefore seek out the places where nettles can always be gathered; if we continuously pick the young leaves, there will be a constant supply for months. Perhaps some of my readers feel that they have no time to find and prepare these plants and would like to buy the juice already extracted. Of course, they can do this; but no prepared medicine can have such a good effect and nothing can be so cheap as the freshly extracted juice from the plant, freshly gathered on the hillside.

As Constipation and Migraine Relief

In citing various natural remedies for the relief of constipation, Dr. Vogel mentions that young spring nettles boiled in milk have helped many people troubled with this condition. He says they should be taken first thing in the morning. In addition he tells us that, "This simple measure also stops migraine which is associated with bilious vomiting. The nettles are wonderful purifiers of the blood stream."

High Blood Pressure, Anemia, and Other Blood Disorders[3]

T. H. Bartram writes on the value of nettles for the treatment of high blood pressure and for anemia:

Here is a remedy with a long traditional reputation for high blood pressure. One ounce of the fresh herb in one pint of boiling water taken in teacupful doses twice daily is known to be considerable help towards reduction of a high systolic pressure. Iron deficiency diseases which have proved intractable to the latest drugs of modern medicine, often yield to this simple herb. It contains an abundance of chlorophyll, and many tons of the plant are gathered yearly for this purpose.

When dealing with some of the anemias, it is necessary to administer copper as well as iron, as the former element facilitates absorption of iron. It is significant that where iron is found in the mineral kingdom, an exceeding small percentage of copper is also present. As with minerals, so with plant life in this instance. In nettles both iron and copper have been isolated. Thus it would appear that the more natural way of dealing with these anemias is to give preparations of

[3] *Health From Herbs*, March 1954, p. 65.

plants containing those elements of which the patient is deficient.

Relieving Hives

Dr. Fox explains that the disease known as hives arises from an impure state of the blood and is generally connected with a disordered condition of the stomach and bowels. A rash appears on the skin and there is more or less inflammation, attended with painful itching or tingling. The rash disappears and reappears suddenly, sometimes in one part of the body and sometimes in another. For this disorder Dr. Fox says:

> Obtain if you can, the juice of nettles, and give a teaspoonful three times a day, and lay a little on the part as well; if, however, the bowels are relaxed too much, diminish the dose. . . . Wash the body down night and morning with water and marshmallow soap. Should the bowels be confined it will be necessary to administer an occasional aperient.

Nettle Therapy in India and Pakistan

Approximately 2000 plants are mentioned in the Ayurvedic, Unani, and Tibbi systems of medicine. In the vast subcontinent of India a wealth and variety of medicinal plants has resulted in a mass of popular remedies which are in common use today just as they were centuries ago. The drug-yielding plants of India and Pakistan are still generally used in crude form even though pharmaceutical researches are increasing in these countries.

In the Ayurvedic, Unani, and Tibbi systems of medicine, nettle is classified as diuretic, astringent, hemostatic, anthelmintic (expels worms), lithotriptic, and antiperiodic. It is generally given as a decoction for kidney disorders, and hemorrhages, especially of the uterus and kidneys. It is also employed for the treatment of jaundice and consumption. For excessive menstruation, gravel, intermittent fevers and ague, fresh nettle tea made from the young tops is administered. The juice taken in one to two tablespoonfuls is considered very effective in arresting bleeding from the lungs, nose, uterus and other internal organs. Sometimes the pulverized dry herb is used as a snuff to check bleeding from the nose. Nettle tea taken first thing in the morning is employed to purify the blood, strengthen the system and to clear the skin. The seeds are classified as diuretic, astringent and tonic.

The Inherent Power of Herbs to Heal

A plant such as nettle, which is repeatedly cited in every corner of the globe as a remedy of similar depth and scope, owes its reputation to only one thing—its inherent healing power. While everything else in the world changes, the therapeutic value of herbs remains consistently the same. One day men and women everywhere will fully realize that the gentle influence of Nature's medicine is the only real antidote for the afflicted body and the distressed mind.

5

SAGE: THE HERITAGE HERB
FOR GOOD HEALTH

The common garden sage is a well-known culinary herb used especially in poultry dressings and sauces for fish. At one time it was employed in the brewing of ale. It is a perennial plant reaching about two feet in height, bearing blue flowers variegated with purple and white. The leaves are of a grayish-green color sometimes tinged with purple or red. There are several varieties but all possess medicinal properties.

Former Uses

The Latin name for sage (*Salvia officinalis*) is a derivation of *salvere* meaning "to be in good health." In former times the plant was used medicinally for so many ailments that a 14th century writer asked, "How can a man die who has sage in his garden?" John Wesley claimed that the use of sage tea had fully answered his expectations as a remedy for palsy. He said, "my hand is as steady as it was at fifteen." Theophrastus, Pliny, and other early writers speak of the plant. According to Hippocrates it was "written that after a pestilence the people of Egypt were told to drink sage tea to make their women fertile and thus replenish the population." Folk-sayings relating to the alleged healing virtues of the herb were numerous. For example:

> Sage soothes the nerves and by its powerful might
> Pagets and palsies often puts to flight.

In herbal lore the use of the plant was associated with the health of the spleen. It was venerated as a sacred herb capable of increasing the life span and exerting a rejuvenating action on the eyes, brain, and glands. Gerard wrote that he had found sage effective for "quickening of the senses and memory, strengthening the sinews and restoring health to those suffering from palsies of moist cause, removing shaking and trembling of limbs." The plant was also employed for the night sweats of tuberculosis. To assist digestion, it was added to sweetmeats following a heavy meal. Cardiac cordials were once made of sage flowers mixed with cinnamon and brandy.

Father Kneipp, the famous European healer, gives the following information on the use of the herb:

Those who have a garden near the house, will not forget when replanting it, the pretty ornamental sage plant. I have often seen the passers-by take a leaf and rub their teeth with it. This proves that sage has a cleansing power.

Old, suppurating wounds, if washed with a decoction of sage, will quickly heal.

Sage tea will remove phlegm from the palate, throat, or stomach.

Sage boiled as tea in wine and water, purifies the liver and kidneys.

Powder from this medicinal plant, sprinkled on the food like pepper, sugar or cinnamon, operates against the given complaints in the same manner as the tea.

AN EXPLORER'S EXPERIENCE WITH SAGE AS HIS LIFE SAVER

During his travels through the interior of Africa, Le Vaillent gives an account of the plant medicine used by the natives. He reports that these primitive people administered a herbal remedy which cured him of quinsy after he had considered his case hopeless.

Due to severe swelling of the throat and tongue, Le Vaillent could only communicate by signs. For almost a week he had despaired of his life, and his breathing had become so dangerously impeded that he expected to suffocate at any moment. He was visited during the evening by a party of natives who took an interest in his condition and pledged themselves to help him.

A hot herbal poultice was bound to his throat, and additional covering placed over this to retain the heat as long as possible. As soon as the poultice began to cool it was immediately replaced with another, and the hot poulticing continued throughout the night. In addition a gargle was prepared from the same plant and used repeatedly. By daybreak the inflammation and swelling had greatly subsided and Le Vaillent could breathe more freely. He says that both methods of using the herbal remedy were continued, and by the third day he considered himself completely well.

Determined to examine the plant which had restored his health, he was astonished to find that, "Nothing in the country was more common; it grew all around the camp and was to be met with in every direction." Le Vaillent says that the herb was a species of ordinary sage, about two feet in height, with a balsamic taste and fragrant odor.

What Sage Generally Contains

In pharmaceutical writings, sage is listed among the natural antiseptics. It contains a volatile oil, tannin, resin, and a bitter principle. The oil is composed of pinene, camphor, salvene, and cineol. Brieskorn and Schlumprecht (*Arch. Pharm.*, 1951, 284, 239) discovered ursolic acid in sage leaves. Sage oil contains bactericidal properties (Brieskorn, *Arch. Pharm.*, 1950, 283, 33).[1]

THE FINDINGS OF SCIENTIFIC STUDIES OF SAGE

Sage is highly regarded as a medicinal agent in many European countries, especially Germany. In *Pflanzliche Arzneizubersitungen*, Czetsch-Lindenwald reported that the predominant and best known effect of sage is the secretion-inhibitory action produced by the volatile oil.[2] This action was known in the old days, and breast-feeding mothers used sage tea as a domestic remedy to dry up the milk when weaning the child. Records show that the old-time family physician also recommended it for this purpose. As an example, Dr. W. Fox wrote: "Whoever has inflammation or gatherings

---

[1] Osol-Farrar-Pratt, *The Dispensatory of the United States of America* (25th Ed.).
[2] *Ibid.*

or sore breasts, can by this herb cause the milk thoroughly to leave in a few days."

Scientific experiments were described by Köcher in which he succeeded in almost entirely counteracting the excessive sweating produced by a drug called *pilocarpine* by the administration of sage extracts. Delphaut *et al.* (*Compt. rend. soc. biol.*, 1941, 135, 1458) reported that the temperature of normal guinea pigs as well as the artificially induced fever of other guinea pigs was reduced by the employment of sage extracts.[3]

According to medical literature the volatile oil of sage has been found to possess spasmolytic properties. When a drug was used on rats to induce contractions of the intestines the effect was immediately relieved by an emulsion of sage oil, or the tincture. However, only a slight beneficial action was observed by the use of the aqueous extract of sage.[4]

Modern Uses

Sage has been found to have an action on the cortex of the brain which is said to be beneficial in mental exhaustion, strengthening the ability to concentrate. It has also been found to insure relaxation in cases of general hypersensitivity and cerebrospinal irritation. According to Dr. A. Comstock, an infusion of the Rocky Mountain variety acts as a powerful diaphoretic (stimulating perspiration) when taken hot, and as an active diuretic (stimulating secretion of urine) when used cold.

Sage is also said to be distinctly tonic and of value in the treatment of fevers. Medical herbalists employ the herb in conditions of tonsillitis, quinsy, and ulceration of the mouth and throat. For these purposes a preparation is made by pouring a half-pint of hot malt vinegar over one ounce of sage leaves. A half-pint of water is added. This is taken frequently in wineglassful doses and is also used as a gargle.

Extracts and infusions of sage are currently employed in Europe for night sweats and neurasthenia. The tincture and volatile oil are used for bronchitis, inflammation of the throat, and to inhibit lactation in weaning. A considerable number of sage preparations are employed in various European countries as gargles, mouthwashes, and to check ex-

[3] *Ibid.*
[4] *Ibid.*

cessive flow of saliva. Also it has been used for the treatment of bleeding gums.

The following item appeared in *Health From Herbs:*[5]

Garden sage, a simple aromatic astringent, has recently undergone a series of tests. As most herbalists know, it makes an excelent gargle for sore throats and needs no introduction into the treatment of aphthous ulcers. It has been used with success for pharyngitis, Vincent's angina, stomatitis, and glossitis (inflammation of the tongue).

A bactericide and fungicide (antiseptics) of subtle and penetrating power, it scores a definite victory over penicillin-resistant substances and common oral pathogens. It is singularly helpful in oral thrush (a fungus disease of the mouth).

REPORTED MISCELLANEOUS USES OF SAGE

Bartram tells us that an infusion of sage made by steeping a handful of the leaves in one pint of boiling water and covering until cool, is a remedy for laryngitis, pharyngitis and also for catarrh. He advises one wineglassful of the strained infusion three times daily between meals. Bartram says that this remedy is of special value for sores of the tongue or mouth (buccal ulcers), and tonsillitis. In his opinion:

Tonsils should not be removed unless it is really necessary. They are the center of lymphatic protection of the throat. They are one of nature's guards against infectious disease. Seven of the vocal muscles originate in the sheath of the tonsils. When extirpated, the undue relaxation of these muscles shortens the vocal range much impairs pharyngeal control and vocal resonance.[6]

As a Gargle

Dr. Skelton recommends the following herbal formula for use as a gargle:[7]

Garden sage	one ounce
Cayenne (in powder)	one drachm
Boiling water	one pint

[5] July–August 1967, p. 111,
[6] *Grace,* Autumn 1960, p. 74.
[7] *Science and Practice of Herbal Medicine.*

Infuse twelve hours, strain, filter, and add tincture of blood-root,[8] one ounce. In inflammation and ulceration of the throat from quinsy, etc., this is one of the best gargles that can possibly be employed.

As a Hair Tonic

Many people use sage as a hair conditioner and/or to darken gray hair. Two heaping teaspoonfuls of sage and two of ordinary tea are placed in a pint container and filled with boiling water. This is covered and heated gently in an oven for two hours. The longer it is permitted to remain in the oven the darker the solution will become. When the steeping period has ended, the liquid is strained. A tablespoonful of brandy or vodka is added to preserve the preparation if it is to be kept for more than a few days. This cold infusion is rubbed into the roots of the hair every night. Used externally, a simple infusion of sage combined with equal parts of rosemary is said to stimulate the growth of the hair.

HEALTH VALUE OF CHIA SEEDS FROM SAGE

Under the name of *chia*, the seeds of one or more varieties of sage were employed as food by the Indians of California, Arizona, New Mexico, Nevada, and Mexico. The most important of the chia-yielding sages is known as *S. columbaria*. When hunting in the rugged mountains of the wilderness, the Indians carried a supply of the seeds and ate them for energy and endurance. It is said that the red man could subsist on them alone for days if necessary. The seeds were also eaten to help fortify the body against the exhaustive effects of the blistering desert heat.

A few years ago a health-minded group in Los Angeles decided to put chia seed to a strenuous field test. Separating themselves into two groups, one team adopted a diet fortified with chia seeds, while the other group ate anything they pleased. The test was one of endurance, a 36-hour hike to the top of Mount Wilson and to the woods beyond. The group of eight men and four women who had used chia seeds finished the hike without a single dropout, four hours and 27 minutes ahead of the competing group that did not use

[8] *Sanguinaria canadensis.*

the seeds. Only five members of the competing 12 member team were able to finish the hike.

Paul C. Bragg, Ph.T., noted physical culture authority, declared: "This test proved definitely that the little chia seed has a special nutritional something. What this 'something' is has to be discovered by the biochemist."

Use of Chia Seeds Persisted for Centuries

Whether or not the biochemist ferrets out the secret of chia seeds, they have been ministering to the needs of mankind for centuries. The Spanish invaders of the New World found that chia was a popular therapeutic food of the Indians. The seed was so highly valued during the time of Montezuma II that it was accepted as payment for taxes! In his account of the Portola Expedition of 1769, Cortanso mentions an Indian practice of toasting chia. Some of the earliest Mexican natives cultivated the seed as an important cereal. Chia was listed among the foods of the Old West in Bancroft's Compendium of 1883.

In her book, *The Wild Flowers of California* (1897), M. E. Parsons quoted a Dr. Bard who stated, "One tablespoonful of chia seeds was sufficient to sustain for 24 hours an Indian on a forced march." Dr. Bard also reported that the seed is "exceeding nutritious and was readily borne by the stomach when that organ refused to tolerate food." For internal inflammation such as colitis, the Indians added the ground seeds to their diet. They also used the seeds in the form of a poultice for healing wounds.

Chia's Power-Packed Nutritional Values

Although chia seeds were used for centuries as an endurance and energy food by the Indians, it is only in recent years that modern man has begun to appreciate their nutritional value. Chia seeds are remarkably rich in certain minerals such as potassium, copper, calcium, phosphorus, iron, magnesium, iodine, and an unknown factor yet to be identified. They are particularly high in the vitamin B complex and also contain protein and vitamins E and D. (Chia seeds can be bought in health food stores and some herb companies carry them in stock.)

MANY WAYS OF PREPARING CHIA SEEDS

It is difficult for the body to assimilate any kind of seeds in their whole form. For this reason chia seeds are ground or soaked before using and can be added to the diet in a number of different ways. For example, a mucilaginous drink may be prepared by steeping a single teaspoonful of the seeds in a tumblerful of cold water for 12 hours (overnight). This beverage is ready for use by morning and may be sweetened with honey. From one to one-and-a-half teaspoons of the ground seeds may be sprinkled over salads or mixed with salad dressing; it can also be stirred into a bowl of soup or into a cup of cottage cheese; a half teaspoonful can be added to scrambled eggs just before the eggs are removed from the skillet. As a spread, it may be mixed with margarine or butter. From one to one-and-a-half teaspoons of the ground seeds can be added to each cup of liquid used in pancakes or other batters. About two teaspoonfuls may be mixed with half a pint of yogurt. These are just a few examples. No doubt you will find many other ways in which you can fortify your diet with valuable, nutritive chia seeds.

Make the Test Yourself

The cultivation and harvesting of chia seeds is now becoming a full-time industry in Arizona and adjacent states. Paul C. Bragg, the famous health authority, says:

> Make the chia test yourself. See if adding chia seeds to your diet doesn't give you the extra "push" that will let you finish every busy day of your life with a hop, skip, and a jump. Chia seed is for everyone—no age limits. All can enjoy this little bundle of "go-power."

Once again mankind is discovering the botanical riches of the deserts, woods, and fields. Nature is still man's greatest apothecary.

(*Additional Reference:* "Chia Seed, Energy-Building Food of the Ancients, Regaining Popularity," *Naturopath,* April 1966.)

6

THE ONION: BULB OF VALUABLE
NATURAL MEDICINALS

The onion (*Allium cepa*) is a member of the lily family and is one of the oldest vegetables known to man. It has been cultivated since the remote past as references in Hebrew and Sanskrit literature indicate. Because of the sheaths which envelop the bulb, the Egyptians regarded it as a symbol of the universe. In giving an account of the different deities worshipped in Egypt. Lucian remarks that "the inhabitants of Pelusium adore the onion," while Pliny tells us that "the Onions and Garlic are among the Gods of Egypt, and by these they make their oaths."

It has been suggested that it was probably an act of ascetic self-denial which caused the Egyptian priests to abstain from the use of onions as food. This sacrifice was considered so great by the common people that they regarded the priests with awe.

FOLK CUSTOMS ASSOCIATED WITH ONION

The ancients connected certain aromas with the supernatural, and employed incense, cloves, musk and other fragrant botanicals for invoking good luck, as counter-charms against witchcraft, and to influence conjurations. Because of its strong penetrating odor, the onion was cut into slices and suspended or placed in every room for purging or protecting the home from "evil spirits." In the morning all the slices were immediately removed, burned, and replaced with fresh ones. This method was also used during the epidemics and plagues to prevent contagion. In 1897 Dr. Fernie wrote:

The onion has a very sensitive organism and absorbs all morbid matter that comes in its way. During our last epidemic of cholera it puzzled the sanitary inspectors of a northern town why the tenants of one cottage in an infected row were not touched by the plague. At last, someone noticed a net of onions hanging in the fortunate house, and on examination all these proved to have become diseased. But whilst welcoming this protective quality, the danger must be remembered of eating an onion which shows signs of decay, for it cannot be told what may have caused this distemper.

Folk Customs Still Followed Today in Some Locations

The practice of placing onions around the home as a disease preventative has persisted to this day. People who follow this folk custom firmly maintain that sliced onions do indeed act as traps, absorbing dangerous germs that would otherwise be attracted to the humans in the house. They claim that as long as the onions are burned every day, all is safe; but whether there is an epidemic in the neighborhood or not, these believers insist an onion that has been bruised, peeled, or sliced for more than a few hours should never be eaten.

One Doctor's View

It is interesting to note that a British physician of modern times has suggested that the practice of hanging sliced onions in rooms as a means of preventing influenza should be scientifically investigated for biochemical validity. Writing to the *British Medical Journal* (11–16–65) Dr. A. J. Pearson of Catterick, Yorkshire, said: "Occasionally these old customs do have a grain of truth behind them."

THE MEDICINE BULB

Long before the advent of aspirins, tranquilizers and other modern drugs, the onion was a vital standby as a food medicine in almost every household. Folk remedies calling for the use of this humble vegetable were very popular and could be found in various periodicals, almanacs, magazines and books. Gleaning through a number of these early publications we find that onions were used domestically for almost every ailment imaginable ranging from bronchitis to insect stings. A few examples may be cited.

VARIOUS FOLK REMEDIES USING ONIONS

An onion is roasted, split, and applied to *suppurating tumors.*

For treating a *jammed finger or toe,* one tablespoonful of olive oil is poured over one or two large grated onions. This is applied as a thick poultice around the injured part. It is said that the pain will subside in a few minutes and any complications which may have otherwise set in will be prevented. Poultices of pulped onions generously salted was another old-time method of treating such injuries.

To remove *calluses* the bulb is cut in half, placed in a jar filled with strong wine vinegar and left to steep for about three hours. The onion halves are then securely bound to the calluses just before retiring at night and allowed to remain until morning. This method is repeated for several nights. Each morning the top layers of the calluses (which have softened) are removed.

A piece of onion with a little salt added is applied to *scalding burns* to draw out the heat.

Onions pounded with a mallet are applied as *poultices for ulcers, boils, abscesses, and insect stings.*

For *protruding piles,* two cups of finely chopped or grated *green* onions are mixed with wheat flour and fried in animal fat until the mixture resembles a salve. A thick layer of the warm unguent is spread on a cloth and bound to the affected area just before bedtime. The poultice is removed in the morning and another prepared that evening and applied again before retiring. It is said that this remedy will relieve the condition in two days.

The water in which onions are boiled is drunk as a tea to *eliminate retention of fluid in the system.*

A finely chopped onion mixed with sugar is spread on a cloth and applied to *sprains.*

To remove brown spots or blemishes from the skin, one-half teaspoonful of onion juice is mixed with one teaspoon of vinegar and used as a wash.

For rheumatism accompanied by shooting pains, bran is boiled in water and the painful part soaked in the solution for 15 minutes just before retiring. As soon as the soaking period has ended, several onions are separated into "leaves" and spread evenly on the affected area and bound with a cloth. The patient then arises around midnight, removes the poultice and applies water to the rheumatic part. The onion poultice is then bound in place again and allowed to remain until morning. This remedy is repeated every night until results are obtained.

Severe headache is treated by pulping three or four onions which are generously salted and mixed with olive oil. The mixture is spread on a cloth and bound to the head. This has been reputed to relieve a headache in two hours.

For itchy feet (*athlete's foot*) onion juice is rubbed between the toes two or three times every day until the condition clears.

Warts have been said to eventually disappear when treated perseveringly with raw onion dipped in salt.

For the *relief of bronchitis, asthma, or other respiratory disorders* a raw onion is sliced and eaten, or the fumes inhaled. As an accessory treatment, crushed onions are spread over a warm flannel which has been sprinkled with camphorated oil and this is applied to the chest and back.

Even *baldness* has been treated with onions, provided the hair roots are still alive. For this purpose ten parts of onion juice are mixed with ten parts of crude cod liver oil and five parts of raw egg yolk. This is beaten together thoroughly and applied to the scalp once a week. Other recipes have simply advised rubbing the scalp with a fresh slice of onion once or twice every day.

Onion Remedies of the "Family Physician"

The onion occupied an honored place in the *materia medica* of a number of old-time family physicians. Dr. Fernie gives his opinion of the medicinal value of the bulb in his book, *Herbal Simples*. He says that onions used in small amounts assist digestion and stimulate circulation, but when eaten freely they disagree. A syrup made from the juice of an onion mixed with honey is an excellent remedy for phlegm when the lungs are congested and breathing is difficult. In addition he says:

Onions, when eaten at night by those who are not feverish, will promote sleep and induce perspiration. The late Frank Buckland confirmed this statement. He said, "I am sure the essential oil of onions has soporific powers. In my own case it never fails. If I am much pressed with work and feel that I am not disposed to sleep, I eat two or three small onions and the effect is magical."

When sliced and applied externally, the raw onion serves by its pungent and essential oil to quicken the circulation and to redden the skin of the particular surface treated in this way; very usefully so in the case of an unbroken chilblain, or to counteract neuralgic pain; but in its crude state the bulb is not emollient or demulcent. If employed as a poultice for earache, or broken chilblains, the onion should be roasted, so as to modify its acrid oil. When there is a constant and painful discharge of fetid matter from the ear, or where an abscess is threatened, with pain, heat, and swelling, a hot poultice of roasted onions will be found very useful and will mitigate the pain. The juice of a sliced raw onion is alkaline, and will quickly relieve the acid venom of a sting from a wasp or bee, if applied immediately to the parts. . . .

Drs. Wood and Ruddock also wrote of the remedial use of the onion. Here are a few brief excerpts:[1]

Croup. The French remedy for croup is onions. Cut them into thin slices, sprinkling each slice with a layer of sugar. This will soon yield a syrup, of which a teaspoonful should be taken about every 15 minutes until relief is obtained.

Bronchitis.

Simple syrup—three tablespoonfuls
Onion juice—two tablespoonfuls
Dose: One teaspoonful before meals.

Or, slice the onions, sprinkle sugar over them; let stand an hour or two, then mash and press out the juice. Dose: one teaspoonful three times a day and before retiring at night. In severe cases, every three hours.

MODERN HEALTH USE OF ONIONS

Properties Contained in Onions

Raw onions contain an acrid volatile oil, phosphorus, cal-

[1] *Encyclopedia of Health and Home.*

cium, magnesium, sulphur, sodium, potassium, iron, starch, acetic and phosphoric acids with phosphate and citrate of lime. They also contain vitamins A, B, C, and traces of iodine, zinc and silicon.

A plant hormone, *glucokinin*, which resembles insulin in its ability to reduce the sugar level was discovered in the onion by Collip and Külz. This has been confirmed by other scientists. Onions have also been found to contain a substance which stimulates the digestive secretions of the pancreas.

Medical Use of Onions

Dr. Alfred Vogel of Switzerland gives an account of the medicinal use of onions in his book, *The Nature Doctor*. He tells us that raw onions chopped or grated and applied as a compress on the neck can often relieve or completely dispel the pains of headache, toothache, earache, and inflammation of the eyes, especially after a chill. Onion compresses applied to the soles of the feet are helpful when a patient is feverish with head congestion. Dr. Vogel also cites the following:

> *Colds.* A "streaming" cold, the symptoms of which are bland lachrymation and excoriating nasal discharge, will always be helped by onions. Their Latin name is *Allium cepa* and as such they are well known to every Homeopath. What you have got to do to get rid of that type of cold is simple enough: just cut a slice from a fresh, raw onion and immerse it quickly in a glass of hot water. Do not let it remain in the water for longer than a second or so. Take little sips of this water throughout the day. If the above-mentioned symptoms correspond with your own, your cold will soon have left you. In addition, you may cut an onion in half and put it on your bedside table so you can breathe in the smell during your sleep. An onion poultice bandaged around the neck is good too, and the sniffing of salt water, lemon juice or calcium powder up the nostrils also often helps to terminate a cold.

Onion Therapy by an English Doctor[2]

As a treatment of bronchitis, Dr. Eric Powell of England tells us that onion poultices applied to the chest are excellent.

[2] *Fitness And Health From Herbs,* December 1963, p. 42.

He also says that onions are very antiseptic and good cleansers of the system but they are not as effective or powerful as garlic. He points out that he has known of cases of severe lung disorders which have been successfully treated with onions. Some people cannot eat this vegetable however, without suffering from gas. But Dr. Powell assures us that this effect will not occur if the onion is taken homeopathically where in some instances it is even more effective for a "certain type of cold."

The cold to which Dr. Powell refers here is the same type previously mentioned by Dr. Vogel, that is, a cold characterized by watering of the eyes and a constant watery discharge from the nose. For this disorder, Dr. Powell recommends taking onion in the homeopathic form third potency: "Dose: five pills every hour until well." He considers the onion so effective when these particular symptoms are in evidence that he tells us that even a few sniffs at a cut bulb have often brought prompt relief. It is his opinion, however, that the onion will have no effect on any other type of cold.

In addition he says, "Onions, raw, cooked or potentized are also most helpful in cases of urinary weakness when urine control is difficult. They act as a tonic to the bladder sphincter muscle."

Onion Therapies in India

The onion is included in the Ayurvedic and Unani systems of medicine in India. The juice of onions mixed with honey is given to counteract seminal weakness. A few drops of the juice are placed in the nose to arrest nosebleed. Onion or garlic is used as smelling salts for fainting spells. A decoction made from the bulb is given as a diuretic in strangury. (Strangury is a condition characterized by a frequent and urgent desire to urinate; the urine is passed with great difficulty in drops and in painful spasms.) A compress made of roasted onions is applied for protruding or inflamed piles. Onions are also used for prolapse of the anus, scurvy, skin diseases, coughs, colds, and boils.

Onion Therapies Used by a French Doctor

A French army doctor used fresh onion juice to treat grippe patients by giving them 200 cubic centimeters of the juice in hot tea, divided into three doses, each day. This treatment was administered as soon as the disease had first started. In two days the fever was gone. There were no fatalities among the 80 patients who were given the onion treatment.

Because of the strong diuretic action onions produce, some French doctors have employed them as a three day treatment for the elimination of fluid in the cardiac and pleural sacs. This treatment has also been used in some cases of dropsy caused by kidney or liver disease.

MYSTERIOUS M-RAYS FOUND IN ONIONS

Some years ago, Professor Gurwitch, a Russian electro-biologist announced that a peculiar type of ultraviolet radiation called "mitogenetic" radiation was emitted by onions. These radiations appeared to stimulate cell activity in general and produce a rejuvenating effect on the system. Garlic and ginseng were also found to emit the same radiation.

Professor Lakhovsky, another Russian electrobiologist who had also studied M-Rays, stated that a type of wild garlic which grows in certain parts of Siberia is eaten by aged men in the belief that it rejuvenates them.

It may be pointed out that for a very long time onions have figured prominently as a home remedy in India against coughs and colds by suspending them near the patient. That the beneficial effect might have been due to M-Rays was of course not imagined.

Other researchers have found that a similarly charged electrical field is also produced by penicillin.

A WARNING ABOUT OVEREATING ONIONS

Experiments conducted by scientists have shown that anemia can be induced by overeating onions. A group of volunteer medical students consumed over two pounds of cooked onions every day for five days in addition to their regular diet. At the end of this period all showed symptoms of anemia which was confirmed by laboratory examination. Within one week after ending their self-induced onion binge all the experimenters had successfully recovered. Similar experiments with animals have demonstrated the same anemic effect. Moderation in all things including eating onions is one rule that should never be violated.

7

HEALING PLANTS FROM THE SEA

A report from Reuters appeared on the front page of the *San Francisco Chronicle*, January 2, 1968. It was printed as follows:

March of the Fearless Hares

Thousands of fearless and hungry hares were reported on the march in far eastern Siberia.

The Soviet news agency Tass quoted a report from the area saying the hares trooped through the streets of settlements in the Kamchatka peninsula "showing utter disregard for the frenzied barking of dogs."

When they reached the coast of the Sea of Okhotsk, "the hares ravenously attacked sea kale (a kind of plant in the cabbage family) washed ashore by the tide," Tass said. Then they "marched back to the tundra in the same organized manner," the report said.

Experts were quoted as saying the hares were believed to be suffering from "an acute mineral hunger."

Instinct does not reason, it obeys and is none other than the ever-present life principle which causes plants to turn towards the sun and animals to seek their proper food. This marvelous instinctive wisdom directed the desperate hares to the richest source of minerals in the world—the sea. Consequently the animals were certain to find either some potent coastal plant such as sea kale or any one of a variety of seaweeds washed upon the beach.

For years nutritionists have pointed to sea vegetation as a rich source of minerals and vitamins which as yet has scarcely been tapped. Due to overcropping, erosion, and the widespread use of chemical fertilizers our food today does not contain the minerals and vitamins that it once did. In general the total mineral content of sea plants is from ten to 20 times higher than any land-grown food.

SEA ALGAE

Seaweeds are known under the collective name of algae. Over 435 varieties have been discovered and these are generally grouped into three kinds depending on color—the brown, the red and the green. Seaweeds have no roots such as land plants do, nor do they have branches and stalks in the same sense. They cling to submerged rocks, wharves, or pilings by means of "holdfasts" and have nothing that resembles seeds, flowers, or fruits.

That seaweeds are extremely rich in vitamins, minerals and trace elements is not surprising. For ages, rain waters have washed precious topsoil into tumbling rivers and streams which have emptied their valuable contents into the seas. Soluble mineral salts eroded and leached from soil, rock, and forest humus possess the constituents necessary for life, both in the sea and on land. The proportion of minerals in the sea water on which algae thrive has been found to be almost identical with that in human blood.

SEAWEED AS FOOD AND MEDICINE

The use of seaweed as food and medicine is not new. Emperor Shen-ung wrote of their value as early as 3000 B.C. It is said that one of the books written by Pythagoras over 2500 years ago dealt with the value of the sea onion as a medicine. During the time of Confucius a poem about a housewife cooking seaweed appeared in the *Chinese Book of Poetry* written between 800 and 600 B.C. In that era seaweed was regarded as such an exquisite delicacy that it was offered as a sacrificial food to the gods.

The ancient empire of Japan has also known of the importance of seaweeds for a very long time and the harvesting of marine crops is a thriving industry in that country today. The people of Japan refer to seaweed as "Heaven Grass" so great is their regard for its nutritional and medicinal value. Diving girls (*ama*) of coastal villages probe marine gardens of offshore lagoons where the algae used for food and medicine abounds. These mermaids are graceful, hardy divers with superb physiques and have become a proud Japanese tradition. The people of Japan say that women, rather than men, are engaged in diving for "Heaven Grass" because they are better suited to withstand the icy temperatures of the seas and can hold their breath much longer under water.

Many varieties of "Heaven Grass" are used in the Japanese diet depending on the flavor and nutritional value desired. One of their favorites is called *Asakusa Nori* which comes in thin sheets. It is dried, crumbled and sprinkled on food or toasted by holding it over a flame for a few seconds. This plant is unique among the seaweeds as it is almost entirely salt-free. Another favorite delicacy of the Japanese is called *suski* which consists of fish and rice wrapped in seaweed. This blend has become so popular that the vacuum-packed tins in which it is sold are now labeled in English as well as Japanese. Other varieties of sea vegetation are prepared as noodles and served in soups or with rice. Seaweeds are also used in the Japanese diet as ingredients in relishes, cakes, puddings, and beverages.

USES OF KELP

One of the most commonly known of the brown seaweeds is kelp (*Fucus vesiculosis*) which is also called bladderwrack. These are long whip-shaped plants which range from five to ten feet in length (along the Atlantic coast) to the giant kelp of the Pacific which reach a length of several hundred feet. In the Southern hemisphere these plants form submarine forests of enormous size.

Professional guides in the land of Tibet always carry a small supply of kelp with them. When ascending to heights at which the air becomes rarefied causing difficult breathing and labored straining of the leg muscles they take a pinch of dried kelp and feel a burst of new energy. They say the strength of the gods is in the plant.

Iodine Source

One of the most important of the trace elements present in kelp is iodine. This mineral is essential for the proper functioning of the thyroid which manufactures the hormone *thy-*

roxin. If an adequate amount of iodine is not provided in the diet the thyroid gland is forced to overwork and becomes enlarged in an effort to make up for the deficiency. This enlargement is known as goitre. In ancient times burnt ashes of the sponge were given to drive out the "evil spirit" which caused swelling of the neck (goitre). The sponge as well as seaweed contains iodine!

"Goitre Belts"

Iodine comes from the sea and is distributed over nearby land areas by windswept sea sprays and rainfall. Foods grown near the seacoasts contain considerable amounts of iodine but the same foods grown in the central part of the United States, or other land areas which are remote from the seas, are deficient in this precious trace material. Localities where the condition of goitre is common are called "goitre belts." According to the *Food and Life Yearbook of Agriculture*, "Lack of iodine in the water and food supply is considered the chief if not the only cause of simple goitre." This enlargement is also seen among coastal dwellers who dislike seafood and whose diets are not provided with sufficient amounts of iodine-bearing vegetables or other foods containing this important mineral. Some doctors have successfully treated conditions of simple goitre solely by the administration of kelp.

A NUTRITIONALIST'S VIEWS ON HEALTH VALUE OF IODINE

Adelle Davis,[1] the noted nutritionalist, tells us that:

In Japan, where seaweed is used as food, abnormalities of the thyroid are non-existent; and the average daily intake of iodine is approximately three milligrams. In contrast, hundreds of thousands of Americans have such underactive thyroids, caused in part by iodine insufficiency, that they must take thyroid medication.

Adequate iodine is absolutely essential to health, and it, of all nutrients, is probably most easily lost in the urine. Iodized salt should be used exclusively, but to

[1] *Let's Get Well* (New York: Harcourt, Brace & World, 1965), p. 402.

eat enough salt to supply three milligrams of iodine daily is certainly not advisable. In my opinion, the diet of every person, especially anyone who is ill, should be supplemented with one teaspoon of granular kelp daily unless a prescription for iodine can be obtained.

USING IODINE FOR OBESITY CONTROL

Obesity is rarely seen among the Polynesians and other races who incorporate seaweeds as a regular part of their daily diet. T. J. Lyle, M.D.,[2] says:

> This plant [kelp] has a reputation as an anti-fat, claiming that it diminishes fat without in any respect injuring the health. It influences the mucous membranes and the lymphatics. It is a gently stimulating and toning alterant. It is one of those slow, persistent agents that require time to accomplish the desired results. It is stimulating to the absorbents and especially influences the fatty globules. Its best action is observed in individuals having a cold, torpid, clammy skin and loose flabby rolls of fat. It is an agent that gives better results in cases of morbid obesity than in those cases of a healthy character. . . .

Dr. Powell[3] of England points out that kelp has a regulating effect and says that, "while it aids in the reduction of fat it may be taken with perfect safety by the thin, as it is a normalizer." He adds: "Indeed, I have known thin people to put on weight when taking Fucus [kelp]."

H. E. Kirschner, M.D., tells us that ocean water is one of the richest sources of the vital life-sustaining mineral elements known to science. He says:[4]

> I shall present just a few in the following list: Aluminum, barium, bismuth, boron, calcium, chlorine, chromium, cobalt, copper, gallium, iodine, magnesium, manganese, molybdenum, phosphorus, potassium, silicon, silver, sodium, strontium, sulphur, tin, titanium, vanadium, and zirconium—nearly thirty in all!

Isn't it wonderful that a Wise Providence has placed

[2] *Physio-Medical Therapeutics, Materia Medica and Pharmacy.*
[3] *Health From Herbs,* November 1957, p. 413.
[4] *Nature's Healing Grasses* (Riverside, Calif.: H. C. White Publications, 1960).

all of the above-named minerals in common seaweed, or kelp? And what is still more wonderful, the plant, in extracting and assimilating these vital mineral elements from ocean-water, miraculously converts them from unavailable, *inorganic* substances into *organic minerals* which the body can utilize for health!

Seaweeds also provide abundant amounts of vitamins A, C, and D, and are rich in the vitamin B complex. In addition they contain the anti-sterility vitamin S and anti-hemorrhagic vitamin K.

Dr. Kirschner says that for many years kelp has demonstrated its value as a remedy for human disorders which result from deficiency conditions. He adds that it has been particularly successful in relieving glandular disturbances which frequently result in such ailments as goitre, anemia, rickets, stomach trouble, headache, kidney disorders, eczema, constipation, asthma, neuritis and low vitality.

VARIOUS WAYS OF USING KELP IN THE DIET

According to Dr. Kirschner, kelp may be taken in a variety of ways. In its powdered form it can be added to salads, cottage cheese, soups, fruit juices, or sprinkled on baked potatoes. Or it can be used as a salt substitute for seasoning; as an ingredient in bread or cookies; in easy-to-take tablets, as a nutritional mineral supplement; as a vegetable gelatin for making desserts; or in flake form as one of the "live foods" in the popular therapeutic "Green Drink."

Beneficial Effects Noted on the Body

With regard to the uses of this valuable seaweed, Dr. Kirschner writes:

> We are indebted to the late Dr. Guyon Richards, famous authority on Radiesthesia, for discovering the beneficial effects of kelp on the reproductive organs— the prostate gland, uterus, and testes and ovaries. Dr. Richards is also to be credited with much of the information we now have relating to the remedial and normalizing action of kelp on the thyroid, the sensory nerves, meninges, arteries, pylorus, colon, liver, gall bladder, pancreas, bile ducts and the kidneys. Few

remedies, in fact, have such a wide range of action on diseased organs of the human body. . . .

With so many of my fellow Americans suffering from various forms of stomach disorder, and chronic constipation, with its resulting *toxemia*, what a blessing is in this simple remedy—*kelp*. We physicians now know that a host of physical disorders, and even some forms of insanity are due to *toxemia* (toxic substances coming from a foul, polluted colon). These poisons accumulate in the colon and are absorbed into the blood stream, causing such serious complaints as rheumatism, nervous disorders, kidney trouble and severe headache.

For those of my readers who may be suffering from arterial trouble, it is good to know that "kelp is an arterial cleansing agent, and gives 'tone' to the walls of the blood vessels. Hence it is helpful in some cases of arterial tension (high blood pressure). Some practitioners believe that kelp helps to remove deposits from the walls of the arteries, and restores their elasticity, thereby lengthening the life span."

What a debt of gratitude we all owe to such persevering pioneers as Philip R. Park, and other devoted researchers in the field of health, who have brought the benefits of life-sustaining kelp to us in so many attractive easy-to-take forms. These fine products can be found on the shelves of all leading health food stores and up-to-date natural food centers. As a physician, my advice to you is: "Put *kelp* on your shopping list today."

CARRAGEEN

Carrageen (*Chondrus crispus*), commonly known as Irish moss, is a small sturdy seaweed from six to twelve inches long that grows on submerged rocks beneath the level of low tide. In shape it somewhat resembles the parsley plant. The color of carrageen varies from green to a reddish-purple, depending on the season of the year and other factors, such as location and the amount of light available. When dried it is considerably darker. Commercial harvesters remove carrageen from submerged rocks with special rakes. An experienced raker can sometimes harvest a thousand pounds at one low tide.

Reported Uses of Carrageen

This plant has a broad spectrum of uses. In addition to the high vitamin and mineral content characteristic of seaweeds, carrageen also possesses remarkable emulsifying properties. Its semi-clear jell is used as a base for culture media in hospitals and bacteriological laboratories due to its ability to remain solid with a firm, smooth surface at the high temperatures required for cultivating various species of bacteria. Other jellies melt under requisite conditions. Its emulsion for photographic plates is also superior to that of ordinary gelatin.

Carrageen is employed as a component of some of the baby food puddings, laxatives, cough syrups, hand lotions, toothpastes, shaving creams, and jellies. Medicinally it is classified as a demulcent, pectoral, and nutrient. In reference to its employment as a remedy, the 17th edition of the U.S. Dispensatory states:

> It has been particularly recommended in chronic pectoral affections, scrofulous complaints, dysentery, diarrhea, and disorders of the kidneys and bladder. It may be used in the form of a decoction, made by boiling a pint and a half of water with half an ounce of the moss down to a pint. Sugar and lemon juice may usually be added to improve the flavor. Milk may be substituted for water when a more nutritious preparation is required. It is recommended to macerate the moss for ten minutes before submitting it to decoction and any unpleasant flavor that it may have acquired from the contact of foreign substances is thus removed.

Using Carrageen for Peptic Ulcers

Peptic ulcers have been prevented in laboratory animals by feeding them an extract made from carrageen. It was reported that this seaweed extract called *carrageenin* apparently interferes with the formation of ulcers by blocking overaction of pepsin in the stomach. These tests lend support to the theory that it is not acids but increased secretions of pepsin that causes stomach ulcers. It was found that the extract was more effective when added to the animals' drinking water.

Carrageen in the Diet

The preponderance of alkaline salts in carrageen is of

particular value in the diet of convalescents, the aged, invalids, and children. It is low in calories and possesses easily assimilated plant phosphorus, calcium and other valuable elements. Phosphorus is a constituent of every known cell and tissue in the body. Calcium is essential to sound teeth and bone structure, helps regulate heart action, assists digestion, and aids the functioning of the kidneys and other vital organs. A lack can cause leg cramps and poor muscle tone. Calcium is said to be needed in abundance during pregnancy.

The demulcent (soothing) properties of carrageen were officially recognized during World War I when gelatin derived from animal sources was unobtainable or very scarce. When properly washed and prepared, carrageen forms a semi-clear jell with only a slight flavor of its own. It is considered an excellent substitute for animal gelatin and is used to stiffen or jell blancmange, puddings, custards, and fruit molds. It is also employed to thicken soups, sauces, broths, and oriental dishes.

Carrageen Recipes[5]

Blancmange

Ingredients: one-third cup carrageen, three cups milk, one-quarter teaspoon salt, three teaspoonfuls of sugar and one teaspoonful of vanilla (or two or three bay leaves or a small amount of lemon juice) for flavoring. Method: Immerse carrageen in water for 15 minutes, drain, pick over and add with salt to milk. Cook in double boiler for 30 minutes, or in an enamel pan from ten to 15 minutes while stirring. The milk will then appear a little thicker than when put on to cook, but if cooked longer the Blancmange will be too stiff. Add sugar and flavoring; strain, and fill individual molds previously dipped in cold water. Chill and serve with stewed fruit and cream.

Irish Moss Jelly

Soak one handful of Irish moss in cold water; then stir in one quart of boiling water, and let it simmer until dissolved; add the juice of two lemons, one glass of wine, and a little cinnamon. Sweeten to taste and strain into molds.

[5] *Botanical Catalog* (Hammond, Ind.: Indiana Botanic

Mousse

Steep one-half cup carrageen in cold water for 15 minutes. Strain and put carrageen into enamel pan with one pint milk. Bring slowly to a boil, and allow to simmer very gently for not more than 20 minutes, stirring occasionally. Now stir in one teaspoonful of brown sugar or honey, and any flavoring desired. Strain liquid into a bowl. While it is still warm, stir in the freshly beaten yolk of an egg, and finally fold in the stiffly beaten white of an egg. When almost set, decoration may be added if desired. Cover closely and serve cold.

Beets in Jelly

Ingredients; one large or two medium-sized cooked beets, one pint water, one tablespoonful lemon juice, two or three peppercorns, one-quarter oz. carrageen, seasoning. Method: Cut the beet into rounds and arrange it in individual molds. Put the water, lemon juice, peppercorns, seasoning, and soaked carrageen into an enamel pan. Bring to a boil and cook for five minutes. Strain this onto the beets, and when set, serve with a green salad.

Soothing Beverage

Wash two oz. of carrageen in cold water, then put the washed moss over a low fire with two quarts of cold water, and simmer until reduced to half the quantity; it is then to be strained. A large teacupful of this should be taken every morning upon arising, without sugar or milk. However, should the subject be able to digest milk with facility, as much as one-third teacupful of boiled milk may be mixed with it. If it be found unpleasant without sugar, a very small quantity may be used; it is decidedly better, however, to dispense with sugar. In cases where the stomach at its first meal would be over-excited by tea or coffee, and chocolate would be too heavy, a cup of this decoction is exceedingly useful, and two or three hours afterwards, a regular breakfast may be taken. . . . In such cases, also, a cup of the same beverage may be taken with benefit at night and then a small portion of sherry wine, or a little brandy may be added to it, with enough sugar to make it agreeable.

As food only, carrageen is exceedingly nutritious,

and by no means disagreeable when made into soup with meat and vegetables; it is, in fact, quite equal to the far-famed bird's nest soup of the Chinese.

from *The Domestic Dictionary & Housekeeper's Manual*, 1842.

A Cosmetic Cream for a Glowing Complexion

Irish moss, one oz.; distilled water, ten oz,; glycerin, two oz.; boracic acid, one drachm; eau de cologne, one oz.

Wash the Irish moss in a little cold water, then boil gently in ten ounces of water, in a closed vessel, and strain. Add the glycerin and boracic acid, previously dissolved in one ounce of water, and cool, and finally add the eau de cologne.[6]

FURTHER VALUE OF ALGAE

Scientific tests have demonstrated that an oil obtained from certain seaweeds possesses 1000 times more of vitamins A and D than are contained in the same amount of cod liver oil. These findings tend to support the views of many scientists to the effect that the vitamins found in fish originally come from the sea vegetation on which the fish feed.

Algae—A Source of Zinc

Seaweed contains valuable amounts of zinc. This precious trace mineral is concentrated in the thyroid, sex organs, liver, and pancreas. A recent study demonstrated conclusively that an insufficient amount of zinc in the diet can cause sterility. Other studies have shown that disorders of the prostate are often traced to a deficiency of zinc; cancer and leukemia victims are found lacking in this mineral; an inadequate supply may be related to diabetes.

Dr. Walter J. Pories, Major, USAF Medical Corps, has found that zinc deficiency seems to be one of the causes of atherosclerosis. Twenty-five patients with this disease were treated with oral supplements of zinc. Dr. Pories found that all the patients have improved leg warmth and exercise tolerance and there has been no further progression of the disease.

[6] Meyer, *The Herbalist,* p. 210.

According to Pories, further trials with zinc therapy are warranted in patients with inoperable vascular disease.

Intestinal Worms

Several investigators in the Philippines used a type of seaweed called *Digenia simplex* to destroy intestinal worms. The powdered seaweed was made into a tea and found to be 73 percent effective. It was said to be non-toxic and could be given to patients without first preparing them in any way for the treatment. Scientists in the Philippines recommended further study of this matter.

Search for Anti-Cancer Properties in Seaweeds

According to a recent announcement,[1] different varieties of seaweeds will be grown and studied for possible anti-cancer agents. Under grants totaling $61,569 from the U.S. Public Health Service, two research firms will cultivate algae in germ-free environments. The plant extracts will be tested on animal cancers according to the National Cancer Institute.

[1] *Health Bulletin,* July 29, 1967, Vol. 5, No. 30.

8

HERBAL HEALTH SECRETS OF THE AMERICAN INDIANS

When the early pioneers reached the shores of the New World over 2000 tribes totaling almost one million Indians inhabited the land from the Pacific coastal regions to the Atlantic. It would be impossible therefore to cover the *materia medica* of each and every tribe in the short space of one chapter. Such an endeavor would require volumes. Under the circumstances, only a fraction of the countless Indian plant remedies may be cited. In addition, the limited space allotted toward the end of this chapter affords only a passing glance at the expanding scientific interest and research into a very few of the numerous Indian medicinal herbs.

OBSERVATIONS ON AMERICAN INDIAN HERBAL LORE

Frontier doctors, settlers, and soldiers fully agreed that the Indians not only recovered from wounds that would have proved fatal to the white man, but that they also recovered from ordinary wounds far more quickly than did white men. In reference to the Natchez Indians, De la Vente wrote: "I have seen many who have received four or five bullet or arrow wounds through the stomach and who are so perfectly cured of them that they do not suffer any inconvenience. Through the knowledge of simples [herbs] which they have received from their fathers they will cure hands, arms, and feet that our best surgeons would not hesitate to cut."

Gunshot wounds of the bladder, invariably fatal to the white man of Colonial times, were seldom fatal to the Indian. In cases of this nature, Indian patients were discharged from military hospitals to die among their own people, yet they recovered rapidly as soon as their medicine men attended them. Such reports could be cited almost indefinitely as all early observers were so astonished by the Indian ability to survive disastrous wounds that hundreds of cases have been recorded.

Through repeated contact with the Indians, the settlers became convinced that the natives knew much more about plant medicine than did the physicians of Europe. They concluded, therefore, that the practitioners of various tribes fully deserved the title of "doctor" and personally engaged their services whenever possible. Du Pratz demonstrated his enthusiasm and respect for the Natchez Indian herbalists when he wrote:

How skillful are the native doctors of Louisiana! I have seen them make surprising cures on our Frenchmen, on two, among others, who were placed in the hands of a French surgeon established at this post. These two sick persons had to take strong remedies, but after having been treated for some time their heads were so swollen that one of them escaped from the surgeon with as much agility as would a criminal from the hands of justice if he found a favorable opportunity. He went to find a Natchez doctor who healed him in eight days. His comrade remained with the French surgeon, where he died three days after the flight of the first, whom I saw over three years afterwards enjoying perfect health. There is no one in the colony who is ignorant of the facts which I have just presented. These physicians have made a great number of other cures the narration of which would demand a special volume.

WHITE CAPTIVE LEARNS INDIAN MATERIA MEDICA

It was a frequent practice among Indian warriors to capture white children whose parents had been slain during an Indian raid. These children were taken to the camp to which the raiding party belonged and were generally adopted by an Indian family who had lost a son or daughter. There was no discrimination and the children were treated and raised as members of the tribe. By the time the young captives reached maturity they had become so deeply attached and accustomed to the Indian way of life that they seldom returned to their own race. They lived as Indians, thought as Indians, and in some instances became so adept in the practice of the Indian healing "arts" that they served the tribes as medicine men. Others were satisfied to learn only as much of the Indian *materia medica* as the average warrior or squaw knew, which in itself was considerable. The government eventually offered to ransom a number of these captives and some were finally persuaded to return to civilization. A few others who desired to abandon their primitive way of life managed to escape. It is from these "White Indians" that we have learned much regarding the healing methods employed by the early native Americans.

John D. Hunter was a white captive. He was taken prisoner at an early age by a raiding party of Indians belonging to, or allied with, the Kickapoo nation. During his life as an Indian, Hunter belonged to many different tribes and traveled as far west as the Pacific coastal regions. He returned to his own race in 1816 when he was around 20 years of age. He confessed that adjusting to civilization was no easy task and says that "the struggle in my bosom was, for a considerable time doubtful." He became educated and later wrote a book called *Memoirs of a Captivity Among the Indians of North America.*[1] It was published in 1824 and became an immediate success.

Hunter's Observations

In writing of his life and experiences among the Indians, Hunter includes his observations of their *materia medica*. He says: "The Indians are far from being ignorant of the treatment of their diseases; they have a rich variety of remedies, from the simple to those which are very active; and experience has given them skill, on most occasions, how best to apply them." He informs us that the Indians generally employed their herbal medicines in conjunction with other methods of treatment such as sweat baths, and/or fasting, massage, friction, special diet, and so forth, depending on the type of ailment they were treating. In some instances however, the plant remedy alone was used.

[1] Reprinted by the Lee Foundation, Milwaukee, Wis., 1964.

Hunter tells us that due to the severe winters and heavy snows of many areas, the red man often suffered from frozen limbs or frostbite. In these cases, plasters made with the resin of sap-pine were applied to frozen members of the body. This remedy was reputed to be highly effective. Pleurisy was treated by placing skins of hot ashes over the area; copious and prolonged sweating was then induced by means of sweat baths and the administration of sudorific herb teas. According to Hunter, once the patient began perspiring freely, the pain in his side and his difficulty in breathing soon abated.

Indian Herbal Remedies Cited

In recording the following list of Indian herbal remedies, Hunter explains that he did not attempt to give the technical names of the different plants. He also states that some of the English names which he applied to the various herbs were conformed either to their Indian meaning or to their particular appearance or qualities. Only a partial list of the Indian herbs cited in Hunter's book is reprinted here:

Tut-Te-See-Hau—*It expels the wind.*

Anise grows in great profusion in moist shaded soils. The roots are perennial, and possess a very agreeable taste and aromatic smell. They are frequently eaten in traveling, are considered good to remove flatulency, and are sometimes given in combination with other drugs to render them less disagreeable to the patient.

Hon-Kos-Kao-Ga-Sha—*It stops the blood flowing out.*

Astringent root. This is a shrubby plant, growing in abundance in the edges of the prairies and hill-sides through the western country. Its principal virtue consists in its astringent properties, which it possesses in very high degree. It is one of their favorite remedies in stopping bleeding from wounds; the dried root is powdered and put on the mouths of the bleeding vessel, and a bandage bound over it. The Indians have great confidence in it. They use it very much, both internally in form of tea, and externally as a wash in female complaints. But by far the most efficacious purpose to which this root is applied, is to stop the spitting of blood; an affection which frequently exists amongst them, in consequence of their long and hurried

marches. They seldom travel without it; a half teaspoonful in cold water is the dose. I know it to be a
highly valuable article in their Materia Medica.

Shen-Don-Shu-Gah—*Bitter red berry.*

Dog wood. They give the bark of this tree, in combination with bitters of various kind, in fevers of the
low type, and when there is great prostration of
strength; I believe, however, they value it mostly in
form of poultice, as a corrector of ill-conditioned sores.

Ton-Ga-Shin-Ga—*It gives strength to a child.*

Gentian wild. This plant has commonly four or five
branching roots, which are about the size of a man's
finger. The stalks, to the number of five or six, grow
to a height of two or three feet, and bear yellow pulpy
seeds or berries, which adhere closely to the stalk, at
the junction of the leaves, which are nearly oval-shaped
and rough. The Indians make great use of the root in
cases of debility; especially when accompanied with
affections of the stomach. They most commonly make
use of it in decoction, though they sometimes take it
in substance. They combine it with dog-wood and
wild-cherry bark; and give it in cold infusion in inter-
mittents, while the fever is off. Thus prepared, it is
also given for the palpitation of the heart and in
dropsies.

Ne-Lash-Kee—*The name of the tree.*

Mountain Birch. This tree is found on the north
sides of mountains and cliffs on western streams in
abundance, and attains to fifty or sixty feet in height.
The Indians make use of the inner bark as a remedy in
colds, coughs, and diseases of the pulmonary organs.
They usually administer it in decoction. Many of the
frontier settlers in the western territories value it very
highly as a table beverage.

Ne-Was-Char-La-Go-Ne—*Good for colds or cough.*

Pipsissewa. This plant is too generally known among
the people of the United States to require any description by me. It is held in considerable esteem by the
Indians, and is used as an anodyne and sudorific, especially in diseases of the breast, colds, etc.

Kee-Chi-He-Ja-Ka—*Gift of the Great Spirit, Sau-kies.*

Sap pine, or healing gum tree of the traders. This tree grows on a cold soil to the height of twenty or thirty feet, and sends off long spreading branches; it is an evergreen of the pine family. On its trunk are numerous small protuberances, which contain a medicinal resinous juice, which is somewhat pungent to the taste and smell. It is held in high estimation, in the treatment of breast complaints and coughs; it is also a favorite remedy for languid ulcers. They give it internally in the first diseases, and when applied to ulcers, it is spread on thin membranes or skins, and laid over the affected part. It relieves pain, arrests inflammation, reduces the swelling, and disposes the parts to heal.

Mr. Spencer, with whom many of my western friends are well acquainted, assured me, that during a trip up the Mississippi to the Red Cedar Lake, he contracted, from exposure, an excruciating pain in his limbs and the small of his back, which interrupted his usual avocations. An Indian of the Chippewa tribe prescribed this medicine in doses of about a common teaspoonful, three or four times in the course of the day. He also applied a plaster to his loins; and this treatment he declares relieved him in a very short time from all his sufferings. Applied externally to the parts affected, it is said to be an excellent remedy in rheumatism. The Chippewas, Sau-kies and Fox Indians, place so much confidence in this medicine that they seldom travel without it. I know very little about it myself, though its merit in the above-named diseases is too well established among the Indians, traders, and hunters, to be questioned by me.

(Indian Term Uncertain)

Slippery Elm. It grows in considerable abundance on the western waters and in other rich lands. The inner bark is the part used. In colds and bowel complaints its properties as a demulcent are considered valuable; it is also much used as a cataplasm or emollient in ulcers and swellings. But though it may deserve some reputation as an article of medicine, its greatest value consists in its nutritive qualities. I have subsisted for days on it, while traveling through the country of unfriendly tribes. The elm bark will support life for a great length of time.

Tut-Tus-Se-Ga-O-Ga-She—*To expel wind.*

Spikenard. This spikenard is one of the most luxuriant of the forest plants: it grows in the beds of hollows in hilly districts in great abundance, and if it possesses half the virtues ascribed to it by the Shawnee Indians, it merits a high rank in the Materia Medica. They give it with a view to expel wind from the stomach, to stop coughs, and to relieve pain in the breast and asthma.

Modern Usages

A comparison may be drawn between the Indian usage of the herbs cited by Hunter and their modern employment and evaluation. Limited space will permit only a brief examination of a few of them that may be better known.

ANISEED

SYNONYM: Anise

Anise (*Pimpinella anisum*) is one of the oldest plants known and has been employed both as a spice and as a domestic medicine. Pliny, Dioscorides, Theophrastus and other early writers mention it. It was used by the ancient Egyptians and later cultivated in the imperial German farms of Charlemagne.

A hot tea prepared from aniseed and taken in doses of a teaspoon to a tablespoon (repeated often) is still a popular domestic remedy today in many parts of the world for expelling or preventing gas in the stomach and bowels. It is also used for stubborn, dry coughs, and for colic in infants and older youngsters.

Anise contains sugar, ash, a volatile oil, a mucilage factor, and a fixed oil. Medical herbalists classify it as carminative and pectoral. The volatile oil is said to loosen bronchial secretions, which gives the plant merit as an expectorant. Accordingly, it is used in lozenges and cough syrups.

V. A. Skovronskii, a research scientist, discovered effective diuretics in anise, caraway, and fennel seeds. They are considered especially safe because they are commonly employed as simple flavoring agents. Diuretics are generally prescribed for patients suffering from an accumulation of fluid in the body, and pronounced swelling due to various diseases of the heart, lungs or kidneys.

PIPSISSEWA

SYNONYMS: Prince's Pine, Ground Holly.

In addition to Hunter's remarks regarding the use of this herb, the following information may be cited:

Certain Indian tribes prepared a tea made with pipsissewa (*Chimaphila umbellata*) and employed it for a variety of genito-urinary disorders such as nephritis, chronic cystitis, and urethritis. It was also used for consumption, scrofula and rheumatism, and to re-establish the menstrual flow after childbirth. The remedy passed from the hands of the Indians to those of the early settlers where it retained its popularity for years before being adopted by the medical profession.

The leaves of pipsissewa were scientifically examined as early as 1860 by Fairbanks who found that they contain starch, sugar, pectic acid, resin, tannic acid, fatty matter, chlorophyll, lignin, a yellowish coloring matter, and a substance which he called *chimaphilin*. Peacock (*A.J.P.*, 1892) conducted a careful analysis of the plant and obtained the yellow crystallized principle *chimaphilin* in pure form.

Recent scientific research with the plant has shown that it possesses antibacterial power. The alcoholic and water extracts have been found to contain *in vitro* antibiotic activity. Two hundred and nine Nova Scotian plants were tested for antibacterial power against *E. coli* and *Staph. aureus*, by Bishop and MacDonald.[2] Pipsissewa (*C. umbellata*) was reported to be one of the ten most active plants.

SLIPPERY ELM

SYNONYMS: Indian Elm, American Elm, Rock Elm, Sweet Elm, Red Elm.

Slippery elm (*Ulmus fulva*) is regarded today as one of nature's most excellent demulcents and is employed for its ability to neutralize stomach acidity and to absorb noxious gases in the body. It is also recognized for its soothing action

[2] C. J. Bishop and R. E. MacDonald, *Canadian Journal of Botany*, 1951.

in minor peptic irritations of the stomach and intestines. When the powder is prepared as a gruel it forms a wholesome food, considered especially valuable for invalids and infants. Either the gruel or the tea is very soothing and well tolerated by delicate stomachs. Many preparations of the powdered bark are now sold in modern health food stores as bland and nutritious foods.

As a herbal tea, slippery elm is generally prepared by mixing two teaspoonfuls of the powder in a half cup of cold water. This is placed in a container and shaken thoroughly for about ten seconds. One pint of boiling water is then added and the mixture well stirred. The beverage may be flavored with lemon juice, or a little cinnamon.

The gruel is made by heating a half pint of milk and sprinkling one-half to one teaspoonful of powdered slippery elm into the liquid. This is beaten thoroughly with an egg beater or electric mixer, then brought to a boil and stirred until it thickens. It may be sweetened with honey. Some people prefer to beat up an egg with one teaspoonful of the powdered bark. Boiling milk is then poured over the mixture which is stirred well and sweetened to taste.

Medical herbalists classify slippery elm as demulcent, emollient, diuretic, and pectoral. They recommend the powdered bark in the form of a poultice for burns, ulcers, chilblains, and skin diseases. For inflammation of the bowels, they advise a preparation of one ounce of the powder in one pint of boiling water to be used as an injection with a rectal syringe after the decoction has been strained and cooled (warm). It is claimed that this remedy has succeeded after all others had failed. A tea prepared from the bark is recommended as an excellent wash for chapped hands. As a soothing gargle, *Hill's Family Herbal* states: "Slippery elm boiled in water makes one of the best gargles that can be supplied by the whole list of medicines. It should be sweetened with honey."

Herbalists prescribe the unsweetened tea to be taken three times a day as an aid in the treatment of gastric catarrh, gastritis, enteritis, and mucous colitis. Because of its strengthening effect on the body and its soothing action on the lungs, they consider it valuable for the debilitating conditions of bronchitis, coughs, and other pulmonary complaints.

INDIAN REMEDIES RECORDED BY LIGHTHALL

John Lighthall was born in Illinois in the year 1856. He was one-eighth Indian. As a boy, Lighthall loved every tree, flower, and bush, wondering what kind of roots they had and what they might be good for. At 11 years of age, he left home and went to Kansas and the Indian Territory where he formed a warm attachment for the native way of life. He became intensely interested in watching the Indian doctors, and his greatest joy was to assist them in gathering Nature's remedies. Lighthall was deeply impressed with the fact that the herbal formulas of the medicine men were remarkably effective and never harmed the patient. He decided that what was good for the natives was also good for the white man and spent 13 years filling his mind with Indian medical knowledge, acquainting himself with all the herbs and various methods of preparation.

Lighthall then traveled to Wyoming and other sections of the country finally arriving in Minnesota with a band of Indian ponies. Here he became friendly with a celebrated physician named Dr. Neff. During a tour of digging ginseng, Dr. Neff said, "Mr. Lighthall, you are a botanist and understand the medical properties so well, if you will bring them before the people you will do a great many sufferers good and cure them." Lighthall took the physician's advice and put his knowledge to use, successfully treating the sick according to the Indian theory of herbal medication. In 1883 he published a book called *The Indian Household Medicine Guide* in which he listed many of the plant remedies. A few excerpts from this book are given as follows:

Poplar

This [Poplar (*Populus tremuloides*)] is a very valuable remedy, and should be used more than it is, and would be if everybody knew of its valuable properties. It is a plant common to this country, and is best gathered in the fall of the year.

Medical properties and uses. There are two kinds of barks, white and yellow; one is as good as the other. It is a fine tonic, and should be used in cases of general debility with feeble digestion. It is good for convalescents when the appetite is deficient. My brother, some years ago had a severe spell of continued fever. After the fever broke, his convalescence was very slow; he had no appetite, and was swarthy, weak, and melancholy; the smell of victuals was that of disgust rather than a pleasure. Our family physician, and a good one, gave him tonics, but without the desired effect. I chanced to be at home at the time, and my mother being alarmed about his condition, asked me if I could recommend anything in our line of practice that would be good for him, give him an appetite and build him up. I recommended equal parts of the inner barks of poplar and dogwood and sarsaparilla root, cut up fine and put in a quart bottle until it was half full, then add whisky till full, and take a large table-spoonful, or a common swallow, before each meal. She did so, he took it, and in four weeks gained 15 pounds. It immediately increased his appetite, strengthened his nerves, and restored his complexion to its natural color.

I will give you another Indian formula:

Rattle Root, one part; Prickly Ash Bark, two parts; Poplar Bark, two parts; Sarsaparilla Root, two parts; Dogwood and Wild Cherry, one part. Fill a quart bottle one-half full of the above finely cut up, and add whisky till full. Dose, from a teaspoonful to a tablespoonful before meals. This will help rheumatism, give an appetite, strengthen the nerves, and purify the blood.

Blue Flag

We find that many of our writers describe this (*Iris versicolor*) as one of our most important plants. Eclectics have held it in high favor, that is, when they knew it to be in a form in which it retained all of its medical properties. From the fact that it has been before the public for the past 15 years in an improper form, it has been ignored by a great many of our physicians. There is not a tincture genuine unless made from the green root.

Medical properties and uses. Blue Flag is a stimulant to the glandular system, consequently a fine remedy for all blood diseases. It promotes excretion. It has a special affinity for the thyroid gland, that lays just below what is called the Adam's apple of the throat, which, when enlarged, is called goitre. It is a very valuable remedy in the treatment of scrofula, and all species of glandular and blood diseases. The dose of the tincture, prepared as I have before directed, is from 5 to 15 drops four or five times a day.

Elecampane

Elecampane (*Inula helenium*) is one of our many harmless, mild tonics. The root is the medical part of the plant, and by many highly appreciated. It is mild and slow in its effects, consequently should be continued a long time in order to accomplish the object for which it is taken.

Medical properties and uses. Elecampane is a mild tonic to the mucous linings and to the skin. It has been found by the Indian doctors to be of benefit in many skin diseases. It has a special affinity for the bronchial tubes and lungs in general. It is indicated where there is pain in the breast with considerable expectoration. It is better used with other remedies of similar properties. I will now give you an Indian formula:

Elecampane Root .... one-half pound
Spikenard Root .... one-half pound
Comfrey Root .... one-half pound

Mash the roots well, boil in one gallon of water until it is down to a quart, put in a half gallon jug or bottle, add eight ounces of alcohol and a pint and a half of strained honey. Dose, a teaspoonful every two hours.

Butternut

The inner bark is the part that possesses the medical property, and should be gathered when the sap is going down, or in other words, in the fall of the year. It is a bark that is truly worthy of notice, from the fact that its medical properties are peculiar from those of others it is classified with. I am acquainted with a California physician, by the name of Dr. James E. Mure, who appreciated this remedy above all remedies for certain conditions of the system, and those conditions were chronic constipation of the bowels, slight bilious derangements of the stomach, or in other words, slight bilious attacks. He gave this remedy in a number of cases with good results. The tincture of butternut bark has been one of my favorites in many cases of bowel troubles of a constipated character. I should certainly be at a loss without this medicine in my assortment of remedies.

Medical properties and uses. In large doses the butternut is cathartic in its action; and this is a peculiar fact in reference to its cathartic action over and above any other cathartic remedy we have in the world. I will give it in plain language. When calomel, may-apple root, colocynth, jalap, senna, gamboge, and such cathartics are given, after the cathartic action, constipation usually follows, and sometimes to a sad extent; but this is not the case with butternut. It is a fine laxative and cathartic, and constipation seldom, if ever, follows its cathartic effects. Where piles are produced by constipation it is almost a certain cure. I pronounce it the king of constipation. For all bilious conditions, and conditions of constipation, take the inner bark of the butternut tree and cut it in fine pieces, and fill a quart bottle full of the pieces, then add equal parts of water and 98 percent alcohol, and after 14 days' standing it is ready for use. The dose of the tincture is three or four tablespoonfuls a day until the bowels become loose and regulated, then lessen the dose according to the necessity of your case or your condition.

Red Clover

I shall speak briefly on this valuable plant (*Trifolium pratense*). Its medical properties, so far as my experience has gone, and the knowledge I have obtained from various authors, are especially adapted to troubles of the respiratory organs, such as irritation of the vocal cords, windpipe, and bronchial tubes. It is a twin sister to honey—taste the blossom, and it has a taste similar. A tea made of the blossoms is the best form to use it in.

Medical properties and uses. Good for asthma, hoarseness, colds, coughs, and irritation of the general respiratory tract. Make a strong tea of the blossoms, and take a common swallow every hour or two. Best to take it hot. Make a strong syrup of the blossoms, mix it with the juice of roasted onions and strained honey, and you will have a fine cough syrup, good for croup, colds, bad coughs, hoarseness, and all troubles pertaining to the lungs, windpipe, and bronchial tubes.

Sarsaparilla

The root is the part that we use, and should be gathered in the months of July and September. It is better to prepare it immediately after digging, but it will retain its virtue a number of months after digging. The root is one of our most valuable remedies, and of great value to the medical profession. Physicians have praised it through every classical publication in the land. Sarsaparilla (*Smilax officinalis*) is a remedy that is undoubtedly alterative in its action. It can be taken freely in the form of an infusion or decoction without fear of doing harm. To make a tincture of it, fill a bottle half full of the finely cut root, add equal parts of water and alcohol, and let stand 14 days, shake well each day. Dose, a tablespoonful four or five times a day. In all bad cases of blood disease and eruptions of the skin, a half pint of the strong tea of the root should be taken in connection with the tincture every day. Let the patient bathe the whole body twice a week with pure water, rubbing the skin after bathing well with a rough towel. Do not charge your stomach with nuts, knick knacks, and fat meats, and you will find, inside of four weeks, that sarsaparilla is a blood purifier and alterative. I saw a case of scrofula caused by bad vaccine virus. The flesh seemed as though it would fall from the bones, and the physicians that were in attendance gave her up and said she would have to die. The mother made a strong syrup or tea of sarsaparilla root and made her drink it instead of water. It did the work. She got well.

Medical properties and uses. The medical properties of this plant are generally known as alterative and blood purifying. . . . It acts kindly and freely on the kidneys, gently stimulating the sudoriferous glands as well as the sebaceous glands of the skin. It increases the appetite, and gently counteracts a constipated condition of the bowels. When taken freely for a considerable length of time it will overcome a majority of our many troublesome skin and scrofulous diseases in general. When a person takes it freely they will find it will act on the kidneys similar to watermelon, and the sweat from the skin will be of a greasy, waxy nature. Try it if you don't believe it.

NOTE: In mentioning the use of alcohol for the preparation of tinctures, Lighthall is referring to pure alcohol, *not* rubbing alcohol. When pure alcohol is difficult to obtain, it is generally substituted by either vodka, brandy, or any similar spirit.

MODERN USES OF PLANTS CITED BY LIGHTHALL

For reasons previously given regarding the Hunter list, only a few of the herbs cited by Lighthall may be compared to their modern usage:

Blue Flag

SYNONYMS: Flag Lily, Iris, Water Flag, Liver Lily, Snake Lily.

Blue flag is an ingredient of many blood purifying compounds and is chiefly employed as an alterative. Chemical analysis of the plant has determined the presence of gum, tannin, resinous matter, acid and starch. Its therapeutic action is cited as alterative, cathartic, stimulant, and diuretic.

Blue flag is employed in European countries for skin diseases, certain types of deafness, and for noises or ringing in the ears. Dr. Eric Powell states that it is an excellent thyroid normalizer which may be used in place of kelp, especially for cases in which the blood is disorganized.

Butternut

SYNONYMS: White Walnut, Oil Nut.

The bark of butternut (*Juglans cinerea*) has proved to be an excellent laxative which operates without griping or irritation, and without debilitating the alimentary canal. It is regarded as valuable in cases of habitual constipation, and other bowel complaints, particularly dysentery. Only the inner bark is used. When first uncovered it is pure white, but with exposure to light and air it turns yellow, then finally brown. The color change is due to its content of organic elements. The odor is slightly aromatic, the taste bitter and somewhat acrid.

Butternut bark contains juglandic acid, volatile oil, tannin, fixed oil, ash, resin, and potassium, with traces of calcium, sodium and aluminum. It is classified as cathartic, tonic, and vermifuge. It is employed either in the form of a tincture, extract, syrup, or pills and does not bind after operating. It is also used in modern times as a remedy for worms, particularly in children.

Butternut bark was extensively employed during the Revolutionary War by Dr. Rush and other physicians attached to the army.

Elecampane

SYNONYMS: Velvet Dock, Elf Dock, Scabwort.

Elecampane is one of nature's richest sources of inulin. It also contains a bitter principle, volatile oil, wax, ash, acrid resin, and *helenin*. The alkaloid *helenin* was found to be a powerful bactericide and antiseptic. One authority stated that a few drops of one part in 10,000 destroys ordinary bacteria immediately.

Elecampane is often used in the form of lozenges and syrups for coughs and colds. It is generally employed in combination with other herbs (for example, those cited by Lighthall) for respiratory disorders such as asthma and bronchitis, and in catarrhal conditions of the nose and throat. Dr. Kuts-Chereaux reports that although elecampane is not a definite anti-tuberculin, it does considerably control the mucous discharge and excessive cough. In addition he states that it improves the appetite, and promotes a general state of well-being.

Dr. Fernie writes that at one time the root was candied and sold in London for asthmatic complaints. In traveling near rivers, he says a piece of the root was sucked or chewed as a preventative against polluted air and poisonous exultations.

Many years ago Dr. Chase reported the case of a young lady who was suffering from asthma. Physicians told her parents that the case was hopeless. An old lady, however, suggested a herbal formula that reputedly saved the young woman's life. Dr. Chase states that the same remedy is also excellent for any type of cough. It is cited as follows:

> *Asthma.* Elecampane, angelica, comfrey, and spikenard roots, with horehound tops, of each one oz.; bruise and steep in honey one pint Strain. Dose: A tablespoon, taken hot every few minutes, until relief is obtained, then several times daily until a complete healing is effected.

The action of elecampane is cited as alterative, expectorant, tonic, stimulant, and antiseptic.

SCIENCE CONTINUES THE STUDY OF INDIAN HERBS

A number of herbs used as medicines by the Pacific Northwest Indians are being probed by modern science. Work on the project is being conducted by the Oregon State University School of Pharmacy under a three year $125,700 grant from the U. S. Public Health Service. The program includes the cooperation of authorities in pharmacy, botany, and medicine at Oregon State as well as several other institutions and universities throughout the country.

During the first two years, 66 extracts were tested for pharmacological activity from such plants as alum root, bitter cherry, wild columbine, wild peony, ocean spray, creek dogwood, and shelf fungus. All were used as remedies by the Indians and research is showing that some of the herbs possess medicinal value. For example, one plant extract produced a smooth-muscle relaxing action. Two alkaloids and several trace alkaloids were found in another plant. Seventeen extracts from nine plants have been submitted to the National Cancer Institute to be checked for possible anti-cancer properties.

Study on several additional plants has just begun. The huckleberry, whose leaves have been claimed as a treatment for diabetes, is one of them. All plants under study have been recommended by Dr. David French, professor of anthropology at Reed College, Portland. The scientists believe that although there are many new synthetic drugs, natural products play an important part in the practice of American medicine.

SCIENTIFIC RESEARCH ON INDIAN BIRTH CONTROL PLANT[3]

For centuries the Shoshone Indian squaws of Nevada used a water extract of a plant popularly known as millet, gromwell, or stone seed, for birth control. Its botanical name is *Lithospermum ruderale*. It is a relative of *Lithospermum arvense*, a plant found in the dry regions of Indiana and other states of the Midwest.

Two Indiana University professors are examining the plant and have already discovered clues to the entire hormone

[3] *Science News Letter*, May 1, 1965.

producing mechanism of the endocrine gland system. Although they feel that their research of the plant could lead to a better oral contraceptive, they emphasize that the most important aspect of their studies is the knowledge it is revealing on fundamental body processes.

Mice and chickens were tested with a water extract of substances from the *Lithospermum ruderale* plant by Dr. William Breneman, an endocrinologist and professor of zoology. It was observed that the extract produced powerful inhibitory effects on hormones such as oxytocin which suppresses blood pressure and controls contractions of the womb.

The substance was found to be one of a group of unstable compounds known as polyphenols by Dr. Marvin Carmack, professor of chemistry. These studies have been made possible by grants from the U. S. Public Health Service.

Indian Herbal Remedy Found Effective in Diarrhea

J. A. Blue, M.D., writing in the *Journal of Allergy* (Sept. 1965) said that when the Indians and early settlers suffered from diarrhea they used a tea made from the Canada fleabane (*Erigeron canadense*). This plant is also known by the common names of fireweed, colt's tail, and horseweed. Dr. Blue reported that it worked when diarrhea "proved so baffling and defied the best modern remedies to relieve it. . . ."

Records of Eye Cataracts Successfully Treated with Herbs

Non-surgical treatment of cataract by the employment of plant extracts was reported by Dr. Edgar R. Palarea of Guatemala.[4] This investigator claims that disappearance of the cataract occurs in from 14 to 28 days. He employs the same treatment as that used for hundreds of years for eye afflictions by the native Indians. Dr. Palarea began experimenting with the plant extract on cats and dogs. He says the results were so successful that he used the remedy on humans. The extract was obtained from a plant known in his country as *St. Apollonia.*

Our own American Indians also relied on various herbs for the treatment of eye complaints. Densmore records the

[4] *Health From Herbs*, February 1955.

following example in *Uses of Plants by the Chippewa Indians:*[5]

> BOTANICAL NAME: *Rosa* (Rose), species doubtful.
> BOTANICAL NAME: *Rubus strigosus* (Red Raspberry).
> PART USED: Inner bark of the root.
>
> How prepared: These two remedies are used successively, the first for removing inflammation, and the second for healing the eye. They are prepared in the same way, the second layer of the root being scraped and put in a bit of cloth. This is soaked in warm water and squeezed over the eye, letting some of the liquid run into the eye. This is done three times a day.
> Remarks: It was said that these would cure cataract unless too far advanced, and that improvement would be shown quickly if the case could be materially helped.

Honey was used by some of the Indian tribes for the treatment of cataract. One drop was placed in the eye daily and the remedy persevered with for several months.

Indian Poison Oak Remedy

The following interesting item appeared in *The Naturopath*, (August 1966):

Oregon Octogenarian Tells of Indian Neighbor and Amazing "Weed" Cure

Poison oak is no fun for anyone, least of all a seven year old boy. Henry Chapelle, who lives in the French Prairie area of the Willamette Valley near Woodburn, Oregon, had his first discomforting experience with the poison plant shortly after he had moved west with his family back in 1887. An Indian woman took one look at his swollen face, steamed up a batch of "weeds" and supervised application of the concoction. The itching, Chapelle recalls, stopped instantly and in a short while all evidence of the poison oak had disappeared.

Through the years that followed, Chapelle says he encountered poison oak again and again. Always, he adds, the Indian remedy came to the rescue. . . .

For years Chapelle has conducted a search to iden-

[5] Frances Densmore, 1928, *Bur. Amer. Ethnol. Ann. Rept.* (1926–27), 44:275–397.

tify the plant. This spring he found out after submitting the "weed" to pharmaceutical specialists at Oregon State University. According to Curator Kenton L. Chambers, Herbarium, Department of Botany at the State University, the name of Chapelle's plant is *Gnaphalium purpurium*. The University, which is currently conducting an extensive study of Indian herbs and medicines, is very much interested in the French Prairie man's experience with the plant.

Chapelle, who is respectful of the tremendous progress of modern science, regards with even greater awe, however, the amazing medical knowledge of a simple Indian woman by the name of Mary DeLore who took one look at a little boy's swollen face back in 1887 and promised simply: "Me fix um."

Modern scientists, most botanists agree, have much to learn from the herbal knowledge of the American Indian.

9

MISTLETOE: MYSTIC HERB OF
THE DRUIDS

Many customs which are still practiced today, apparently with little meaning, originally had a mystic association in times past which has been forgotten. This is true of the ivy, holly and mistletoe as decorations during the Christmas season. The use of mistletoe is older than Christianity.

In former times the mistletoe was a mystic plant, and was highly venerated by the Gauls. As the oak was sacred to them, their priests (Druids) lived in oak forests, used oak leaves and boughs in religious ceremonies and made their sacrifices under an oak tree. When the mistletoe was found growing on an oak, it was believed to be a gift from the Divine. A ceremony was performed annually in which the priest, clothed in a long white robe, ascended the tree and carefully removed the plant with a golden sickle. It was caught in a white cloth and divided into shares which were distributed among the bystanders. The pieces were kept as charms or sacred relics and were also used in the form of a potion as a remedy against poisons and disease.

According to Norse mythology it was a branch of the mistletoe which slew the god Baldur, while in other Scandinavian legends it was regarded as a symbol of life and resurrection. Its symbolism in the latter instance is believed to have originated from the appearance of its green leaves entwined around a bare tree in winter time which gave the impression that the tree had regained its foliage.

Distinguishing Between Two Varieties of Mistletoe

In this chapter we are dealing solely with the European mistletoe known botanically as *Viscum album*. It is a half-parasitic plant which attaches itself to certain trees such as the apple and poplar, drawing its nourishment from them. The Latin name *Viscum* is from *viscus*—birdlime, a sticky substance which forms in the leaves, berries and stalks.

The American variety or *false* mistletoe is also a half-parasitic plant and is known as *Phoradendron flavescens*. In many instances it has proved destructive to the trees upon which it attaches itself. It is not as ornamental as the English mistletoe.

Mistletoe—A Remedy Based in Antiquity

The use of mistletoe as a remedy for circulatory and nervous disorders dates from antiquity. In former times it was a traditional remedy for epilepsy and records show that as far back as 3000 B.C. the Persians employed it for this purpose. Hippocrates claimed that it was an excellent remedy for the spleen. In this connection it is interesting to note that in modern Europe some physicians have expressed the opinion that treatment of the spleen should be considered when dealing with the condition of epilepsy.

Culpeper referred to the traditional use of the plant when he wrote that mistletoe "made into powder and taken in drink by those that have the falling sickness, heals them if used 40 days successively." A French medical work printed in 1682 stated that mistletoe may be taken "in decoction against all sorts of nervous maladies, such as epilepsy, convulsions, and irritations, while it gives tone to the nerves, if taken morning and evening and re-establishes the circulation of the blood." In 1770 a pamphlet entitled *The Treatment of Epilepsy by Mistletoe* was published by Sir John Colbatch in which the plant was credited with great curative properties and cited as a specific for epilepsy. Other practitioners testified that the plant was also an effective tonic in conditions of St. Vitus Dance, hysteria, neuralgia, nervous debility and similar ailments.

In the centuries that followed, the medicinal use of the plant was all but forgotten until 1907 when Rene Gaultier became interested in the results obtained by the healers of

Cologne in which mistletoe was successfully employed in cases of tuberculous hemoptysis. He studied the plant and demonstrated its anti-hemorrhagic properties.

Constituents in Mistletoe

Modern studies have shown that twice as much potash and five times as much phosphoric acid has been found in the wood of the mistletoe as in that of the foster tree. Over the past few years German research has demonstrated that the plant thrives best on poplar which produces the highest percentage of *viscotoxin*. Mistletoe contains choline and acetylcholine-tyramine substances. These two constituents are becoming more widely known and used for the regulation of high blood pressure and circulatory troubles. In Germany alone the yearly amount of from 170 to 190 tons of mistletoe is employed for remedial purposes.

MODERN USES OF MISTLETOE

Dr. German J. de Rovira of Barcelona, Spain, gives the following information on the value of *Viscum album* (mistletoe):[1]

In his thesis in Paris (1911) Lestrat proved that the action of Viscum album was more effective than that of nitrate of soda, with the advantage over trinitrin of being non-toxic. These properties can be of good benefit in arteriosclerosis and high blood pressure. The role played by high blood pressure in arteriosclerosis is well known with its manifold manifestations: headaches, vomiting, sight disturbances, buzzing of the ears, etc. In these cases Viscum album by decreasing the blood pressure and tonifying the heart muscle sets up a considerable improvement and frequently a complete cessation of all these incidents.

In Menopause

During the menopause, often there is an increase in the blood pressure originating disturbances—so frequent at this stage of feminine life—like palpitation, tachycardia, suffocation, dyspnoea of effort, abnormali-

[1] "Therapeutic Uses of Viscum album," *Health From Herbs,* August 1957, pp. 311–12.

ties in the peripheral circulation, against which Viscum
album is very effective. According to Payne and Lang,
Viscum album is a tonic to the uterus and can be employed in uterine atony.

In Congestive Hemorrhages

It is recorded also as being used since long ago as
an anti-hemorrhagic in cases of hemorrhages post-
partum, epitaxis, and tubercuolus hemoptysis, as well,
as proved by Chobard and Gaultier, as in intestinal
hemorrhages occurring in typhoid fever.

In Chronic Nephritis

Specially useful in interstitial nephritis of arterio-
sclerotic patients with retention of nitrogen. . . .

Administration form

In maceration, in aqueous extract, pills, syrup, in
solution and in powder. . . .
To decrease the blood pressure two to four degrees
in ten days, three grams of Viscum album in powder
should be taken before breakfast, every morning, and
three other grams every night before retiring, with
some fluid (water, milk, broth, etc.). . . .
Once the blood pressure is normalized the doctor will
prescribe "sustaining" treatment with one and one-
half to three grams every day or every other day, or
every three days, according to the requirements of the
case. Of course, the cause for the high blood pressure
should be found and removed if possible, and then a
hygienic mode of living and a suitable hygienic diet
will do much in the patient's benefit, so that he is not
forced to depend upon Viscum album continually and
for long.

Additional Recorded Uses of Mistletoe

T. Bartram, F.N.I.M.H., M.R.S.H., F.H.A.,[2] tells us that:

It [mistletoe] can deal with many a stubborn headache, even migraine. Natural tranquilizer. Three heaped
teaspoonfuls to half pint cold water may be brought to
boil, and simmered for two minutes. Strain when cold.

[2] *Grace*, Vol. 2 No. 4, Winter 1961, p. 179.

One wineglassful three times daily after meals will help alleviate "nerves" and high blood pressure.

Dr. Vogel of Switzerland cites the value of the fresh extract of mistletoe in the treatment of hardening of the arteries and high blood pressure.[3] He says that the extract combined with hawthorne (*Crataegus*) and wild leek will "safely arrest the progress of this tragic accompaniment to old age." He points out however that salt and too much protein must be eliminated from the diet if best results are to be obtained.

Dr. Vogel also calls our attention to other conditions which indicate the use of mistletoe as a remedial agent:

Mistletoe extract ("Visca-drops") is also indicated in headaches which are accompanied by dizziness, in spells of vertigo when there is a tendency to fall backwards, in people whose gait is wavering, who are afraid of open places, get attacks of "pins and needles" in the limbs and suffer from cold feet. Used in conjunction with the heart remedies the "Visca-drops" will benefit you in sudden attacks of palpitations which are coupled with vascular spasms, difficult breathing and nightly attacks of asthma. Five drops, three to five times daily will suffice.

He also reports that patients suffering from pains in the joints due to chronic arthritis were given homeopathic injections of mistletoe with beneficial results.

Neuritis Symptoms

Neuritis is an inflammatory condition of the nerves or nerve sheath. Doctors explain that although it can affect any part of the body it is generally situated in the main nerve of the face, leg, or arm. It may be caused by any number of things such as a cold, rheumatism, inflammation of some part of the body that also affects the nerves, or debility due to illness. Sciatica, facial neuralgia, and neuritis in the arm are all types of this disorder. When the sciatic nerve and branches are affected, the pain extends from the buttocks down along the thigh to the knee and foot. When the arm is affected, the pain is felt from the back of the neck and top of the

[3] *The Nature Doctor*, p. 187.

shoulder, on down the arm to the wrist or fingers. Sometimes there is a tingling or numbing sensation.

Mistletoe is one of the plants included in a herbal combination recommended by H. Darwent, M.N.I.M.H., as a remedy for neuritis as follows:[4]

> *Treatment.* If the pain is almost unbearable apply warm poultices. If the pain is in the face apply the poultice to the back of the head or in front of the ear. For a severe pain in the shoulder, arm or fingers, apply the poultice to the spine in line with the collar bone. For the buttocks and leg apply the poultice about three inches from the bottom of the spine. Poultices applied to the parts mentioned will soothe the inflamed nerve where it branches from the spinal cord.
>
> This formula is very helpful; drink the doses warm and often to commence with. It has an immediate soothing action on the inflamed nerves and will gradually build up the whole nervous system.

> | | |
> |---|---|
> | Hops | one-half oz. |
> | Burdock herb | one-half oz. |
> | Scullcap | one-half oz. |
> | Bogbean | one-half oz. |
> | Mistletoe | one-half oz. |
> | Senna as required | [as a laxative] |

> Mix well and put half the contents in two pints of cold water, bring to the boil and simmer for 15 minutes. Strain when cold and take half a teacupful four times a day, after meals.

TRANQUILITY WITHOUT DRUGS

In an article entitled "Safe Treatment for Nervous Stress and Anxiety Tension,"[5] Jon Evans, eminent English psychologist and practitioner of homeopathic and botanic medicine, expresses concern over the increasing number of people who are taking orthodox tranquilizers and similar drugs for "nerves." He says:

> Doctors have neither the time nor facilities to give personal attention to the distressed patient who is more often than not, handed a prescription for some form

---

[4] *Health From Herbs*, March–April 1967, p. 79.
[5] *Health From Herbs*, March–April 1967, p. 74.

of barbiturate drug. Many of these medicines have dangerous side effects and are habit forming. Rather than help the patient they do nothing but dull the senses, impair the digestion and bludgeon the symptoms into submission.

Evans goes on to say that, by contrast, the practitioner of natural therapeutics can play a highly important part in the treatment of nerve stress and mental anguish. He will listen patiently and sympathetically to the patient's problems and offer practical suggestions and advice. In addition he will prescribe herbal remedies which will feed and repair the worn nervous system. Evans assures us that these herbs can be used with complete safety and adds:

They relieve tension, remove depression and restore the normal activities of the vital forces. In all cases they have a healthy influence upon the body. Nervous strain, insomnia, shock and overwork respond to the wondrous properties of chosen herbs relegated to the viscera, nerves and brain.

Evans tells us that in his professional practice he has used several plant remedies which have been highly successful in dealing with a weakened and disordered state of the nervous system and says that they may also be used as domestic remedies. Among them is mistletoe which he lists as follows:

Mistletoe. A nervine, antispasmodic and tonic. It is a useful heart tonic because it raises a low pulse, strengthens the beat, and has a sedative effect upon the solar plexus. An infusion of one oz. of the plant to a pint of boiling water. A tablespoonful dose several times a day. I have found this remedy more effective when combined with valerian root and vervain. An infusion of one-half oz. of the three herbs to one and one-half pints boiling water.

CANCER

A complicated preparation of mistletoe called *Iscadore* is employed in the treatment of cancer patients at a research clinic headed by Dr. A. Leroi at Kirschweg, Arlesheim, Switzerland.[6] According to the Arlesheim research team,

---

[6] William Gordon Allen, *Enigma Fantastique* (Mokelumne Hill, Calif.: Health Research, 1966), pp. 57–58.

hundreds of case histories gathered over a number of years show interesting results on many types of cancer in many areas of the body.

Recent progress reports by the clinic have shown that psychological treatment becomes every bit as important as physical treatment. Researchers at Arlesheim discovered that the fear of cancer is as dangerous as cancer itself. After the treatment with *Iscadore* the research team goes to great lengths to establish the correct psychological post-*Iscadore* therapy for the patient. Through years of experience they have found that the psychological conditioning of the patient and his immediate family is most vital.

10

THE HUMBLE PARSLEY: A
TREASURY OF NATURAL REMEDIES

The ancient Greeks believed that parsley had a special relation to the honored dead as the herb was said to have sprung from the blood of their slain heroes. When a friend died, it was customary for persons of prominence to inaugurate games to render the event honorable and noteworthy. Although different prizes were awarded, the garlands presented to the victors were generally made of parsley as a tribute to the departed.

Because of this symbolic association, the plant was regarded as something ominous and foreboding. Plutarch tells of how a few mules laden with parsley threw a whole Greek army into complete panic when they were on the march against the enemy. In other countries, however, the herb was connected with nuptials, and brides wore a chaplet of flowers and parsley on their heads. Bridegrooms were crowned with a garland of the herb as a symbol of victory, while singers and dancers at the happy occasions wore sprigs of parsley, rosemary and myrtle. Roman charioteers placed the herb on their banquet tables and included it in the diets of their horses to make them swift-footed and strong.

As a Popular Garnish

The name "parsley" comes from two Greek words *petros* and *selinon* from which the Latin *petroselinum* was derived. This became corrupted by degrees into petersilie, percely, persil and finally parsley. This humble herb has maintained its popularity as a garnish since earliest times. Pliny states that there was not a sauce or salad served without it. The ancients believed that parsley had the power of absorbing the inebriating fumes of wine and therefore prevented intoxication. It was used medicinally for a variety of illnesses but more particularly for gravel, bladder and kidney stones, and other disorders of the urinary system.

HEALTH VALUE OF PARSLEY

Early herbalists wrote that the use of parsley would "fasten loose teeth, brighten dim eyes and relieve a stitch in the side." Culpeper said that the leaf "laid to eyes that are inflamed with heat or swollen, helps them greatly if used with bread and meal."

Today, modern science tells us that parsley is extremely rich in vitamins A and C. Night blindness is successfully treated with vitamin A, and the health and vigor of the gums (necessary to keep the teeth tightly secured) depend on vitamin C. So the early herbalists were certainly on the right track even though they knew nothing of the existence of vitamins.

Parsley Generally Neglected as a National Source of Good Health

Although thousands of tons of parsley are produced each year, only a small percentage of this is actually eaten. When a catering service conducted a survey it was found that over 90 percent of the parsley served as a garnish was left untouched. Yet this humble plant contains 22,500 units of vitamin A per ounce. Carrots, which are highly touted for use in night-blindness, contain only 1,275 units per ounce. Parsley provides four times as much vitamin C as does an equal weight of oranges. Its iron content far surpasses that of spinach which contains only 1.2 miligrams per ounce while parsley contains 5.763 miligrams. The herb also contains more calcium and phosphorus than most vegetables. In addition, parsley is a good source of manganese, potassium and vitamin B_1.

Dr. Henry Sherman of Columbia University experimented with test animals by increasing the amounts of vitamin A in their diets. He found that the life span of the animals was extended to about ten years beyond the so-called normal, and these were *not* senile years. Dr. Sherman feels that the importance of vitamin A is greatly underestimated and believes that adults should have 16,000 units each day, which is four times more than the recommended minimum daily requirement.

Dorothy H. Anderson, M.D., also of Columbia University reported tests conducted on animals in which a vitamin A deficiency contributed to the condition of hernia. Dr. Anderson found that when vitamin A was given to the animals it reduced susceptibility to this ailment. Since hernia afflicts many older people it would seem wise to include parsley in the daily diet as it may prove a valuable preventative.

Reported Usage in Kidney and Bladder Trouble

In addition to its vitamin and mineral content, parsley also contains sugar, mucilage, starch, volatile oil and *apiol*. The herb is classified medicinally as diuretic, aperient, and emmenagogue. It is reputed to act as a solvent for uric acid when used as a tea or eaten after meals. Because of its emmenagogic action it is prescribed for suppressed and painful menstruation. R. D. Pope, M.D., has done considerable research on this plant and says that it is "excellent for the genito-urinary tract, of great assistance in the calculi of the kidneys and bladder, albuminaria, nephritis and other kidney trouble. It has properties essential to oxygen metabolism and in maintaining normal action of the adrenal and thyroid glands."[1]

One doctor who made a trip to Holland was surprised to find that the people there were using parsley tea with very good effect for urinary trouble and prostate pressure. When he returned from his trip he began recommending parsley tea to his patients.

Reported Usage for Diabetes, Prostate, and Rheumatism

Cyril Scott, the popular English author of a number of books and articles on natural healing methods, tells of cases of diabetes which have responded well to the use of parsley tea. He writes:[2]

[1] H. E. Kirschner, M.D., *Nature's Healing Grasses,* p. 97.
[2] *Grace,* Summer 1961, pp. 60-61.

According to medical orthodoxy, diabetes is caused by a defect in the so-termed "islands of Langerhans [secrete insulin]," and is really due to a deterioration of the pancreas. But it remained for the exponents of the "Biochemic System of Medicine" to discover the cause of that deterioration, namely a deficiency (chiefly) surphate of soda in minute and therefore assimilable quantities. The 6x attentuation is likely to be the most useful—two tablets, dry on the tongue, between meals thrice daily until all trace of sugar has disappeared, and then an occasional dose to prevent a recurrence. As the disease comes from a certain chemical deficiency, the system that makes good that deficiency would seem to be the best to employ. . . .

I am not in a position to say whether *parsley* is especially rich in sulphate of soda and other types of soda, but it seems highly probable in view of some spectacular cases which have recently come to my notice. The following, which concerns an acquaintance of mine, may be cited first.

Gentleman in His Sixties

This person was in great distress because he was unable to pass water. The doctor was called in, and a catheter had to be used several times. The doctor told him that he was suffering from prostrate trouble, and would have to undergo an operation. But it was then discovered that he had sugar in his urine, and it would be dangerous to operate while the diabetic condition was present. In consequence, injections of insulin were given. Finally, the patient's osteopath advised him to try parsley tea. The result was astonishing. Not only was he able to urinate freely, but in a very short time all trace of sugar had vanished from his urine. After first drinking the parsley tea, a lot of offensive substance came away in his urine. But the latter soon became normal, and the erstwhile patient is now in fine fettle, and able to play his rounds of golf with enjoyment. . . . There is no more thought of an operation.

Scott says that the other cases of diabetes which came to his attention were those uncomplicated by prostate trouble, and these too, responded favorably to the use of parsley tea. He also mentions that the tea seems to have a beneficial action in some types of rheumatism. He refers to an elderly man who could barely hobble around with the aid of two canes. The man started drinking parsley tea on the advice of a friend and became well enough to discard the canes. Scott concludes his article by saying, "Without making too extravagant claims for this homely potherb, it is obvious that it must contain some very valuable properties beneficial in a number of ways for humans."

Controlling Weakness of the Kidneys and Bladder

Dr. John Skelton, M.D.,[3] suggests the following herbal combination which includes parsley as one of the ingredients:

DIURETIC POWDER

Buchu .... one oz.
Queen of the meadow .... one oz.
Uva Ursi .... one-half oz.
Parsley root .... one oz.
Ginger .... one-half oz.

Mix until the whole is well incorporated. Infuse two ounces in a quart of boiling water, mix well; when cool, strain and bottle for use. Dose, a wineglassful four times a day.

This is very useful in obstruction of the urine, and weakness of the kidneys and bladder.

PARSLEY AS IT ACTS ON THE BRAIN

A reader wrote to a health magazine,[4] stating that for years he has worked at account books all day and sometimes during the evenings as well. He asked what was the best thing to eat to help strengthen the brain. Here was the answer:

Parsley. Nothing like it for stimulating those jaded cerebral cells. How? First take it raw in salads or with your hot meal. A refreshing summer drink may be made by bringing to the boil in a saucepan a handful of fresh parsley in one pint of water. Remove saucepan on boiling. Do not simmer. Strain. Drink one wineglassful two or three times daily. Just the thing to make the trial balance come right, first time.

[3] *Science and Practice of Herbal Medicine.*
[4] *Grace,* Autumn 1963, p. 669.

PARSLEY PIERT

Parsley piert (*Alchemilla arvensis*) is not related to the common parsley, however its medicinal action is somewhat similar. It has an astringent taste, but no odor and is classified as diuretic, demulcent, and refrigerant. Gerard says, "Our herb women in Cheapside know it by the name of Parsley Breakstone," and the plant has maintained its reputation to this day as a general remedy for gravel, kidney and bladder stones, and other complaints the urinary system.

Urinary Disorders

Potter's[5] gives the following information on the medicinal use of parsley piert:

> Used in cases of gravel, kidney, and bladder complaints. It acts directly on the parts affected, and will be found exceedingly valuable even in seemingly incurable cases. Several London doctors prescribe this remedy regularly. The infusion is taken in teacupful doses three times daily.

Cystitis

Cystitis is an inflamed condition of the bladder and is generally associated with catarrh of the urinary system. Mucous membrane lines the passages to and from the bladder itself. If the membrane becomes inflamed it produces excess mucous in the attempt to keep harmful germs and salts from injuring the system. This together with pus formed as the body destroys the invading germs may cause the urine to become cloudy and slightly thicker than normal. There is a dull aching pain in the lower part of the abdomen which increases with pressure when the urine is retained for awhile. In very acute cases pain is also felt towards the small of the back. The desire to urinate more frequently is experienced and the urine is voided with great difficulty and pain, sometimes only in dribbles. The difficulty and pain slowly increases and may finally become so severe that the patient suffers intense agony each time he tries to urinate and a

[5] R. C. Wren, F.L.S., *Potter's New Cyclopaedia of Botanical Drugs and Preparations* (7th Edition; London: Sir Isaac Pitman & Sons Ltd., 1956).

catheter has to be employed. In the condition of cystitis the urine is generally very acid whereas normal urine is only slightly so.

Physicians mention several causes of this disorder such as infection spreading from other organs of the body, for example, sinusitis, septic tonsils, and chronic ear catarrh. However, the main cause is said to be due to invasion of the urinary system by the colon bacillus either directly or through the urethra. Because the female urethra is very short, the condition of cystitis is much more common among women. Doctors therefore stress the necessity of cleanliness and strict hygiene at all times, especially after urination or bowel evacuation.

A Case History of Cystitis Healed

Arthur C. Hyde, a practicing medical herbalist of Leicester, England, mentions a case history involving cystitis.[6] The patient complained of frequent urination associated with severe scalding which was accompanied by pain in the bladder region. The urine was thick and gave off a strong odor. These symptoms had been getting steadily worse during the past ten days and had proved extremely depressing and wearying.

Hyde says that he found that the patient was subject to head catarrh and, in addition to her present affliction, was also suffering from sinus trouble. He says her whole body seemed to be in an exhausted state. On examining a sample of the patient's urine both chemically and microscopically he found that the acidity was high and there were copious pus cells containing ingested colon bacilli.

Hyde advised the patient to keep warm and rest as much as possible for one week, using a light diet with very little solid food, but large quantities of liquids. He suggested that she consume freshly prepared barley water every day, and told her to flavor it with black currant juice which is a rich source of vitamin C. In addition he prescribed a herbal combination which included parsley piert and within a week of following this advice and taking the herbal formula the most distressing symptoms had cleared. Not very many days after that the patient reported complete relief from the trouble.

Hyde says:

[6] *Health From Herbs*, July–August 1967, p. 114.

The herbal medicine prescribed for this case contained remedies to ensure free urine flow, to kill the invading organisms, to soothe the mucous membranes, and to combat acids; also to help clear sinus catarrh. It was composed of tinctures of the following:

Buchu leaves	(*Barosma betulina*)
Uva-Ursi leaves	(*Arctostaphylos uva-ursi*)
Parsley Piert herb	(*Alchemilla arvensis*)
Marshmallow root	(*Althea officinalis*)
Meadowsweet herb	(*Spirea ulmaria*)
Yarrow herb	(*Achillea milleforium*)
Prickly Ash bark	(*Xanthoxylum americanum*)

An infusion of the following selection from the above herbs may be taken for cystitis due to a chill or bacillary infection:

Prickly Ash	two drachms
Buchu leaves	one-half oz.
Uva-Ursi leaves	one-half oz.
Parsley Piert	one-half oz.
Marshmallow root	one oz.

Allow to infuse in a pint of boiling water for 15 minutes, strain and take three teaspoonfuls in a wineglass of hot water every two hours.

PARSLEY AS A NECESSARY FOOD AND NATURE'S MEDICINE

Hippocrates, the most renowned of the ancient physicians, and author of the Hippocratic Oath, was the first to employ various foods for healing the sick. He said, *"Let foods be your medicine and medicine your foods."* The practical knowledge for health which he gave to the world has been followed by the wise for centuries.

Scientists tell us that the nerves, glands, blood, bones, cartilage, and so forth are all composed of elements provided by the food we eat. Since the health and proper functions of the body depend on getting the necessary vitamins and minerals, it becomes vitally important to learn how to select and prepare our food. About 40 years ago, H. C. Fuller of the U. S. Bureau of Chemistry said: "Few people stop to think of the future when they sit down to a meal. And as there seems to be no prospect of educating them to become their own dieticians during the next 50 years, there will be indigestion, constipation, anemia, obesity. . . ."

We should reject the popular conception that the sprig of parsley which adorns the plate at mealtime is nothing more than a decorative garnish to be left untouched, and resolutely keep in mind that it is one of our most valuable foods and natural medicines. As we have seen, this humble herb contains blood cleansing and tonic properties. It stimulates digestion and aids in keeping the organs of the urinary system in good health. Parsley is credited from antiquity with having a beneficial action on the gall bladder, liver, spleen and has been used as a folk medicine for menstrual irregularities and cramps. It is reported to supply a rich amount of vitamin A, so necessary for the health of the eyes and optic nerve system. The vitamin C content in parsley helps to strengthen the body's resistance to infection and to maintain the tissue health of the bones, teeth, and gums. Vitamin C is also necessary to the normal healing rate of wounds and to prevent bruises from discoloring the skin for too long a period of time.

Let us resolve to make this valuable herb a staple in our daily diet. Chopped parsley can be sprinkled into soups, broths, egg and vegetable dishes. Salad dressings, sauces, meat loafs, broiled hamburgers, fish, salads, are all natural and delicious ways to eat parsley. One-half cup of the chopped herb added to a four-pound stew could provide up to 10,000 units of vitamin A alone.

11

SASSAFRAS—"CHIEF MEDICINE" PLANT

Sassafras (*Sassafras officinalis*) was used as a medicinal agent by the Indians long before Ponce de Leon reached the shores of Florida in 1512. The first detailed description of this American tree and its remedial employment is credited to Nicholaus Monardes, a Spanish physician of Sevilla in 1574. His information, however, was not gained from actual experience but from a careful review of government records and by personal consultation with travelers.

Several years prior to 1574 the Spaniards, on the advice of a few remaining Frenchmen in Florida used the plant in conditions of fevers and other diseases resulting from exposure to putrid swamp air and from drinking polluted water. The French had obtained their knowledge of the medicinal virtues of sassafras from Indians who called the plant *pavame*. For reasons unknown to Monardes, the French had named it *sassafras*. When the Spaniards first landed in Florida they believed the tree was the same as the cinnamon tree of Ceylon because of its strong spicy aroma.

USE OF SASSAFRAS BY THE INDIANS

Indian medicine men regarded sassafras as one of the chief remedies of their *materia medica*. The Iroquois Indians prepared a tea from the root-bark and used it for the treatment of rheumatism, as a tonic after childbirth, and to purify the blood. It was also employed as a tonic to the stomach and bowels, and as a remedy for bladder, kidney, and throat ailments. The Mohawks extracted the pith from the young shoots of sassafras and soaked it in water. This solution was carefully strained and used as an eye bath for inflammation of the eyes. Soups were flavored with a yellow powder which was obtained from the dried leaves.

John D. Hunter gives the following account on the Indian use of sassafras:

Shi-Kee—*Name of the tree.*

Sassafras. The Indians make a drink of the young blossoms and bark from the roots of sassafras in the spring of the year. The bruised leaves are applied as poultices and are deservedly prized. The pith, or medullary part of the sprouts steeped in cold water, forms a wash for sore eyes. They smoke the dried bark of the root, and prize it very highly.

We find these remarks in Lighthall's *Indian Household Medicine Guide:*

Sassafras. The bark of the root is the part used in medicine and domestic use. The Indians of many tribes dig it and use it as a tea. If it were used by civilizations instead of store tea and coffee, the stomach and digestion of civilization would be much better, and the owner more happy and hopeful.

Medical Properties and Uses. It is a blood thinner and purifier. It acts gently on the kidneys. Make a tea of it, and drink it either warm or cold at meals, instead of tea or coffee, and during the day instead of water, when you have bad blood.

Early Description

C. S. Rafinesque, A.M., Ph.D., was intrigued by the herbs and plants he found growing in the New World. Our knowledge of the early American flora is considerably derived from the studies and teachings of this great man. He prepared the first comprehensive work of its kind of which we have any record. In his book, *Medical Flora: or Manual of Medical Botany of the United States of North America* (1830), he gives a complete description of sassafras and its early medicinal uses:

Found from Canada to Mexico and Brazil. Roots, bark, leaves, flowers, fragrant and spicy. Flavor and smell peculiar, similar to fennel, sweetish subacrid, residing in a volatile oil heavier than water. The *sassafrine*, a peculiar mucus unalterable by alcohol, found chiefly in the twigs and pith, thickens water, very mild and lubricating, very useful in opthalmia, dysentery, gravel, catarrh, etc. Wood yellow, hard, durable, soon loses the smell; the roots chiefly exported for use as stimulant, antispasmodic, sudorific, and depurative; the oil now often substituted; both useful in rheumatism, cutaneous diseases, secondary syphilis, typus fevers, etc. Once used in dropsy. The Indians use a strong decoction to purge and clean the body in the spring; we use instead the tea of the blossoms for a vernal purification of the blood. The powder of the leaves used to make glutinous gombos. Leaves and buds used to flavor some beers and spirits. Also decmed vulnerary and resolvent chewed and applied, or emmenagogue and corroborant for women in tea; useful in scurvy, cachexy, flatulence, etc. Bowls and cups made of the wood; when fresh, it drives bugs and moths. The bark dyes wood of a fine orange color called "*shikih*" by Missouri tribes, and smoked like tobacco.

SASSAFRAS AS THE EARLY "WONDER DRUG"

Sassafras soon became a popular brew among the early colonists who used it as a "spring tonic" and as a home remedy for sore throat and colds. Squaws peddled the botanical in the settlements, and hawkers (medicine sellers) and traveling supply wagons always carried a stock of the root with them. In 1657 the French at Onondaga stated that they had found the leaves of sassafras every bit as effective for the treatment of wounds as the Indians had claimed.

Shortly after its discovery, explorers, soldiers, and sailors wrote such glowing accounts of the tree that sailing expeditions to the New World were undertaken to collect the bark, wood, and root for shipment to Europe. Early records show that an English merchant, Martin Pring, arrived on the American coast in 1603 with two sailing vessels. He built a temporary storage hut for sassafras, enclosed it with a barricade and placed a guard around it while he and others in his party engaged themselves in gathering the plant from the woods. As early as 1582 sassafras was already well-known in Frankfort-on-the-Main and in Hamburg in 1587. Spain and France were also well acquainted with the fragrant botanical from the New World and later it became known in Europe as the "wonder drug" of the 16th century. Highly exaggerated and fantastic remedial claims were made for sassafras, many of which proved groundless. However, it has retained its popularity as a health beverage to this day and its medicinal value in some areas has now been scientifically acknowledged.

Research Findings in Sassafras

There was a scientific interest in the plant around the turn of the century when it was found that people who drank sassafras tea were more resistant to colds and severe throat infections than those who did not. Medical research was started but was interrupted by the advent of World War I. By the time studies were resumed many years later, modern antibiotics had been discovered.

According to Dr. Reinsch, the bark of the root contains a volatile oil, resin, wax, camphor, fatty matter, a decomposition product of tannic acid known as *sassafrid*, tannic acid, albumen, starch, gum, lignin and salts. It has been found to possess general antiseptic power in various instances.

MODERN USE OF SASSAFRAS

Sassafras tea emits a spicy spring-like essence, and has maintained its popularity as a beverage for almost 400 years. "Sassafras bars" are built near popular health resorts where the tea is served either cold or piping hot. In many homes throughout the nation this hearty American brew is still used as a home remedy "spring tonic." Another favorite domestic use of the plant consists of a hot infusion of the bark which is employed as a sudorific in combating colds.

Potter's New Cyclopaedia[1] classifies the medicinal properties of sassafras as diaphoretic (producing perspiration), stimulant, and diuretic. Its use has been recorded as follows:

Parts Used: Root and bark of the root.

Medicinal Use: Used with success in eruptions of the skin, rheumatism, gout, etc. A decoction is beneficial

[1] Wren, (7th Ed.), p. 270.

as a wash for the eyes in ophthalmia, inflammation, etc. An infusion of one oz. of crushed bark in one pint of boiling water is taken in doses of a wineglassful, repeated frequently. Is generally given in combination with other remedies.

Skin Diseases

According to a journal of organic medicine,[2] sassafras combined with certain herbs forms a powerful remedy for skin diseases such as eczema, dermatoses of untraceable origin, impetigo, herpes zoster and ecthyma, acne, boils, and pityriasis. The journal states:

> These complaints are well covered by the following:
> Red clover flowers, two oz.; burdock root, one oz.; blue flag root, one oz.; sassafras bark, one-half oz.
> *Method.* Place one-quarter of the mixture in one pint of cold water, bring to the boil, simmer for 20 minutes, strain when cold.
> *Dose.* One wineglassful three times daily, until improvement is apparent.

Arthritis and Rheumatism

The following information is reported from a health publication:[3]

> *Arthritis.* This widespread octopus requires little introduction as its stranglehold is only too painfully apparent today.
> In this era martyrs do not die at the stake, but suffer from what is sometimes ten times worse. If those disturbing twinges have not yet tightened into the vise-like grip of this scathe, the following may prove to be just what you need to avoid its clutches.
>
> *Recipe.* One oz. prickly ash bark; one oz. sassafras bark; one oz. wood betony herb.
> Boil the barks in three pints of water for 20 minutes, and pour the whole of the hot liquor on the wood betony. Strain when cold.
> Dose: one wineglassful three or four times daily.

[2] *Health From Herbs*, February 1955, p. 58.
[3] *Health From Herbs*, October 1954, p. 315.

At bedtime, taken hot, it will be helpful to induce sleep. Some like it with a quarter teaspoonful of ginger added (which is good for flatulence) and a little honey to taste.

Do not forget this is Nature's medicine. She will not be hurried. Do not be disappointed if creaky joints of several years' standing are a little tardy in responding. Perseverance does not go unrewarded.

Dr. W. Fox gives this classification and use of sassafras:

Anti-scorbutic, alterative, stimulative, tonic, and aperient.

Sassafras is useful in rheumatism and all eruptive diseases. Aged people troubled with rheumatism will find it a useful drink—an infusion of the bark being drunk instead of common tea.

Practical Tips on Sassafras

If you are unfamiliar with botanicals, purchase them only from firms who know quality. The good grade of sassafras is red in color and consists of the peeled outer bark of the root only. Collecting the outer bark involves considerably more time and expense. Inferior grades are chipped, light in color, and consist of the outer bark as well as the often predominant and worthless inner wood.

When making apple sauce or canning pears, some people add a piece of sassafras bark for its delightful flavor.

To protect dried or fresh fruit from troublesome little insects, place a few small pieces of sassafras bark in the fruit bowl.

Sassafras Enters the Space Age

In spite of the numerous quick-acting drugs that are sold over the counter today, numerous people still prefer the patient virtues of simple herbs. We have seen how readily sassafras was adopted by many countries once the Indians had introduced the tree to the white man. To this day it has retained much of its early favor, especially as a spring tonic. Aside from providing a pleasant aromatic beverage, this medicine bush of the American Indians contains many valuable therapeutic properties as recorded in a wide range of usage.

Although we are now in the space age, the charm and healthful living in using sassafras is still with us, offering the comfort and epicurean delight of more leisurely eras.

12

THE "GREEN HOPE" IN THE FIGHT AGAINST CANCER

The second leading cause of death today is reported to be cancer, and it is on the increase. Yet, according to the National Cancer Institute, National Institutes of Health, more people are being cured of it than ever before. About 870,000 persons are under treatment for the disease at all times and upwards of a billion dollars annually is spent for the cost of hospitalization, doctors, nurses, and drugs. The cancer problem is an incredible enigma of paradoxes, hopes, frustrations, successes, and disappointments. Let us briefly examine some of the factors connected with the problem.

When searching for the solution to any disease, science follows the formula of prevention—seek out the cause and remove it, but unfortunately this approach does not work in general with cancer. This is because scientists have determined that cancer is not just one disease but many and that there are probably hundreds of different causes including environmental factors which elude identification. As Dr. Walter Alvarez explains: "Because there are so many different types of cancer, we can hardly expect one 'cure.' Chemists may have to discover 30 cures or vaccines for 30 cancers."

In all cases the cancer process seems relatively similar although there are a number of different types of cancer. The disease is reported to start when one cell or a group of cells stops functioning normally and begins an unrestricted growth which crowds out and destroys the normal cells. To complicate matters, the cancer cells often break away from the original location of the disease and travel to other parts of the body through the blood stream. This breaking away and lodging in other areas is called metastasizing.

Some of the Causes

Cancer researchers believe they have had considerable success in identifying a great number of the various causes of the disease. Certain chemicals, viruses, smoking, radiation, continued physical irritation, and air pollution—these are external causes. Within the individuals themselves there can be factors which may predispose to cancer, such as immunological characteristics, genetic predisposition, and hormonal patterns which all apparently play a part.

Many years ago a high percentage of scrotal cancer was found among males working as chimney sweeps. Certain chemicals in the soot of the chimneys was determined to be the actual cause and steps were taken to prevent the soot from becoming lodged in the sweeps' scrotal skin. Cases of scrotal cancer were then reported to have dropped dramatically.

Dr. William B. Shimkin, U.S. Public Health Service cancer researcher, says that other causes of cancer are associated with various occupations. For example: lung cancer is found among workers who inhale radioactive ores, chromates, iron and asbestos. Bladder cancer occurs frequently among aniline dye workers who handle such chemicals as betanaphthylamine. Workers who inhale or ingest radium are susceptible to bone cancer. Skin cancer is reported to have occurred among workers who handle the distillation and fractional products of oil shale, coal, petroleum and lignite. These and other factors are responsible for some 150 forms of cancer that are now undergoing study.

Cancer Research Accelerated

Notable advances have been made in the fight against cancer. Scientists are widening the front, examining every possible new angle to the problem. In the last 15 years cancer research has been dramatically speeded up. A special diet has been credited in some cases with bringing about a degree of remission in a number of terminal cancer patients. Dr. Albert B. Lorincz, professor of obstetrics and gynecology at the University of Chicago, made the first report of "objective remission" in cancer patients treated by the diet, at a meeting of the American Medical Association's 116th Annual Convention. In Tokyo, Dr. Saffiotti announced a study indicating that vitamin A inhibits lung cancer induced in animals subjected to benzpyrene. He pointed out that this discovery could "possibly lead to results of practical significance for the prevention of lung cancer."

Task force projects have been set up as new areas of research. These are listed as follows:

The Acute Leukemia Task Force, largely responsible for the Special Virus-Leukemia Program recently launched.

The Lymphoma Task Force, which will study the possibility of increasing the cure rate for Hodgkin's disease and promoting widespread use of successful treatment techniques.

The Chronic Leukemia and Multiple Myeloma Task Force, also scheduled to delve into the survival of patients with those conditions.

The Breast Cancer Task Force, which faces one of the most formidable problems in cancer research. Mortality rates for breast cancer victims have generally remained unchanged for the past three decades.

The greatest hope for cancer patients against which radiation and surgery are ineffective is chemotherapy—treatment with drugs. Since 1957, the government has paid out hundreds of millions of dollars for cancer research in which 257,000 materials have been screened. A small number of these substances have shown promise against various types of cancers and have been evaluated first for safety in lab animals and then for safety and effectiveness in hospital patients across the nation.

Dr. Shimkin says: "The full application of known methods of diagnosing and treating cancer would further increase the salvage rate from our present 30 percent to 50 percent. Thus, in effect, we have the necessary knowledge to reduce cancer mortality in the U.S. by some 25 percent."

THE SEARCH FOR CURATIVE POSSIBILITIES IN HERBS

Scientists are not overlooking the botanicals in their search for anti-cancer agents. Plants used for thousands of years as folk remedies are yielding substances effective against tumors in laboratory animals and against human cancer cells in test tubes. University of Wisconsin researchers revealed that extracts of *dogbane, woody nightshade,* and *milkweed* have yielded four active compounds. These results stem from a major research program at the University of Wisconsin, School of Pharmacy, headed by Dr. S. Morris Kupchan, one of the pioneers in exploring the plant kingdom for anticancer drugs. Several thousand of the over one-half million plants in the world have been tested during the past six years. From these, Wisconsin researchers have turned up over 150 plants whose substances have shown anti-tumor activity.

"We're using folk medicine and herbalism as a source of leads," Dr. Kupchan said. "One of the plants we're studying —*Solanum dulcamara,* also called 'bittersweet' or 'woody nightshade'—was recommended by Galen in 150 A.D. as a treatment for tumors, cancer and warts." An extract of red milkweed was found effective in test tube experiments against human cancer cells. The scientists fractionated the extract to isolate the anti-tumor substance and eventually a single crystalline compound, *calotropin,* was produced. *Withaferin,* from the Central American shrub, *Acnistus arborescens,* was said to "look very good" in experiments conducted by this team. Research on Indian dogbane, also called Indian hemp, led to the discovery of two other anti-tumor principles, *cymarin* and *apocannoside.* Dogbane is botanically known as *Apocynum cannabinum.* The juice of this plant was used in folk medicine against growths and warts which appear on or near the genital organs.

Dr. Kupchan points out that many of the plants under study are not included in the "witch doctor's" pharmacopoeia. For example, a wild flower called meadow rue, *Thalictrum dasycarpum,* is found growing near the university campus. It contains *thalicarpine,* an alkaloid that has an inhibitory effect on intramuscular tumors in rats. *Elephantus elatus,* a plant native to Florida is another which has demonstrated anti-cancer properties.

Dr. Kupchan explains that the botanical approach to cancer research supplements the work of other researchers. He says: "Medicinal chemists have nearly exhausted the possibilities of improving known cancer drugs by chemical modification." He concludes that, "New approaches to cancer treatment could come from clarifying the structures of plant-derived tumor inhibitors."

ADDITIONAL PLANTS UNDER STUDY

Following is a partial list of other plants which have shown promise as cancer fighting agents. It includes the research and findings of foreign countries as well as those of the United States.

Australian Scrub Ash

Drs. G. H. Svoboda and Gerald A. Poore of the Lilly Research Laboratories in Indianapolis reported that an antitumor substance has been extracted from the bark of the Australian scrub ash (*Acronychia baueri*). The alkaloid called *acronycine* is said to be a new type of chemical structure which attacks various types of leukemia and some tumors. The substance inhibited 12 out of 17 types of tumors in mice. It is still in the early stages of investigation.

Bamboo Grass

German scientists have become keenly interested in a Japanese cancer drug known as Bamfolin. It is a yellow powder obtained from a type of bamboo grass which has been used in Japan as a medicinal agent for centuries. According to the *German Tribune*[1] some cases of cancer were said to be effectively treated with the drug. No side effects were observed. Bamfolin however is still in the preliminary stage of chemical testing and only on a minor scale at that. Professor Fritz Scheller cautioned against over-optimism saying that the material would not be available for several years. The Japanese discoverer readily admits that the reason Bamfolin is effective is not known. In some cases the material acts quickly and with lasting effect, however, in others the initial improvement ceases and in some cases it does not work at all.

Beets

Dr. Siegmund Schmidt of Bad Rothenfelde, Germany, has reported effective results with the use of beet juice in the treatment of cancer. He states that: "This therapy suggested by Dr. Ferenczi [Nobel prize winner] and myself was at first

[1] June 9, 1964.

smiled at. But we found that in all cases of tumorous diseases and leukemia, the juice of *Beta vulgaris* (beets) produced favorable results. The juice from at least one kilogram [about 2.2 lbs.] of raw beet is taken daily before meals over the whole day. It may be mixed with curd or yogurt or some fruit."

Dr. Schmidt also mentions a powder prepared from beets which was administered to cancer patients and says: "I saw favorable effects in 15 patients who suffered from leukemia and in 30 patients suffering from cancer." He also suggests its use as a means of prevention before the cancer flares up in what he calls "pre-cancerous" conditions. On this basis the use of beet juice could possibly be considered as a preventative of some types of cancer.

Dr. Schmidt maintains that, "Through daily doses of beet juice, it is also possible to reduce the toxic effects of ionizing radiation. . . . The good results of my method of treatment can best be established by the Scheller test (Munich, Frundsberg-str.). Tests with animals have proved the favorable effects of *Beta vulgaris*."

The German physician also draws attention to the fact that Professor Wilstatter successfully isolated the material in beets as the agent producing the improvement, classing it among the group of Anthocyans. He says that this substance regulates the "oxygen fermentations." Dr. Schmidt adds:

I wish to state that a treatment with *Beta vulgaris* seems to be indicated for patients suffering from cancer and which should be applied in connection with the usual cancer therapy. I noticed above all that the toxic effect of the cystostatics were considerably reduced. I could administer essentially higher doses of cystostatics over a longer period, resulting in a mitigated progress of the disease and a prolongation of the patient's life.

I am very grateful to Professor Dr. Trub, head of the Association of the Social Insurance Institutions of North Rhine-Westfalia for the Fight Against Cancer, that he has taken up my suggestions. In several hospitals *Beta vulgaris* in the form of juice or powder was administered as mixed beverages with buttermilk, red wine or curd.

In the *Therapie der Gengenwart*, No. 8, 1962, Professor Dr. Trub reports as follows: "In the course of our model test we found that the patients could stand the cystostatics much better after having received red beet juice . . . the unfavorable side-effects were less frequent. Through individual observations we could furthermore establish that the red-beet juice should be of a minimum concentration with a specific gravity of 1.04 in order to be effective." He then describes the case of a woman with an advanced cancer who was treated with trenimon and beet juice. She was soon able to leave the hospital, walking with a walking stick. He then speaks of 75 cancer patients helped by this therapy.

Brewers' Yeast

At one time brewers' yeast was used only in breweries but is now available in pure form from health food stores for use as a food supplement. Brewer's yeast is not the same as uncooked yeast cakes or raw dried bakers' yeast. It is a plant product which has been specifically produced for food. It is a rich source of complete protein and contains all the elements of the vitamin B complex.

Experiments involving the effect of diet in relation to cancer of the liver were conducted over a period of many years at the Sloan-Kettering Institute for Cancer Research. To determine whether or not brewers' yeast was effective as a preventative of liver cancer, three groups of rats were all placed on cancer inducing diets for 150 days. The diet consisted of rice mixed with *butter yellow*, a chemical dye known to cause cancer (this coloring substance was banned from food products many years ago). In addition, 3 percent brewers' yeast was included in the diet of the first group while the second group received 6 percent and the third 15 percent. Within 150 days all the animals in the first two groups had developed cancerous livers. By contrast all the rats in the third group which had received 15 percent brewers' yeast had normal healthy livers at the end of the 150 days.

Dr. Kanematsu Suguira and his co-workers conducted further experiments to determine if brewers' yeast would cure liver cancer once it had taken hold. From results based on these and other experiments, Dr. Suguira believes that although 15 percent brewers' yeast added to an animal's diet will not destroy malignant tumors which have been allowed to develop to any degree, early stages of cirrhosis can be halted and successfully treated by this method.

In another experiment on lab animals it was found that 10 percent dessicated liver (which was substituted for the brewers' yeast) would also tend to prevent liver cancer.

Although these experiments were conducted solely with animals, Dr. Suguira feels that, "These dietary influences may yet prove to play a very large part in the causation, prevention and treatment of human cancer."

Calaguala

The fern Calaguala was used as a folk remedy for centuries by the aborigines of northern Honduras. University of Honduras scientists have recently announced that an extract from the fern has been successfully used on patients with advanced cancer at San Felipe Hospital. No serious side effects were observed.

Calvatia giganteum

From the giant puffball mushroom known as *Calvatia giganteum* comes an extract known as *calvacin*, an antitumor agent which has been found effective against 14 types of cancer in animals. The discovery was reported by researchers from Sloan-Kettering Institute, Michigan State University, and from Armour and Company.

Camptotheca acuminata

A U.S. Department of Agriculture researcher reports that the substance taken from the wood, bark, and twigs of a rare Chinese tree holds promise for arresting leukemia in humans. In tests on laboratory animals the extract known as *camptothecin* was shown to be effective against leukemia. It was identified and isolated by Dr. Monroe E. Wall of the Research Triangle Institute, Durham, North Carolina.

The only natural source of this substance is the *Camptotheca acuminata* tree, but scientists are now trying to synthesize the material. Some 1,000 seedlings of the rare tree were planted at the Agricultural Research Service's Plant Introduction Station at Chico, California. These are expected to produce good amounts of the raw material for continued testing.

Garlic

Japanese scientists Motonori Fujiwara and Toshikazu Natata are tackling the cancer problem from the angle of immunity. The principle of immunity has been known for a very long time and basically consists of taking a diseased cell or virus and treating it in a special way so that it does not produce the disease, but still retains its ability to form antibodies. In that way the person or animal into which these disease producing organisms are introduced acquires the ability to produce antibodies which fight against that particular disease.

The Kyoto University researchers took Ehrlich ascites tumor cells and treated them with an extract of freshly ground garlic (*Allium sativum*). They reported that, "Mice injected with these tumor cells developed a strong immunity to the same type of tumor cells." However, tumor cells treated with an extract of *boiled* garlic and injected into the mice did not bring about immunity. The mice in this control group all developed cancerous tumors. In another experiment mice were injected with 100,000 live tumor cells two weeks after the final garlic extract inoculation and the scientists announced that "none of the mice developed tumors within a period of 100 days."

Similar lab experiments in which garlic extract was employed have been conducted here in the United States. When injected with garlic-treated cancerous cells no deaths occurred for a period of six months among the mice treated. Austin S. Weinberger and Jack Pensky of Western Reserve University then experimented further. Mice were inoculated with live cancerous cells and then given injections of the garlic extract. It was found that the garlic delayed the development of the malignant tumor and in some cases prevented its formation. In every case, however, it was essential to continue the garlic treatment as it was observed that the tumors grew rapidly if this was not done.

Ipecac

This is a tropical plant native to South America. There are many varieties. The Rio Ipecac or Mato Grosso (Brazil); Minas Ipecac which grows in the province of Minas Gerais; Johore Ipecac which bears a close resemblance to the Rio; and the Cartagena Ipecac of Colombia. Two alkaloids, emetine and cephaeline, are found in each of them but in different proportions.

According to researchers, substances extracted from Ipecac could lead to new potent compounds for use against cancer.

Dr. Arthur P. Grollman of the Albert Einstein College of Medicine, Yeshiva University, has successfully traced the chemical action by which emetine (extracted from Ipecac) inhibits the growth of some cells but not others. It arrests the growth of granulomas which are masses of cells that form over wounds as part of the healing process. Dr. Grollman found that emetine destroys certain cells by blocking the chemical process involved in making protein, the cells' nourishment.

Juniper

The well-known red cedar, *Juniperus virginiana*, belongs to an extensive genus of evergreen trees and shrubs. It is found in all regions of the country but particularly from Virginia southward. The botanical name is from the Celtic *juniperus*—rough.

Tumor-inhibitory activity against Sarcoma 180 in mice was demonstrated by the use of an alcohol extract of *Juniperus virginiana*. The extract was also found effective against human carcinoma of the nose and throat carried in cell culture. Podophyllotoxin proved to be the active principle. These findings were reported in a scientific paper submitted by S. Morris Kupchan, Jane C. Hemingway, and John R. Knox (*Journal of Pharmaceutical Sciences*, Vol. 54, No. 4, April 1965).

American Mandrake

American mandrake (*Podophyllum peltatum*) grows in moist thickets, woods and pastures in the Eastern half of the United States and Canada. The plant was well-known to the American Indians who used the root as an emetic, cathartic, vermifuge, and as a treatment for warts. It became an official drug in 1864 and has remained so to this day. An active resin known as *podophyllin* was discovered and extracted from the rhizome during the last century by John King, M.D., of the Cincinnati Eclectic Medical Institute. Mandrake is noted for its cathartic effect and is also employed as a caustic in the treatment of some types of superficial tumors (papillomas). Its action on the liver is greatly recognized and *podophyllin* forms a basis for a number of proprietary "liver pills."

Mandrake contains the promising tumor-arresting principle, *podophyllotoxin*, the same substance found in *Juniperus virginiana*. Oddly enough, mandrake and the juniper are not closely related. Tumor-bearing mice were injected subcutaneously with *podophyllotoxin* and alpha and beta-peltatin.[2] Extensive damage was induced in all six types of the transplanted tumors. In Switzerland, Drs. Albert von Wartburg and Emil Schreier of Sandoz, Ltd., a pharmaceutical manufacturer, have also discovered anti-tumor compounds in the American mandrake.

Periwinkle

Vinblastine sulphate (Velban, Lilly) is the name given to a substance obtained from the periwinkle plant, *Vinca rosea*. Since its discovery, it has been used primarily in the treatment of choriocarcinoma and Hodgkin's disease and is presently under study for other types of cancers. Recently, a team of British physicians has reported that vinblastine shows promise in the treatment of lung cancer. It was revealed in a study of patients treated with the plant drug that the three month survival rate had a "statistically significant advantage" over controls. No apparent advantage was observed however at 12 months. The investigators feel that "higher dosage or longer treatment with this well-tolerated drug might give better results." Patients were given vinblastine intravenously, once weekly.

Vine of the Genus Tylophora

Approval has been given to a drug company by the National Institutes of Health—National Cancer Institute for tests on humans of the anti-cancer agents of a drug extracted from an Australian vine. According to Dr. Koppaka V. Rao, a biochemist with Pfizer's cancer laboratory in Maywood, New Jersey, the plant is a vine of the genus *Tylophora*. It has been found to produce an alkaloid that shrinks tumors in rats. Compounds derived from the vine are chemically known as tylophorinine, tylophorine, and tylocrebrine.

[2] Greenspan *et al.* (*J. Nat. Cancer Inst.*, 1950, 10, 1295) and Leiter *et al.* (1950, 10, 1273).

Violet

The violet (*Viola odorata*) has been used in folk medicine to relieve the pain of cancer and many of the early herbalists claimed that it even cured the disease. Recipes citing the use of the plant for this purpose could be found in a number of the old herb books. Instructions were: One pint of boiling water to be poured over a handful of fresh violet leaves and the infusion allowed to steep (stand) for 12 hours. It was then strained and reheated for use. A cloth dipped into the solution was applied to the affected part and covered with an oilskin. As soon as the cloth became cold or dry it was immediately changed. Some herbalists recommended poultices which were prepared and employed in a similar way. In addition to either of these methods, one pint of the infusion made from dried violet leaves was taken as a tea every day. If the tumor appeared on the inside of the mouth the infusion was taken as a tea and also used as a gargle or mouthwash.

It must be remembered, however, that in the old days there were no scientific laboratories to determine whether or not a tumor was cancerous or benign. So it may be that the good results claimed by the herbalists for the use of violet were not really curing cancer at all. Nevertheless the following comments by Dr. Jonathan L. Hartwell of the National Cancer Institute, National Institutes of Health, are of great interest to us:

> The violet plant, as far back as 500 B.C., was used in poultice form as a cure for surface cancer. It was used in 18th century England for the same purpose. And now, only months ago—a letter from a farmer in Michigan tells me how he used the plant as a cancer remedy. When the remedy was tried on a cancerous mouse here at the Institute, we found that it did damage the cancer.

Russian Research

In Moscow, research scientists Lidiya Kryukova and Alexander Kuzin have discovered in the leaves of sunflower, flax, mint, potato tubers, beans, and other plants which have been exposed to heavy doses of gamma radiation, substances capable of halting the growth of cancerous cells. Very promising results have been obtained when administered to test animals (*Moscow News*, March 30–April 6, 1968).

HOPE SPRINGS ETERNAL

For ages herbalists have maintained that the final solution for conquering every illness would be found within the plant kingdom. The growing scientific trend toward botanical medicine may eventually prove this idea to be a valid one. In the words of the distinguished Dr. Alfred Taylor of the University of Texas:

> In our 20 years of cancer research, we have never had as much success with chemicals invented by man as we are now having with plant extracts. There is not a single chemical agent that will completely inhibit the growth of, or destroy, tumor tissue without causing undue disturbance in non-tumor tissue.
>
> But in plants we have more compounds to work with than scientists can ever hope to synthesize. The plant kingdom contains forms as diverse as oaks and fungi, and variety in form is paralleled by variety in biochemistry. We have scarcely begun to explore this potential.[3]

(*Additional references: Health Bulletin*, September 3, 1966, Vol. 4, No. 36; and October 21, 1967, Vol. 5, No. 42. *Prevention*, October 1956, Vol. 8, No. 10.)

[3] *The Naturopath*, September 1963, p. 5.

13

VARIETY OF USES
OF ROSEMARY

Rosemary (*Rosmarinus officinalis*) belongs to the mint family. It may be called a versatile flower as it has been symbolically associated with joy and sorrow, life and death. The botanical name is from the Latin *ros*—dew, and *marinus*—of the sea, as the plant grows so luxuriously near the seashore. There are several varieties under cultivation in gardens, *Rosmarinus officinalis* being the more common and popular species.

TRADITIONAL BACKGROUND

The ancients claimed that the use of rosemary strengthened the memory, and poets make frequent allusion to the plant which shows a familiarity with this tradition, such as Shakespears's "There's rosemary, that's for remembrance; I pray you, love, remember." (*Hamlet*)

The Romans and Greeks burned the plant as incense during their religious rites and, at banquets, crowned their guests of honor with garlands made from the leaves. Because the herb was used so much as a crowning wreath, it was often called Rosmarinus Coronaria. To the Romans its evergreen foliage was symbolic of the soul's immortality, and rosemary was one of the botanicals employed for embalming their dead. Until comparatively recent years it was customary in various parts of the world to strew the herb on coffins as emblematic of the life to come. This fragrant plant was also a token of the dignity of the marriage sacrament. Those attending a wedding all carried sprigs of rosemary. Several sprays were entwined in the bridal wreath as a silent reminder to the newlywed that she should take with her the fond memories of loving hearts she was leaving behind. Mystically the herb signifies love and loyalty, and was once believed to strengthen the heart as well as the memory.

Christian Traditions Associated with Rosemary

In early times rosemary was greatly associated with the observance of Christmas. This association may have been suggested by the great number of legends connecting the herb with a religious background, particularly with reference to the Blessed Virgin. A quaint old Spanish legend says that when Mary was escaping from Herod's soldiers with the Infant Jesus in her arms, some plants rustled as they passed, betraying the whereabouts of the Holy travelers; but a beautiful rosemary bush quickly stretched out its branches encircling the Mother and Child, hiding them safely in its foliage. Another legend says that Mary spread the frocks of the Holy Infant on a rosemary bush to dry. When she returned to get them she found them dangling from a sunbeam. The herb therefore became "Mary's rose" (although it is not actually a rose) and was said to bless every household with peace and good will if it was included among their Christmas decorations.

Another early Christian legend claims that the bush ceases to grow when it reaches the age of 33, the age of Christ at the time of His crucifixion. From that point on, the plant only grows in width, refusing to exceed the height of Jesus Christ when He lived on earth as a man.

REPORTED HEALTH USES OF ROSEMARY

Rosemary was extensively cultivated in the gardens of the early Monks for use as a medicinal agent. The young tops, leaves and flowers were brewed as a tea and employed for nervousness, convulsions, liver trouble, headache, and stomach disorders. Mixed with honey, the tea reputedly brought relief from bronchitis and asthma. A liniment prepared from the herb was used for rheumatism and gout.

Culpeper devotes considerable space to this plant in his writings. He says it is good for "swimming of the head" (dizziness), weak eyes, weak memory, flatulence, and indigestion. He also recommended its use to sweeten the breath. The herb was prescribed by Arabian physicians to restore the speech after a stroke. Dr. James wrote: "Rosemary is a plant of great service in affections of the head and nerves, helping the apoplexy, palsy, and all kinds of convulsions, pains and dizziness of the head. It strengthens the sight and memory."

In former times rosemary water was called "the bath of life" as the plant was believed to impart liveliness and gaiety if used in the bath. Young ladies claimed that a wash made from the herb was effective for removing freckles, while the Italians stated that rosemary strengthened the memory and prolonged life. An old herbalist advised: "Make thee a box with rosemary [wood] and smell to it and it shall preserve thy youth." The herb was strewn in clothes closets and drawers as a moth repellent. Until recent years, the leaves were mixed with juniper twigs and burned regularly in French hospital wards to purify the air and to check the spread of infection. Around the turn of the century a noted English physician wrote: "Rosemary wine, taken in small quantities acts as a quieting cordial."

Father Kneipp's Heart and Stomach Remedy

According to Father Kneipp, rosemary is a good remedy for the stomach and heart:

Would it not be a shame if this spicy herb escaped the attention of the gatherer for the household apotheca [medicine shelf]?

Rosemary is an excellent stomachic.

Prepared as a tea, it cleanses the stomach from phlegm, gives a good appetite and good digestion. Whoever likes to see the medicine glass, this comforter in illness, shining on his table, let him fill it with rosemary tea, and take from two to four tablespoonfuls morning and evening. The stomach will soon become sensible, that is, will not stick fast much longer in phlegm.

Rosemary wine, taken in small doses, has also proved an excellent remedy against heart infirmities. It operates in a sedative manner, and in cases of heart dropsy it works strongly on removal through the urine. . . .

Against both complaints, three or four tablespoonfuls, or a small wineglassful, of this pleasant drink are taken daily, morning and evening.

The preparation of this wine is exceedingly simple. A handful of rosemary is cut up as small as possible, put into a bottle, and good, well-kept wine poured upon it; white wine is preferable.

Even after half a day's standing, it may be used as rosemary wine.

The same leaves may be used a second time.

What Rosemary Contains

Rosemary contains a special camphor, tannin, a volatile oil, a bitter principle and a resin. It is classified as astringent, tonic, and diaphoretic. Homeopathic physicians employ the wild species of rosemary (*Ledum palustre*) in the treatment of rheumatism. In various parts of the world the common rosemary is used as a stomachic and nervine (acting on the nerves). A medicinal water distilled from the plant is highly esteemed in Hungary as a remedy for nervous disorders. In America and England, a delicate aromatic oil is extracted which is employed in the manufacture of perfumes.

The Memory

Dr. Eric Powell[1] tells us that tests over a lengthy period have demonstrated that there is a lot to the old saying, "Rosemary—that's for remembrance." He says:

There is no doubt that small doses of fresh rosemary help improve the memory. In common with camomile and wild yam it is also of much service in the treatment of congestive headaches and insomnia. It undoubtedly has an affinity for the brain.

Reported Uses for Bone and Joint Pains

The village healers of the Balkans employ rosemary for the relief of aches and pains in the bones and joints. This is claimed to be a highly effective folk remedy. A bottle which holds nine-tenths of a quart is used to prepare the recipe. Three-fourths is filled with vodka and the balance with the flowers and small tops of rosemary. The bottle is then tightly corked and placed in the hot sun for three days. If the sun is not sufficiently hot or if there is no sun out at all, the

[1] *Health From Herbs*, July–August 1967, p. 120.

bottle is kept near a heated stove. The mixture is shaken well three times daily. At the end of the steeping period the liquid is carefully strained and placed in another bottle and two or three grains of camphor are added. The mixture is shaken well as soon as the camphor dissolves. A small amount of this solution is rubbed thoroughly on the aching parts until it is no longer absorbed by the skin—at this point the rubbing is discontinued. The parts are then covered with wool or flannel. At the same time, eight drops of this preparation are taken in one tablespoonful of water. In severe aches and pains this treatment is used three times a day, every day until the desired results have been obtained. For minor pains it is used but once a day.

Ear Disease

Some medical herbalists recommend rosemary in combination with other herbs for the following disorder of the ears:[2]

> *Meniere's Disease.* This was named after the French physician of that name who lived from 1799 to 1862. It is concerned with the ears, and is an inflammatory process and congestion of the semi-circular canals. Symptoms are vertigo (dizziness) pallor and a number of aural and ocular disturbances. Dizziness is perhaps its most trying feature.
> Do not despair. There is a herbal combination of proven worth, and which will not let you down.
> Let sufferers obtain equal parts of these herbs (fine cut); rosemary, wood betony, wood sage, mistletoe, shepherd's purse. Mix. Place two teaspoonfuls in a teacup and fill with boiling water, making yourself a cup of tea. Allow to stand for some minutes, and drink with a little honey and milk if the taste seems a little strange on the palate.

Migraine Headache

According to an article printed in a health publication,[3] a woman who had suffered from migraine headache for ten years was successfully treated with a herbal formula in which rosemary was one of the ingredients. The recipe called for

[2] *Health From Herbs,* September 1957, p. 348.
[3] *Health From Herbs,* October 1954, p. 312.

two ounces of wood betony, one ounce of rosemary, and one ounce of scullcap. After thoroughly mixing the herbs, one-quarter of the mixture was placed in one pint of cold water and brought to a boil. This was simmered for two minutes, then strained and left until cold. "Dose: one wineglassful three times daily." The patient was also suffering from insomnia, but we are told that this was effectively dealt with by "taking an extra dose, hot, at bedtime."

Strength for the Heart Muscles

Dr. Vogel[4] says:

Carry dried currants and raisins about with you in your pocket and chew them slowly as you attend to your work! Your heart muscles will be grateful to you for this, especially if in addition, you chew the tops of rosemary first thing in the morning after breakfast.

The Liver

Swinburne Clymer, M.D.,[5] recommends the use of rosemary for torpidity of the liver. He writes:

In all cases where there is a torpid condition of the liver and a predisposition toward dropsy, this is the remedy to take. It is also excellent when the system is congested with morbid matter. All those who suffer from congestions as indicated by frequent colds, would do well to take rosemary tea at regular intervals of three days each. Rosemary tea is an ideal fall and spring remedy and will readily take the place of the well-known sulphur-molasses combination.

Headache

The following is a popular folk remedy for simple headache: As soon as the headache begins, a small bottle of spirits of rosemary is held close to the nose and the fumes inhaled. In addition, a few drops of this remedy are rubbed well on the temples, forehead, veins of the neck, and behind the ears. It is claimed that the headache will soon be gone.

[4] *The Nature Doctor*, p. 17.
[5] *Nature's Healing Agents*, p. 136.

Hair Health and Beauty

Rosemary has enjoyed a solid reputation since olden times as an excellent hair conditioner. It is prepared as a strong infusion and used externally. In some countries the infusion is combined with borax and employed as a wash to prevent premature baldness. In Mexico, 20 grams of the herb is mashed and steeped in a pint of pure alcohol for one week. The scalp is frictioned with this solution twice a day as a treatment for falling hair.

The following combination is used to give the hair a glossy sheen: Two ounces of rosemary herb, one ounce of raspberry leaves, and two ounces of red sage. Mix well. Place a good amount in a small bowl and saturate with boiling water. Cover and let it stand until cold, then strain. The solution is brushed into the hair once or twice a day. This herbal recipe should be freshly made every few days as it will not keep.

Oil of rosemary is the main ingredient in a number of modern preparations for the hair, such as shampoos, tonics, and hair conditioners. It is also used in making Eau de Cologne, and for scenting cosmetic soaps and perfumes.

ROSEMARY—A VALUABLE AND DELICIOUS CULINARY HERB

We think of culinary herbs in terms of flavor and do not realize that their original purpose was therapeutic. When the ancients began adding more and more meat and heavy foods to their diets, they found to their dismay that they were becoming sick and exhausted. So they conceived the idea of taking their medicine along with their food and included herbs such as rosemary, mint, sage, or ginger to counteract the ill effects. Mint, for example, is usually added to pea soup which undoubtedly enriches the flavor, but of far greater value is the fact that the herb helps correct the tendency of peas to produce gas. Mints are well-known remedies for flatulence. (Rosemary is a member of the mint family).

In a record written in 1782, the author tells of his escape from the Indians, and how he lived on berries, roots, and raw meats during his trek back to civilization. He said: "When food sat heavy on my stomach, I used to eat a little wild ginger root, which put all to rights." An old herb book states: "Sweet marjoram is chiefly used as a condiment in cooking, to diminish by its excitant qualities, the heaviness of pork, goose, and other fat foods." Rosemary and sage were also used for the same purpose. Certain herbs or spices such as cinnamon, garlic, and cloves are powerful antiseptics, and germicides. The Indians fully recognized the true purpose of culinary herbs and combined them with food that was questionable, as well as to improve digestibility and flavor.

Let us adopt the wisdom of the ancients and select our herbal dressings first and foremost with a view to their therapeutic properties. Among its many virtues, rosemary is repeatedly cited as an excellent stomachic. This means that it contains substances which give strength and tone to the stomach, assist digestion, and stimulate the appetite. That the herb is also an excellent flavoring agent is a foregone conclusion.

Rosemary is used in veal, lamb, roast beef, beans, gravies, sauces, poultry and rice. When the dried herb is employed, the leaves are first soaked for several hours to soften them. Since prolonged cooking destroys the delicate flavor of culinary herbs, rosemary should be sprinkled on roasts or other meats that require long cooking about an hour before the food is done.

For those on diets, the plant kingdom offers a wide assortment of herbs which can add more flavor to the vegetables without an increase of calories.

14

HOW TO USE HERBS FOR
BATHING AND BEAUTY BENEFITS

Bathing and the proper care of the skin are far more important to the health of the body than most people realize. Somehow the skin is not generally thought of as a vital organ such as the heart, liver, or lungs. Yet science tells us that if the skin fails to function even for a few hours, all internal organs can break down. The nervous system can become paralyzed and the kidneys, liver and heart poisoned. In severe scalding or third degree burns where two-thirds of the skin is destroyed, death shortly follows as a result of reflex destruction of the internal organs.

If the skin were to be completely coated or covered with a substance through which no air could possibly penetrate, an individual would soon die. He becomes poisoned by his own gases and toxins, and the increased internal temperature causes inflammation of the visceral organs. Tragic accidents have occurred and cases are recorded in which individuals have died in a very short time after their bodies had been covered with impervious material. Many years ago, in a street parade, a child dressed in tin foil was standing on a float as a representation of cupid. The child died of acute inflammation of the kidneys a few hours after the parade ended due to the suspension of the skin as an organ of elimination. The suspension had caused a severe burden to be placed on the kidneys, a demand which the kidneys simply could not handle.

FUNCTION AND DUTIES OF THE SKIN

Let us examine some of the facts relating to the skin and the duties which it performs for the body. The word "pore" is taken from the Greek *poros* meaning "passage." The millions of pores in the skin are important gateways in eliminating waste products from the system. From two to three million tiny sweat glands drain off perspiration through the pores. These glands are each coiled under a layer of fat and constitute a drainage of from two and a half to three miles. Normally about one quart of moisture is excreted during a period of 24 hours. In addition, the sudorific glands secrete and discharge a fine oil which lubricates the skin and hair and also acts as a protective device against invading bacteria.

Temperature, Absorption and Respiration

Another function of the skin is that of aiding the regulation of bodily temperature. It prevents the escape of necessary body heat to a considerable extent. On the other hand when the body becomes overheated through strenuous exercises, external heat, or fever, the skin relieves the tissues by helping the heat to escape. It is also an organ of respiration and absorption, taking in oxygen and exhaling poisons and gases. To some extent food and medication are absorbed by the skin and passed into the blood stream. It is also an organ of touch or sensation and is very closely connected with all the great nerve centers.

Excretion of Body Waste Products

One of the most important functions of the skin is that of excretion of waste products. Experiments conducted by some noted physiologists such as Seguin, Lavoisier, and others, revealed that the skin eliminates more impurities from the body than the lungs, bowels and kidneys combined. A great portion of this waste material is discharged through the skin in the form of invisible gases and is called insensible perspiration. This process continues steadily every day and night. Visible perspiration collects on the surface of the skin and is commonly referred to as sweat. Were it not for this arrangement of removing poisonous waste products from the body, the blood would become more and more toxic until it would no longer be able to support life. Therefore this vital function of the skin cannot be stopped or even checked without inviting serious consequences.

IMPORTANCE OF CORRECT BATHING FOR HEALTH

Since the skin is an organ of excretion and absorption, the importance of bathing cannot be overestimated. Unless a person bathes frequently and properly the impurities deposited on the skin through perspiration accumulate, obstructing the work of the pores, thus interfering with the further elimination of poisons from the body. In addition some of this accumulated waste may be reabsorbed, causing the system to become toxic. Dr. Wilson says, "When the functions of the skin are imperfectly performed the whole body suffers, the heart, lungs, bowels, liver, stomach, the brain, nerves, are imperfectly nourished; and then the vitality is weakened by the noxious matter with which the blood is loaded."

In his *Domestic Practice*, Dr. Johnson also stresses the importance of keeping the skin clean and healthy. He writes, "Not only do solid and fluid matters escape through the skin, but it also throws out gaseous matters, which being retained in the system are equally poisonous as either solids or fluids."

The Ancient Art of Bathing

The ancients recognized the value of bathing, a practice which was followed to a much greater extent than in modern times. Books written by some of the oldest medical authors make constant reference to the use of the bath in eliminating disease and preserving health. Hippocrates, the noted early physician and herbalist, employed the use of water in numerous ways as a means of treating disease. Galen, another early advocate of natural healing methods, considered the bath invaluable. The North American Indians used baths in the treatment of many disorders. The vapor bath was one of their favorites. Mohammed instructed his people to bathe before each of the five daily prayers. History relates that Charlemagne held court in a large warm bath. Moses, who lived to the age of 120, commanded his people to be scrupulously clean, and bathing was incorporated into their religious rites. The Romans, Greeks, Persians and countless others, all praised and glorified the use of the bath as an essential means of maintaining good health.

Ancient Bathing Establishments

In ancient times, stately and magnificent buildings were erected for the accommodation of public bathing. Still in evidence today are the ruins of the great aqueducts which supplied the luxurious Roman public baths with millions of gallons of pure mountain water. Emperors and kings strove for superiority in erecting such establishments. During the reign of the Emperor Diocletian, the Roman baths had a capacity sufficient for 18,000 persons, while the Emperor Caracalla erected baths nearly a quarter of a mile square. At one time, the bathing institutions in Rome numbered one thousand. Marble walls, statues, mosaics and beautiful paintings adorned these vast luxurious buildings.

With the advent of the Dark Ages public baths were abandoned. In the opinion of Michelet, a noteworthy historian, this loss was responsible for the terrible plagues and pestilences of that period.

ADDITION OF BENEFICIAL HERBS TO THE BATH FOR HEALTH

The custom and practice of adding herbs to the bath dates from antiquity and is still presently followed by many people the world over. Our earliest ancestors rubbed flowers and scented herbs on their bodies while bathing in forest pools. Fragrant lemon grass is widely used in the West Indies, Africa, South America and the Orient. The exotic flowers of the Ylang Ylang are rubbed on the body by the South Sea Islanders. The leaves of the chaste bush are used in India to make a warm bath for women after childbirth. Roman soldiers added mugwort to the bath to relieve sore and aching muscles. Saffron was a favorite of the wealthy ruling classes. This plant has always been one of the world's most expensive spices, requiring the three stigma of 75,000 flowers to yield one pound! Joe-pye weed, sumach, and witch hazel were among the many herbs used by the American Indians. In Haiti, orange leaves and flowers are placed in the baths of infants.

The Health Value of Herbal Baths

Herbs added to the bath can greatly enhance and improve its ordinary beneficial effects. In the stress and strain of modern times, with the air polluted by chemicals, smoke, and exhaust fumes, the healthful practice of bathing deserves more attention now than ever before. In addition to the sanitary benefits of the warm herbal bath, certain botanicals greatly assist in keeping harmful bacteria at a minimum. After a hard day's work a good bath frees the millions of pores to "breathe" again, giving a tonic-like refreshment to the body. The natural fragrance of certain flowers and leaves gives the bather a "back to nature" feeling, disposing the mind to pleasant thoughts while the body relaxes.

HOW HERBS MAY BE USED IN BATHING FOR HEALTH

Herbal baths are simple to prepare. For example:

1. The botanicals to be used are placed in boiling water, covered, and allowed to simmer for about ten minutes. The resulting decoction is then strained and added to the bath water or used as a rinse after bathing.

2. An equal amount of borax crystals is added to the herbs and the mixture placed in a nylon, silk, or cheese cloth bag (a clean stocking may be used). This is tied with a piece of string or ribbon to the spout of the bath tub. The water is then turned on. This method may also be used without the addition of borax crystals.

3. A cloth bag may be filled with the herbs, then tied securely and placed right into the bath water.

Temperature of the Bath

Doctors inform us that the temperature of the bath is very important. Cold baths are not recommended for the aged or anyone suffering from artery or heart disease or neurasthenia. In such cases it may be dangerous. Hot baths drive the blood near the surface of the skin, cause the veins to become enlarged and a sense of heaviness is felt in the head. Afterwards the bather is left fatigued and weak. Hot baths should never be used by stout people or those who are afflicted with any type of heart trouble. The practice of bathing in water as hot as the body can stand it has been employed by some as a drastic method of losing weight and has cost many people their lives through heart failure.

The warm bath is the safest and the best. It does not shock the body and always leaves the bather refreshed.

FRAGRANT BATHS

History and legend show that man has always derived great pleasure from the delicately scented perfumes of flowers, herbs and the gums of tropical trees. In 570 B.C. Nebuchadnezzar insisted that flower beds of fragrant herbs be placed in the famous Hanging Gardens, "so that the breezes may spread perfume far and wide." When the tomb of King Tut was opened, an alabaster jar of perfumed oil was found. The oil was still 100 percent potent after the passing of 3000 years. The *Arabian Nights* contains many references to aromatic plants: "She stopped at the stall of a distiller of perfumes and bought ten sorts of waters—rose water, water of orange flower, willow flower, violet and other kinds; she also bought a spray of rose, musk-scented water, grains of male incense, aloe wood, ambergris and musk."

Recipes for Fragrant Baths

Many people thoroughly enjoy a warm bath steeped with the gentle fragrance of aromatic herbs and flowers. Any of the following recipes may be used for this purpose:

1. To ten parts of borax crystals, add four parts of cut (not powdered) orris roots, four parts of Khus-Khus roots, four parts of rose leaves, one part Benzoin, one part sandalwood, one part rose geranium. You may simplify this recipe if you desire, or any other aromatic botanical such as rosemary or your own favorite herb may be added.

2. Select an assortment of herbs such as bay, calamus, rosemary, camomile, marigold flowers, and add equal parts to a large vessel of boiling water. Allow to simmer for about 10 or 15 minutes, keeping the container covered so natural oils are not lost. Strain, and add this decoction to your bath or use as a warm rinse after bathing.

Other Herbs for Fragrant Baths

The following are just a few other examples of an endless variety of herbs that may be used for fragrant baths:

Khus-Khus. The aromatic roots of Khus-Khus were used in the baths of virgins in Jamaica. It is a favorite in the West

Indies and bundles of Khus-Khus are offered in the markets and streets of almost every island. Dried roots are placed in drawers as insect repellants as well as to impart a delicate fragrance to the clothes.

Sandalwood. Fragrant sandalwood is employed as an incense in religious rites in China and India. The Chinese mix sandalwood chips with rice paste to make perfumed candles. According to legend, King Solomon's temple was built of sandalwood.

Lavender. Lavender has been valued for generations because of its deep fragrant aroma. It was a favorite with the Romans who used it to perfume their baths. The name "lavender" comes from the Latin word *lavare* which means "to wash." It is also used for making perfume, sachets, potpourri, lavender water and soaps. The flowers are dried and placed in drawers to scent linen and also as a moth repellent.

Lovage. The flowers are small and yellow. It is grown in gardens for its aromatic oil. The roots will keep for many years. In folklore, it was said that lovage used in the bath would "make one more loveable."

Roses. The rose was the flower-crown of the goddesses long before the period of its present fame. A tradition of India tells of a favorite sultana of Jehanghir who, desiring to please, caused the bath in the palace garden to be filled with rose water. The oil particles soon became concentrated from the action of the sun and began floating on the surface. The attendant, believing that the water had become corrupt began to skim the particles off. During the process the globules burst and emitted such a fragrant odor that the value of preparing this as a perfume was at once apparent. This is alleged to be the first discovery of the method of preparing the celebrated *attar of roses*.

MISCELLANEOUS HERBAL BATHS

Since time immemorial, herbs have been used in the bath for a variety of physical complaints such as nervous insomnia, the relief of sore aching muscles, tension and strain. The following recipes have been gleaned from many sources both past and present.

Relieving Muscular Aches and Pains

The value of this type of bath has been recognized for generations. Excerpts from a few old herbals bear this out: "Balm is often used among other hot [spicy] and sweet herbs, to make baths and washings for men's bodies or legs in the summer time, to warm and comfort the veins and sinews to very good purpose and effect."—"Camomile added to bath water taketh away the weariness and easeth pains."—"Mints are often times used in baths with other herbs, as a help to comfort the nerves and sinews."

Great quantities of mugwort were used in the baths of the Romans for the relief of fatigue and muscular aches and pains. In his writings, Pliny also confirms the reputation of this herb in relieving fatigue. Frances Densmore in *Uses of Plants by the Chippewa Indians* says that mugwort prepared as a strong decoction is "strengthening for a child, also used for steaming old people to make them strong." Wild marjoram is a favorite in France and England.

Note: For best results in using herbal baths for muscular aches and pains it is necessary to soak in the tub for about 20 minutes, massaging the aching muscles until the body feels a comforting glow of warmth over its surface.

Herb Oils for Sore or Strained Muscles

Because of its deep penetrating action, oil of cajuput is considered valuable for the relief of sore or strained muscles. This is *not* used in the bath but applied directly, gently massaging the muscles. Care must be taken that it does not get into the eyes. Eucalyptus or camphorated oil is also used in the same way for the relief of minor muscular aches and pains.

Relieving Nervousness or Tension

1. Valerian is valued for its soothing and tonic effect on the nervous system. One pound of the herb is boiled for 30 minutes and the decoction added to the bath.

2. A bath prepared with lavender flowers is another popular favorite for nervousness. In some countries this bath is also used to relieve the pains of rheumatism and gout.

3. A warm decoction made from equal parts of hops and

meadowsweet is employed as a rinse and poured over the entire body following the regular bath.

4. A decoction of either linden flowers or camomile added to the bath is said to be effective for insomnia. In many lands a tea is prepared from Bahe Bahe or linden flowers and taken directly following the herbal bath. It is maintained that the tea is an additional aid in assuring a good night's sleep. (It may be sweetened with honey.)

5. For the relief of tension and strain the use of a pine oil bath at the end of the day is considered excellent. It helps to stimulate the circulation and refresh the system. One tablespoonful of the oil is added to the bath water.

6. Sweet flag, also commonly known as calamus, is recorded as a valuable plant in the domestic medication of India. The herb is mentioned in the Bible and is one of the constituents of the ointment Moses was commanded to make for use in the Tabernacle. Sweet flag is prepared as a herbal bath by placing one-half pound of the roots and leaves in a container filled with cold water. This is covered and allowed to boil for 30 minutes. It is then strained and the decoction poured into the bath.

Helping to Stimulate Circulation

When the hands and feet are cold and a person is unable to exercise, a warm bath can do much to increase the circulation and bring a comforting warmth to the body. A decoction made with equal parts of marigold, nettle, and bladder wrack added to the bath is a favorite English recipe.

Relieving Dry, Itchy Skin

For dry, itchy skin, an old-fashioned remedy which is still very popular today is the oatmeal bath: Fill a cloth bag with one pound of oatmeal; tie securely and place right in the bath water. Remain in the tub for about 20 minutes gently rubbing the skin with the oatmeal bag.

HERBAL FOOT BATHS

The feet are the most important parts of the body to keep clean for good health. Because of the pressure on the bottoms of the feet, rejected poisons from the system adhere firmly to this area and tend to rapidly form a coating over the pores. Unless the feet are washed frequently and thoroughly, the rejected poisons may be reabsorbed into the body.

Hay-flower and Oat Straw Foot Baths

In his writings, Father Kneipp[1] mentions the use of a foot bath made with either hay-flowers or oat straw. He says:

A sanative foot bath is that made from hay-flowers.

Take about three to five handfuls of hay-flowers (what I call hay-flowers are all the remains of hay such as stalks, leaves, blossoms and seeds, even the hay itself) pour boiling water upon them, cover the vessel, and let the whole mixture cool to the warmth most comfortable for a foot bath. It is of no consequence whether the hay-flowers remain in the foot bath, or whether the decoction only is used.

These foot baths operate by dissolving, evacuating, and strengthening; they are of good service for diseased feet, especially sweating feet, open wounds, contusions of every kind (whether from a blow, fall, etc., or bleeding or black and blue with blood), for tumors, gout in the feet, gristle on the toes, putridity between them, etc.

A gentleman suffering to a great extent from gout in his feet, was freed from pain in an hour by one of these foot baths, together with a foot-bandage dipped in the decoction.

The foot bath with oat straw is closely connected with the preceding one. The oat straw is boiled for half an hour in a kettle and a foot bath is prepared with the decoction which is to be used for 20 or 30 minutes.

According to my experiences, these foot baths are unsurpassed as regards the dissolving of every possible obduration on the feet. They are useful against gristle, gout, corns, nails grown in . . . and against blisters caused by walking. Even sore and suppurating feet, or toes wounded by too sharp foot-sweat, can be treated with these foot baths.

Special Directions for Hot and Cold Foot Baths

Father Kneipp tells us that he frequently advised that the foot baths be taken in the following way: Enough of the

[1] *My Water Cure.*

herbal decoction is prepared to make two separate foot baths. One is used warm and the other cold in this order:

ten minutes in the warm foot bath
one minute ″   ″ cold   ″   ″
ten minutes ″   ″ warm   ″   ″
one minute ″   ″ cold   ″   ″
ten minutes ″   ″ warm   ″   ″
one minute ″   ″ cold   ″   ″

The entire process is done consecutively and takes 33 minutes. It is always ended with the cold foot bath.

Alleviating Corns, Calluses, Bunions

1. The feet are soaked in hot water just before bedtime. After they are thoroughly dried, a small piece of lemon peeling with the pulp intact is bound over the corn or callus and bandaged. This is left on overnight and removed in the morning. This procedure is continued for four or five days, after which the skin growth may be peeled.

2. A foot bath is prepared by adding one cup of yarrow leaves and one tablespoonful of salt to three quarts of hot water. This is used for corns, calluses, and bunions.

3. Castor oil frequently rubbed on calluses is said to soften them. Olive oil has a soothing effect on the skin and is used for dry skin and seed corns. It it also applied to nails that show signs of brittleness or splitting. Gum arabic mucilage applied to corns or calluses every night before going to bed will soften them.

Coping with Athlete's Foot

1. One cup of red clover blossoms is boiled until thick and placed directly on the affected parts for the relief of athlete's foot.

2. Apple cider vinegar applied frequently is said to be another simple, yet effective remedy for relief of athlete's foot.

MISCELLANEOUS HERBAL AIDS FOR EXTERNAL USE

Chapped Hands, Chilblains

Chapped Hands. One-half oz. of rose water, one-half oz.

of glycerin, and one-quarter oz. of witch hazel extract. Mix together and bottle for use. Each time the hands are washed and dried, this solution is rubbed in.

Chilblains. Applications of lemon juice mixed with glycerin is a favorite with many people for the relief of chilblains.

Warts

1. The common dandelion is an old-time folk remedy for eliminating warts. However, it is said to be effective only in the late spring or the summer. The stem of the fresh flower is squeezed until a drop of milky juice appears. The juice is then touched to the wart and allowed to dry. This is repeated three or four times every day. It is said that the wart will soon turn black and fall off, leaving the skin clear.

2. The Greater Celandine is another domestic remedy employed for the treatment of warts. It is used in much the same way as the dandelion, that is, the end of the stalk or leaf is squeezed until a drop of juice appears which is then applied to the wart.

3. Plantar warts have been removed by the use of wheat germ oil. The wart is well saturated with the oil, then bound with a Band-Aid. This process is repeated every night for three or four weeks. (Wheat germ oil may be purchased at any health food store.)

Poison Oak, Poison Ivy

1. The following remedy was known and used by the American Indians as a treatment or preventative of poison ivy. Many people living in the country, who are familiar with its use, claim that it is highly effective. The name of the plant is *Impatiens*, commonly called jewel weed. The fresh stems and leaves are mashed and the juice rubbed on the skin. It is also considered an excellent preventative. The fresh juice is rubbed on the exposed skin before going into any area of the country in which poison ivy may be growing. (The fresh *Impatiens* plant may usually be obtained from a plant nursery.)

2. As a treatment of poison oak or poison ivy several kernels of garlic are crushed and placed between layers of gauze and applied to the affected parts for about a half hour.

Gnat Bites, Insect Repellants

Mosquitoes. A strong decoction of camomile flowers is prepared and used as a wash on the exposed areas of the body. This is said to keep mosquitoes away. Cajuput oil is used in Africa and India as a mosquito repellent. In many parts of the world, the dried leaves of sweet basil are burned for the same purpose. In Australia, the exposed parts of the body are rubbed with the bruised young leaves of eucalyptus. The oil mixed with glycerine is another method employed in that country. Mint oils are also reputed to be good insect repellents.

Gnats. For the relief of gnat bites the following is used: one oz. of quassia chips is placed in one pint of cold water and allowed to steep (stand) overnight. The parts of the skin which have been affected are bathed with this solution. It is also reputed to be an excellent preventative if applied to the exposed areas of the skin before going into any regions infested with gnats. The liberal application of the tincture made from marigold flowers is said to bring relief from gnat bites. The oils of lavender, geranium, or citronella are each claimed to be good insect repellents.

HERBAL BEAUTY AIDS

1. Hyssop prepared as an infusion and used as a wash has been known for centuries for its cleansing and beautifying effect on the skin. The herb is mentioned in the Bible, and David drew a wonderful lesson from the use of it when he said, *Purge me with hyssop, and I shall be clean; wash me, and I shall be whiter than snow* (Psalm 51:7). This plant is native to Asia and Europe and is grown in gardens in our country. An essential aromatic oil extracted from the green portions of the plant is used in making English eau de cologne.

2. The following mixture is packed loosely in cheese cloth bags (four or five inches square):

> five parts oatmeal
> one part almond meal
> one part orris root
> one-half part castile soap

One or two bags may be placed right in the bath. A milkiness and delightful fragrance is released into the water, which has a cleansing and beautifying effect on the skin.

3. Gum benzoin is another favorite beauty aid from the past. The following excerpt is taken from the book *Personal Beauty* printed in 1870:

> Gum benzoin is a fragrant resin which comes to us from the sunny meadows of Sumatra, and is redolent with odors of the Spice Islands, and the mysterious virtues of tropical balms. Its qualities are strange. Mix a little of it with fat, and the latter will not become rancid. Some of the tincture, combined with glycerin, is simply the best application in the world for chapped hands, and for those cracked nipples which afflict some women during nursing. But this apart. We speak of it now as a cosmetic. Two ounces of it to a pint of pure alcohol (free from acrid fused oils and the like) make as fine an application as those can ask, who wish a white, spotless tint and fragrant aroma. Some of it may be used once or twice a day in the manner already mentioned.
>
> About a tablespoonful should be poured into a small tumbler of water. It changes the water to a whitish fluid, which is known in France as *lait virginal*, virgin's milk, and is highly and justly esteemed. None of the cosmetic washes is more agreeable. Some glycerin can be added to the water if desired.

The cosmetic virtues of benzoin are also mentioned in another old herbal entitled *The New Medical Guide*, printed in 1901. We read: "A remarkable wash was said to have been used by the beauties of the court of Charles II. It was made of a simple tincture of benzoin precipitated in water."

The Beauty Recipe of a Queen

The attractive Queen Elizabeth of Hungary was said to have used a recipe consisting of the following: 12 oz. of rosemary herb, one oz. each of fresh lemon peel, fresh orange peel, mint herb, and balm of melissa, and one pint of rose water and spirits of wine. This mixture was allowed to stand for several weeks, and the bottle shaken thoroughly once a day. It was then strained and bottled for use. The solution was rubbed on the skin after bathing, producing a flower petal skin appearance.

Magic Water

The famous French beauty, Ninon de Lenclos, retained her youthful appearance to such a remarkable degree that young men fell in love with her when she was seventy years old. French historians claim to have discovered at least part of the secret formula she used to keep herself looking so young all her life. She allegedly took herb baths that were prepared as follows:

> Take a handful of dried lavender flowers, a handful of rosemary leaves, handful of dried mint, handful of comfrey roots, and one of thyme. Mix all together loosely in a muslin bag. Place in your tub, pour on enough boiling water to cover and let soak for ten minutes. Then fill up the tub. Rest 15 minutes in the magic water" and think virtuous thoughts.

Skin Blemishes and Freckles

1. One cup of centaury herb is placed in two quarts of water to which a small amount of castile soap has been added. This is used as a wash for freckles and skin blemishes.

2. The following is an old-time Parisian lotion which was used for freckles: one oz. of powdered alum and one oz. of lemon juice is added to a pint of rose water. This is bottled and shaken well before using.

3. One-half cup of fresh elder blossoms is placed in a container and covered with cold distilled water (about three-quarters of a cup). The container is covered and allowed to stand overnight. In the morning the liquid is carefully strained. This is used every night and morning as a wash for freckles.

Culpeper also mentions the use of elder for the same purpose: "The distilled water of the flowers (elder) is of much use to clear the skin from sun burning, freckles, and the like." He also adds that the "eyes washed with it lose redness and blood shot . . ."

4. An old French recipe for "refining" the skin:

> Express the juice of fresh cucumbers, bring to the boiling point, skim and bottle. Take one teaspoonful of the juice to two teaspoonfuls of water, and apply to the face night and morning, letting it dry on.

Another source states that cucumber skins are an excellent

skin bleaching agent, when rubbed over brown spot areas.

5. Burdock prepared with distilled water was popular in the old days as a wash for skin blemishes and freckles.

6. The following recipe is used by many people to clear the discoloration (black and blue marks) of bruises and sprains. The affected parts are bathed frequently with a strong infusion of marshmallow herb and comfrey until the discoloration clears.

(*Reference: Botanical Catalog,* Hammond, Indiana: Indiana Botanic Gardens.)

15

HERBS AND THEIR EFFECT ON THE EMOTIONS

Increasing scientific interest has resulted from medical observations pertaining to emotional stress as a cause of illness. When speaking of psychogenic ailments most people believe them to be the result of prolonged stress, but medical men are now finding out that a sudden shock may be equally destructive. Scientists are considering the possibility that in such instances a rather violent mental reaction with corresponding release of hormones may occur which is great enough to cause considerable damage to certain functions of the body.

A French army medical consultant recently found that a number of cases of diabetes developed immediately following an experience of sudden shock. For example, a pilot pulled his plane out of a dive just seconds before it would have crashed. In another case, a man spear-fishing surfaced from a dive to find a motor boat practically on top of him. These men were reported to have suddenly developed symptoms of diabetes.

The French doctor also cites the case of a young mother who suffered shock when she saw her daughter go into convulsions after a smallpox vaccination. The mother was stricken with diabetes shortly after and required daily insulin to control it.

Results of other researchers have shown that sudden fright can cause many other illnesses. Infections of the respiratory system and digestive disorders were especially noted among people who had been in an accident. Another researcher found that a severe accident or shocking experience often causes the thyroid gland to become seriously overactive, causing damaging effects on some body functions.

Ulcerative colitis, migraine, noninfectious skin diseases, irritable colon, and ulcers are a few examples of some of the ailments cited by science which appear to almost always have a psychological element arising from either prolonged stress or brief sudden shock.

IS THERE A MIND–CANCER LINK?

The following item appeared in the *Health Bulletin*:[1]

> *Cancer Has Emotional Aspect.* Medical researchers are investigating the theory that the mind may play a role in certain forms of cancer. Men with poor outlets for passions were found to have a death rate from lung cancer four and a half times that of men with proper outlets, according to research in Scotland and reported last week in *The Times* of London. In this country, Rochester, New York, scientists report that examination of more than 100 leukemia patients showed that the disease often could be traced to "a number of losses or separations with understandable feelings of sadness, anxiety, anger or hopelessness." A comprehensive report on the mind–cancer link was highlighted in the recently published proceedings of last year's New York Academy of Sciences conference, "Psychophysiological Aspects of Cancer."

Other Studies

A five-year study conducted by three physicians revealed that grief is a potent factor in causing a high death rate among elderly widows during the first six months following the loss of their mates. The doctors added: "The grief precipitated by the death is almost certainly associated with changes in the function of the endocrine (gland system) and nervous system."

The following remarks by Dr. Denis Leigh were reported in *The Lancet*:[2]

[1] Vol. 4 No. 36. September 3, 1966.
[2] November, 1966.

Epidemiological research has revealed illnesses in clusters related to life experience. Prisoners-of-war subjected to the harsh regimen of the Far East had more illness in later life than those who were in the European prison camps. Ex-prisoners of the Japanese six years later had twice the rates for cancer, heart disease, and suicide, and three times the rate for all forms of accident. These were not the diseases that would have been predicted. Inquiries in post-war Germany confirmed the pattern: Nazis dismissed from office had higher rates for all forms of illness than Nazis not dismissed.

Scientific Breakthrough

In attempting to understand the effect of the mind on the body, one breakthrough was made when scientists began a study of the hypothalamus, a segment of the brain which controls the primitive reactions to pain, hunger and danger. A pathway from the hypothalamus to the pituitary was found. It was already known that this tiny gland situated at the base of the brain secreted a growth hormone. Further research, however, revealed that a number of other hormones are produced by the pituitary. The front lobe was discovered to yield chemicals that trigger the manufacture of male and female sex hormones, along with other chemicals that cause the manufacture of sperm cells in men and ovulation in women, and they are responsible for many other functions of the reproductive system. A hormone family that governs the thyroid which in turn controls the metabolism is also produced by the front lobe of the pituitary. Another hormone causes changes in the blood sugar resulting in effects like diabetes. Another chemical triggers the adrenal glands to release cortisone-like secretions, while others are apparently involved with the use and storing of fat.

The back and middle lobes of the pituitary are still somewhat of a mystery to science, however they are known to affect rises in blood pressure, contractions of the uterus, and the coloring of the skin. One researcher says: "We have opened a door, and have only had a superficial look at this gland. But clearly we now know one way in which emotion can be translated to an array of bodily changes."

Brief Summary of Findings

We must be certain that we fully understand what scientists are telling us here. In speaking of emotional stress or psychological influence as a cause of physical illness they are not saying that the illness is imaginary. As we have just seen, one segment of the brain controls the emotional reactions of fear and anger, and there is a link between this segment and the pituitary gland. The latter performs a vital function relating to the chemical balance in the body. An emotional upset of any kind can disturb the proper function of the gland to the degree where the chemistry of the body (which is under its control) becomes disordered and disease results.

HOW HERBS HELP EMOTIONS FOR BETTER HEALTH

If the emotions can cause serious physical disorders, then it becomes at once apparent that adequate control over this aspect of our nature is essential if we hope to attain or maintain a proper state of health and happiness. But how can this be done? A mere command cannot dispel melancholy, guilt, regret, impatience, anxiety or any other negative emotion which we do not wish to nourish and of which we would gladly rid ourselves. We need a helping hand to assist us through the emotional trials that beset us so frequently throughout life. Perhaps the hand so generously offered by the late Edward Bach, physician, scientist, and bacteriologist of England is the one for which we should reach.

In 1930 this remarkable man gave up his lucrative practice to devote himself entirely to research work along these lines and to seek plant remedies that would help an individual to gain control over his emotions. Edward Bach was no ordinary doctor. Considered a genius in the field of conventional or orthodox medicine, he had contributed many valuable discoveries to this branch of medical science. In addition to his highly successful private practice, preparing his lifesaving vaccines for shipment to medical men in all parts of the world was another of his busy occupations. So, no one could understand why such a highly esteemed practising physician would abruptly give up his career to search for *flower remedies!* His decision to do so greatly distressed his colleagues and friends who believed it to be a tragic waste of his brilliant talents.

THE DR. BACH FLOWER REMEDIES

Dr. Bach eventually discovered a new system of herbal medicine based on the principle of "treat the patient and not the disease." According to this method the remedies are not prescribed for the physical disorder but for the sufferer's adverse state of mind—his fear, anxiety, sense of failure, regret, or whatever it may be, as Dr. Bach believed these to be the underlying causes of his patients' illnesses. Bach successfully treated patients suffering from a diversity of diseases by giving a specific herbal remedy for a specific emotional state of mind. As the negative emotion disappeared, the physical complaint cleared up and the patient was restored to health.

All of the Dr. Bach remedies but one are prepared from the flowers of wild plants, trees, and bushes. The exception is Rock Water which is obtained from certain wells or springs. A number of these plants are already in standard use by herbalists for their action against certain physical symptoms, but with the Bach method of potentizing, a completely different property is released, the Vital Force or life of the plant is tapped. These potentized remedies attack the disease through their action on the mind and are said to revitalize the whole personality of the patient so that he can easily shake off his anxieties and fears, and with them the disorder from which his body suffers.

Mental States Classified

Dr. Bach originally classified 12 outstanding negative states of mind or moods. Later he expanded this classification to a final total of 38. These included such states as fear, self-distrust, mental torture or worry, discouragement or hopelessness, indecision, and so on. Overlapping naturally occurred and more than one negative state was evident on occasion. He also learned that beneath these adverse emotions were the positive qualities of mind. With help the fearful man could set aside his fear and rise in courage and confidence which was his rightful heritage and true nature; the intolerant would become more understanding and compassionate; and the timid would gain strength and self-assurance.

DR. BACH'S DISCOVERY OF HERBAL REMEDIES FOR COPING WITH MENTALLY-INDUCED ILLNESSES

When Dr. Bach fully realized the importance of the mind with relation to the health of the body he began his search for the herbs which would assist in removing the difficult moods—to heal the inner man, and this search lasted seven years. The first three remedies he discovered were *Mimulus luteus*, a musk-like flower; *Clematis vitalba*, commonly known as Traveler's Joy; and *Impatiens royaleii*. Mimulus was the herbal remedy he used for treating patients whose outstanding state of mind was fear; Clematis was employed for those who lacked sufficient interest in life; and Impatiens for irritability or tension. Later these three flower remedies and one or two others were made known to the medical profession and their description was published in the *Homeopathic World* in February 1930.

Dr. Bach continued his search and later potentized (made potent) the flowers of Agrimony and Vervain. Agrimony was the remedy used for the harassed, worried state of mind so frequently disguised by an outward pretense of cheerfulness. Chicory was found effective for those suffering from over-concern, especially for the affairs of others, and Vervain was given for the tendency to strain and overwork.

The beneficial results obtained with the administration of these, and later from the other flower remedies which comprised the total of 38, far exceeded Bach's expectations.

Specific Properties of Herbs Extracted by the Sun Method

During his search for the flower remedies, Bach was confronted with the problem of how he might extract the specific properties he sought once he found the correct plant. Nora Weeks, author of the excellent book, *The Medical Discoveries of Edward Bach, Physician* (6th ed.),[3] tells us how this inspired physician solved this problem:

> One early morning in May as he was walking through
> a field upon which the dew still lay heavy, the thought

[3] (Ashingdon, Rochford, Essex, England: The C. W. Daniel Company, Ltd., 1963), pp. 49–50.

flashed into his mind that each dewdrop must contain some of the properties of the plant upon which it rested; for the heat of the sun, acting through the fluid, would serve to draw out these properties until each drop was magnetized with power.

Then Bach realized that if he could obtain the medicinal properties of the plants he was seeking in this way, the resulting remedies would contain the full, perfect and uncontaminated power of the plants, and they would heal, surely, as no medical preparations had been known to heal before.

Collecting dew from individual plants, however, would involve considerable time as well as labor, so Dr. Bach filled a glass container with pure spring water and covered the entire surface with freshly picked blossoms from a chosen plant. This was left standing in the full sunlight for several hours. The blossoms were then carefully removed and the water poured into bottles. When half full, an equal amount of brandy was added to preserve the extract.

Dosages were very small (homeopathic). Two drops were taken from the "mother tincture" (first preparation), and placed in another small bottle filled with pure water. This was the bottle used for dosages and if it was to be kept for some time a little brandy was added.

SOME CASE HISTORIES UNDER DR. BACH'S TREATMENT

"Treat the patient and not the disease" was the rule that Dr. Bach followed religiously; treat the indecision, the fear, the hopelessness or the anxiety of the patient and the physical healing would follow. These were his views and convictions, and he put them into practice with marked success. Here are just a few of the many recorded case histories which attest to the effectiveness of his method:

Clematis Remedy:

Key notes: The day-dreamer; the inattentive; the absent-minded. Those who lack sufficient interest in life.

1. A woman 36 years of age had suffered from asthma all

her life. Her baby daughter had died several years before and the mother would sit in front of the child's photograph, crying incessantly for long periods of time. She had no interest in the rest of her family and had retreated into a dream world.

Dr. Bach decided that this state of mind required the Clematis remedy. After the patient had taken the first bottle of the herbal remedy she suffered no further asthmatic attacks. A second bottle of the same remedy was given and she began to take an interest in her home and recapture her joy in life. When seen three years later there had been no recurrence of her previous illness.

2. A 40 year old woman had been suffering from the after-effects of sleeping sickness. The medical doctors could do nothing more for her condition. She tried her best to do a little housework and cooking but could barely drag herself around, frequently stumbling and falling down. Her muscles had become weak, her eyelids half-closed and she had no interest in anything. Dr. Bach administered Clematis for the patient's dreamy, disinterested state of mind. Within two weeks the patient was able to keep her eyes open wider; she walked steadier and did not fall asleep so often. The most remarkable change, however, occurred in her personality. She smiled and laughed, and began making plans about what she was going to do when she fully recovered. The doses were continued and at the end of three months the change was miraculous. She was alert and happy, doing all her own housework, including the washing and cooking, and walking a mile to do her shopping. She told Dr. Bach that she was also now able to walk to and from church, a combined distance of six miles.

3. A young girl of 18 had undergone an operation six months before for the removal of large cysts on the thyroid gland. The cysts were growing back again but it was advised that she must wait until they had grown larger and another operation would then be performed. She was of the gentle, daydreaming type and took very little interest in her condition. Dr. Bach administered the Clematis remedy three times a day for two weeks. Complete absorption of the cysts took place and there was no further recurrence of the disorder.

Centaury Remedy:

Key notes: Timid, shy. These people are often imposed
upon by others because they do not have the
strength to refuse.

1. A 9 year old girl suffered frequent attacks of nosebleed
which occurred at weekly intervals. She was the quiet, shy
type always anxious to please others. Bach first saw the patient during one of her attacks and administered doses of
Centaury, the remedy indicated for the timid state of mind.
The bleeding soon stopped. The herbal remedy was continued
and a week later there was a slight attack which lasted only
a few minutes. There were no further recurrences after that.
When seen three years later the girl was still well and strong
and her change in character was striking. From a weak, intro-
verted, shy youngster imposed upon by her sisters and
brothers she had become an outgoing, self-assured and happy
individual.

2. A young man of 22 had been pale and weak for some
time especially during the past year. There were indications
of a small hernia starting in the groin. Because of his timid,
easygoing nature, others frequently took advantage of him.
Centaury, the remedy for timidness, was given three times a
day, and in two weeks there was marked improvement in
his color, muscle tone, and general health. The patient was
seen six months later still in good health. His personality had
become much more positive and he was able to assert himself whenever necessary. There was no need for a hernia
operation.

Combinations of Remedies Used by Dr. Bach

Because moods change from day to day and sometimes
more frequently, Bach found that in these cases the remedies
needed would also have to be changed accordingly. Different
single remedies or combinations of remedies were administered depending on the various states of mind that appeared
during a course of illness.

Here are two examples:

Example 1. A man was suffering from the aftereffects of

shellshock. He became speechless and shaken when cars passed him on the street; he found closed rooms unbearable, and jumped at the slightest sound. Every night he awoke from terrifying dreams, shouting, trembling and sweating profusely. He was extremely restless, and very frightened that he might do something desperate if he did not improve.

He was in poor physical health, troubled with severe indigestion, nagging backache and constipation.

Dr. Bach gave him a prescription of the following remedies: Aspen for his fear of the unknown; Cherry Plum for his fear of doing something desperate; Rock Rose for terror; Sweet Chestnut for his unbearable mental anguish; Scleranthus for his uncertain state of mind; Agrimony for his restlessness; and Mimulus for his fear of noise and people.

The following week he felt calmer; the backache was somewhat eased and he had slept for three nights without having the terrifying nightmares. The prescription was continued and in one month great improvement was noted. During this period he had suffered only one nightmare; the constipation had cleared up and his digestion was considerably better. He felt much more hopeful and confident, but sudden noises and traffic still troubled him. The remedies Honeysuckle and Larch were then given along with Mimulus, Agrimony, and Aspen. Larch was added to help him acquire complete confidence in himself, and Honeysuckle because he dwelt too much on the past and the origin of his trouble.

It was eight months before the patient was seen again, reporting that he had been feeling so well that he had thought it unnecessary to continue further treatment. All his fear and terror were gone; he was sleeping well and was happier than he had been for the past 20 years.

Example 2. A woman afflicted with acute rheumatism had spent the past two years in various nursing homes and hospitals. When Bach first saw her, her ankles were double their normal size, the hands were very stiff and painful and the patient could hardly manage to get around. There was also considerable pain in the back, neck, and shoulders.

The woman was a courageous soul who had borne her illness and anguish in silence and with extreme patience. For this state of mind, Water Violet was given for two weeks and definite improvement was noted. At the end of one month the patient was able to walk two miles, however, she felt unsteady and unsure of herself. The Scleranthus remedy (for uncertainty) was administered for a few days. A period then followed in which the woman became restless and anxious to be back doing everything for herself. For this state of mind the Impatiens remedy was given.

At the end of two months the patient could use her hands freely and had no more pain. With the exception of a little stiffness and trace of swelling in one ankle, she was completely well.

Dr. Bach's Rescue Remedy

Dr. Bach prepared a combination of three herbal remedies and he named this the Rescue Remedy. He always carried a bottle of this mixture in his pocket for cases of emergency such as great pain, fear or panic, unconsciousness, shock, or accident. Later he added two more remedies, making a combined total of five, but in the meantime he had found the first three to be invaluable as a first-aid measure when no other help was available. The five remedies are:

Star of Bethlehem	for shock
Rock Rose	for terror or panic
Impatiens	for mental stress and tension
Cherry Plum	for desperation
Clematis	for the bemused, far-away feeling often preceding a faint or loss of consciousness.

During the early 1930's a small ship was wrecked off the coast of Cromer during a terrible storm. One man had roped himself to the mast but it was almost five hours before a life boat could manage to reach him. When brought ashore, his clothes stiffened by salt water, he was unconscious, foaming at the mouth, and almost frozen. His condition appeared hopeless. Dr. Bach repeatedly moistened the man's lips with the Rescue Remedy as he was being carried up the beach to a nearby hotel. In a few minutes, the patient regained consciousness and his scattered faculties as well. After a few days' rest in the hospital he had fully recuperated from his terrifying experience.

DR. BACH'S DESIRE TO SHARE HIS DISCOVERIES

Bach was eager to share his discoveries with the medical world and to encourage his associates to adopt the herbal remedies and new method of diagnosing. A few of his faithful friends in the medical profession were already using his system and getting remarkable results. But the majority found it difficult to accept his ideas even though they still regarded him as a genius for his former work as a bacteriologist. So Dr. Bach decided to share his knowledge with the laymen, the sufferers themselves; to explain his method in such a simple way that anyone would be able to understand and use it if they desired to do so. He maintained that the remedies themselves were pure and harmless; there was no danger of overdosing or giving them too often; if the remedy selected was not the correct one, no ill effects could come from its use.

He wrote a small book called *The Twelve Healers and Other Remedies* (10th ed.),[4] in which he names and describes the herbs, along with the 38 emotional states of mind for which he found these remedies effective. A detailed explanation is given on how the herbs are to be prepared, what dosages should be taken, and other relevant information.

The flower remedies, as Bach wrote in his treatise published in *The Homeopathic World*, 1930, would have "the power to elevate our vibrations, and thus draw down spiritual power which cleanses mind and body, and heals."

The Bach Foundation's Work in England

Dr. Bach's work is carried on today at the Dr. Edward Bach Healing Centre at Mount Vernon, Sotwell, Wallingford, Berkshire, England. This Centre occupies the house where Dr. Bach spent the last years of his life and where in the surrounding countryside he found and prepared many of his flower remedies. Patients are seen by appointment and many impressive case histories are on file there. Stock bottles of the 38 remedies are prepared at this Centre and shipped to almost every country in the world. They are reasonably priced and available to anyone.

A quarterly Newsletter is also published which may be obtained by subscription. It is invaluable as a source of

[4] The C. W. Daniel Company, Ltd., 1964.

instruction for those who want to gain a greater understanding of the Bach remedies and how they are used. In addition to answering questions and citing case histories, the different issues also cover all the aspects of the various states of mind and are carefully detailed and thoroughly explained.

A Medical Doctor's Opinion of the Bach Remedies

In his book, *The Pattern of Health*,[5] Aubrey T. Westlake, M.D., of England tells us that at first he found it hard to believe the reports of the wonderful results obtained by the Bach flower remedies. However, he was open-minded enough to give the matter his serious consideration. He says:

> So I proceeded to try the remedies. To make a test as conclusive as possible, I eliminated all other therapeutic factors so that only one factor was operating— the Bach remedy—if anything happened it would presumably be due to the remedy and to nothing else. I treated a variety of conditions in this way, and much to my surprise I became completely convinced that the remedies acted as Dr. Bach claimed; anyhow in acute conditions. . . . As a user of these remedies for 20 years I can affirm that, generally speaking, it is just as simple and just as sure as that, surprising as it may sound.

(*References:* Nora Weeks, *The Medical Discoveries of Edward Bach, Physician.* Sixth ed.; Ashingdon, Rochford, Essex, England: The C. W. Daniel Company, Ltd., 1963. Patricia and Ron Deutsch, "Is Emotional Tension Making You Sick?," *Family Circle,* Vol. 71 No. 3, September 1967, pp. 46–47, 111–5.)

[5] (New York: Devin-Adair Company, 1963).

16

HERBAL SMOKING SUBSTITUTES
FOR TOBACCO

Smoking was introduced to the white man by the Indians; however, the ingredients and methods used by the natives and early settlers greatly differed from those employed today. Smoking by the Indians was originally ceremonial and an important factor in their ritualistic practices. Pipes were in general use, although some tribes also prepared and smoked corn-husk cigarettes. Ingredients consisted of a mixture of herbs blended with only a very small amount of tobacco; consequently, the nicotine content was substantially reduced.

By contrast, modern tobacco is flavored in such a way that it remains 100 percent tobacco. Cigarettes are rolled in chemically treated paper to prevent it from going out.

HERBAL SMOKING MIXTURES

Let us consider some of the recipes used in former times (and in some countries today) in which herbs were or still are used as smoking mixtures. Naturally, the more botanicals added to the tobacco, the less nicotine content the blend will have. Any herbal smoking preparation in which tobacco is entirely omitted will, of course, be completely nicotine-free. It is reported that satisfaction from smoking is not inhibited by using herbals in a smoking mixture.

Angelica

There are many species of angelica but only two are used in domestic medicine, the wild American variety known as *Angelica atropurpurea* and the *Angelica archangelica* which

157

is cultivated in European gardens. Both plants have a warm aromatic taste and fragrant odor. The American angelica, sometimes called masterwort, is smaller, less branched, and paler in color than the European variety. Advertisements offering the seed for sale appeared in the *Boston Evening Post* in 1771.

Angelica is largely employed as a flavoring agent for confectionery and liqueurs. It is extensively cultivated near Clermont-Ferrand in France for the latter purpose. The plant is used in domestic medicine as a carminative, diuretic, expectorant, diaphoretic and stimulant. It is mentioned in a number of old family herbals as a remedy for sore throat, hoarseness, and coughs.

The Laplanders chew and smoke angelica like tobacco. At one time they crowned their poets with a garland made of the plant in the belief that its fragrance inspired them. Hunter tells us that the Indians called angelica "La-Go-Nee-Haw," and says that it always constituted an ingredient in the medicine bag. He adds: "It is chiefly valued, however, as an agreeable commodity for smoking, in which way they frequently use it alone, though they prefer it mixed with tobacco."

Bearberry

Habitat: North America, Great Britain, Central and Northern Europe.

Although the bright red berries produced by the bearberry (*Arctostaphylos urva-ursi*) are tasteless and dry, they formed an important article of diet among the Indians. Bears are also very fond of the berries.

Indians in the Eastern part of the country called the plant *Kinnikinnick*. The word originally applied to any smoking mixture which contained various ingredients such as sumach bark, native tobacco, spice-bush, bearberry, and so on. The name was finally applied only to certain plants used rather than the entire smoking preparation.

The Potowatomi Indians mixed bearberry leaves with their tobacco for a milder smoking blend while the Chippewa combined the leaves with tobacco or red willow as a medicinal smoke for headache. Early French settlers were very fond of smoking bearberry and always carried a pouch of the dried leaves.

Beech (*Fagus*)

A genus of hardy deciduous trees remarkable for their great size and beauty and for their graceful and symmetrical habit of growth. The official name is from *phago*, "to eat," in allusion to the nuts which were once used as food. White beech, *F. sylvestris*, is one of the tallest and most majestic of our forest trees and grows abundantly in the Western and Middle States. Red beech, *F. ferruginea*, is more confined to the Northern States. The attractive and popular European beech is known as *F. sylvatica*.

The leaves of the beech tree were smoked by the Germans as a substitute for tobacco during World War I.

Buckbean (*Menyanthes trifoliata*)

This plant belongs to the gentian family and grows in marshy regions of North America and Europe. Buckbean is not a bean, however, the trifoliata leaves suggest a legume which may be responsible for that part of the name. The herbalists consider the plant a valuable tonic in conditions of rheumatism and skin diseases. The leaves have been employed in many parts of the world as a substitute for hops in brewing beer.

For smoking purposes, buckbean is used alone or blended with other herbs or with tobacco.

Coltsfoot (*Tussilago farfara*)

The official name is from *tussis*, "a cough," in reference to the use of the flowers and leaves as a remedy for pulmonary complaints. The flower may be seen painted on the walls and windows of many pharmacies in France.

Coltsfoot leaves were used as a medicinal smoke by the ancients and are used in modern Germany as a substitute for tobacco. This herb forms the chief ingredient of almost all English herbal smoking blends. One of the best mixtures is said to consist of the following plants, the proportions of which may be changed according to the flavor or mildness desired:

Take of coltsfoot leaves, dried, one lb.; eyebright, buckbean, of each one-half lb.; wood betony, four oz.; rosemary, two oz.; common thyme, one and one-half oz.; lavender, one oz.

Some add rose petals and camomile flowers. The herbs should be rubbed to a coarse powder between the hands. Those who prefer a mild tobacco, may increase the quantity of coltsfoot, which some prefer in the proportion of one-half to the whole quantity.

Here is a recipe for a similar blend which appeared in an English publication:[1]

> two parts coltsfoot
> one-half part camomile flowers
> one-half part thyme
> one part eyebright
> one part betony
> one-half part rosemary

Mix well.

The above mixture is also used in England as a medicinal smoke for coughs.

The following was taken from a very old newspaper clipping of unknown publication:

> Dr. Ambialet suggests mixing with tobacco the dried leaves of the plant known as coltsfoot. This mixture reduces the nicotine content of the smoke proportionately.
>
> He claims that tobacco, mixed with coltsfoot leaves, retains its full aroma and taste. The only perceptible change is an additional flavor like that of Turkish tobacco, which is very acceptable to most smokers.

Corn Silk (*Stigmata maidis*)

Fine, yellowish, silky threads consisting of the stigmas from the female flowers of maize. Employed by the medical herbalists for urinary and bladder troubles.

Corn silk is used as a filler with tobacco or with August flowers.

Cubeb Berries (*Piper cubeba*)

Habitat: Sumatra, Southern Borneo, Java.

In size and color, the fruit somewhat resembles black

---

[1] *Health From Herbs,* October 1953, p. 314.

pepper. The taste is not pungent but aromatic and camphor-
ous which leaves a peculiar sensation of coolness in the
mouth, like that produced by peppermint. The berries add
flavor to tobacco or herbal smoking mixtures. Once it was
widely advertised in the United States in cigarettes as a
medicinal smoke for coughs.

Deer's Tongue (*Liatris odoratissima*)

This native plant of America is commonly known as wild
vanilla or vanilla leaf. It has a stronger fragrance than that
of sweet woodruff. When used in small amounts it adds a
delightful fragrance to smoking mixtures.

Dittany-American (*Cunila mariana*)

A native herbacious perennial, it produces clusters of small
white or purple flowers. A hot infusion of the plant was
drunk freely by the Indians as a sudorific for coughs and
colds. Hunter lists the Indian name of the plant as "Mas-
Tin-Jay"—rabbit, and says: "The leaves are much used for
smoking and chewing among several tribes. It is entirely free
from the narcotic tobacco; and is pleasant-tasted, though it
produces a slight degree of pungency on the tongue."

Eucalyptus (*Eucalyptus globus*)

The eucalyptus is remarkable for its rapid growth, reaching
a height of 50 feet in five or six years. These trees are im-
mense evergreens of the Australian and Tasmanian forests
but have been extensively planted in other regions of the
world.

Cigars made of eucalyptus were displayed at the Paris
Exhibition of 1867 and were recommended as being effective
in promoting better digestion. A pharmacist at Melbourne,
Australia prepared cigarettes from the foliage and advised
their use for bronchitis and asthma. In reference to eucalyptus, the 17th edition of the U.S. Dispensatory stated: "As an
antispasmodic, it has been highly lauded in asthma. In this
affection it is best given by inhalation. Cigarettes may be
made by rolling up the dried leaves, or the vapor from boiling water containing the oil may be inhaled."

Ginseng (*Panax quinquefolium*)

There are two varieties of this plant, the American *Panax quinquefolium* and the Chinese *Panax schinseng*. The official name is from *pan*, "all," and *akos*, "remedy," in reference to the miraculous healing virtues ascribed to the herb by the Chinese. Ginseng root was chewed as a substitute for tobacco by the early colonists and the juice swallowed for its stomachic properties.

Licorice (*Glycyrrhiza glabra*)

Native to the warmer parts of Asia and Europe, it is cultivated in many parts of the world. Because of its demulcent and expectorant properties, licorice is employed in the form of an extract and incorporated in various modern medicaments. It was known to the ancients as early as the third century B.C. for its effectiveness in dry coughs.

Licorice is blended with tobacco as a flavoring and conditioning agent.

Life Everlasting (*Antennaria dioica*)

Habitat: America, Asia, Northern Europe.

This was an old Indian remedy. It was claimed that hoarseness, or irritation of the mouth and throat was relieved by chewing the herb and swallowing the juice. The Indian medicine men always carried so much of this aromatic botanical with them that it gave them an odor similar to that of hickory nuts. The Indians also claimed that the use of the herb cleared and strengthened the voice in a most remarkable manner and created a desire to sing.

Life Everlasting was used in former times as a substitute for the tobacco chewing habit. It was a favorite pipe smoke of the Indians and is also used for smoking purposes in many European countries today.

Marjoram (*Origanum majorana*)

The name comes from *orios*, "a mountain," and *ganos*, "joy," in reference to the natural places of growth. This is a well-known and popular seasoning herb. A favorite saying among those first learning to flavor cookery is "when in doubt try marjoram." The leaves were used in old-time smoking mixtures and to flavor tobacco and snuff.

Mullein (*Verbascum thapus*)

Mullein is a yellow-flowered biennial common in fields, banks and roadsides. Its generic name was first used by Pliny and is thought to be a corruption of *barascum*, "with beards," in allusion to the hairy filaments.

The American Indians smoked mullein in their pipes for the relief of sore throat. During the last century the *Medical and Surgical Reporter* carried this bit of information:

> In that form of disease in which there is dryness of the wind-pipe, with a constant desire to clear the throat, attended with little expectoration, and considerable pain in the part affected, the mullein smoked through a pipe acts like a charm and affords instant relief. It seems to act as an anodyne in allaying irritation, while it promotes expectoration and removes that gelatinous mucus which gathers in the wind-pipe, and, at the same time, by some unknown power, completely changes the structure of the disease. . . .

Dr. A. W. Chase refers to this medical report when he relates the following:

> Since the publication of the foregoing, in the ninth edition, I have been smoking the dried mullein, and recommending it to others. It has given general satisfaction for coughs and as a substitute for tobacco in smoking, exhilarating the nerves, and allaying the hacking coughs from recent colds, by breathing the smoke into the lungs. In one instance, after retiring, I could not rest from an irritation in the upper portion of the lungs and throat, frequently hacking without relief even for a moment; I arose, filled my pipe with mullein, returning to bed I smoked the pipeful, drawing it into the lungs, and did not cough again during the night.
>
> An old gentleman, an inveterate smoker, from my suggestion, began to mix the mullein with his tobacco, one-fourth at first, for awhile; then half, and finally three-fourths; at this point he rested. It satisfied in place of the full amount of tobacco, and healed a cough which had been left upon him after inflammation of the lungs. The flavor can hardly be distinguished from the flavor of tobacco smoke, in rooms.

It can be gathered any time during the season, the center stem removed, carefully dried, and rubbed fine, when it is ready for use. The clay pipe which is to be used, can be readily cleansed [after smoking] by burning out.

Red Raspberry (*Rubus strigosus*)

The botanical name comes from the Celtic word *rub*, "red," in reference to the color of the fruit. This plant contains a good amount of vitamins and minerals. Raspberry leaf tea is highly valued by the medical herbalists who prescribe it as a remedy for preventing miscarriage and for easing the severe pains of childbirth.

Red raspberry leaves, finely cut, are said to be one of the most satisfying mixtures of the many herbs employed for smoking purposes. When burned, they do not emit a herby aroma. The leaves are blended with other herbs employed as smoking mixtures or they can be used alone.

Rosemary (*Rosmarinus officinalis*)

An aromatic low-growing evergreen, native to Southern Europe. The mystic fragrance of this plant is suggestive of ancient ceremonies and rituals. It is smoked with tobacco or herbal mixtures in England where smoking was first introduced by Sir Walter Raleigh. Culpeper said, "The dried leaves taken in a pipe as tobacco, helps those that have a cough." A combination of dried rosemary and coltsfoot leaves rubbed together was used as a medicinal smoke for the same purpose, and also as a substitute for tobacco.

Sage (*Salvia officinalis*)

This plant is a native of Mediterranean countries but is commonly found in the United States and Great Britain. Sage tea was so highly esteemed by the Chinese that they gave the early Dutch traders twice the amount of their choicest oriental teas in exchange for sage.

A pipe mixture consisting of dried sage leaves blended with coltsfoot was smoked in former times in the belief that it secured immunity from contagious diseases. For ordinary smoking purposes the leaves of sage were combined with mullein and mint. In some countries sage is blended with tobacco.

Sassafras (*Sassafras officinalis*)

This tree is well known for its spicy aromatic bark. The custom of drinking sassafras as a spring tonic is of Indian origin. In some sections of the country it is used as a seasoning in sauces.

Hunter says that the Indians "smoke the bark of the dried root and prize it very highly." Rafinesque, in his *Medical Flora* (1830), writes: "The bark dyes wood of a fine orange color called *'shikih'* by Missouri tribes, and smoked like tobacco."

Sumach (*Rhus glabra*)

This species of *Rhus* commonly called smooth sumach, upland sumach, and Pennsylvania sumach is an indigenous shrub ranging from 4 to 12 feet or more in height.

Charles F. Millspaugh, M.D., gave the following information in his *American Medicinal Plants*, printed in 1887:

> The berries of sumach (*Rhus glabra*) when dried, form an article of trade in Canada, known as sacacomi. This when smoked as a substitute for tobacco is said to antidote the habit. The Western Indians make a preparation of equal parts of the roots, leaves and of tobacco, which they smoke under the name of Kinikah.

Another interesting account of sumach berries was cited in the *Historical Dictionary*, 1813:

> It has long been the practice among the natives of this continent, to substitute the sumach berry for tobacco, and the secret has been transmitted to Europe; in consequence of which it became so universally esteemed there by people of fashion and fortune, that large sums were offered to persons of mercantile professions, for this valuable but common production of nature. It has been preferred to the best manufactured Virginia tobacco. The method to be pursued in preparing the sumach berry to a proper state for smoking is to procure it in the month of November, expose it some time to the open air, spread it very thin on can-

vas, and then dry it in an oven, one-third heated. After having completed the progress of the cure thus far, spread it again on canvas, as before; there let it remain 22 hours, when it will be perfectly fit for use.

In writing on the uses of sumach by the American Indians, Hunter says, "They consider it a principal article, next to tobacco, in the stores for the pipe; mixed with about an equal part of tobacco, it forms one of their most fashionable treats." The Tewa Indians dried the leaves and rolled them into cigarettes made of corn-husks or smoked them in pipes. It was also a favorite smoke of the Jicarilla Apache.

Sweet Clover (*Melilotus officinalis*)

From *meli*, "honey," and *lotus*. The genus consists of about 20 species which are generally found in Central and Southern Europe and Western Asia. *M. officinalis* which produces yellow flowers and *M. alba* which produces the white have become naturalized from Europe and are common on the roadsides of the United States. Either of these two varieties was used to flavor tobacco.

Sweet Gale (*Myrica gale*)

From *myrio*, "to flow," it is found on the banks of rivers and streams. This evergreen shrub has a distinctive odor resembling that of bay leaves. The Norwegians mix the leaves of this bush with tobacco for smoking purposes.

Sweet Woodruff (*Asperula odorata*)

Sweet woodruff, also known as Master-of-the-Woods, is a small hardy plant well-adapted to shaded situations among trees. When dried it acquires a vanilla-like fragrance and is considered one of the most agreeable and delightful of all herb teas. Withering, an English writer, said that in his opinion it exceeded the choicest teas of China.

In ancient times, fierce Teuton warriors believed that a spring of this dainty herb was needed to wage a triumphant battle. The herb was fastened to their shield or horned helmet or attached to their animal skin mantle.

Sweet woodruff is used in modern Germany to flavor the famed *Maitrinke* (May Wine), liqueurs, and the like, while the Swiss use it to flavor candies. It is highly prized in European countries as a fragrant addition to pipe tobacco.

Yerba Santa (*Eriodictyon californicum*)

This herb is a native of California. The Spanish considered the tea an excellent remedy for coughs, bronchitis, and hoarseness. The California Indians smoked and chewed the aromatic leaves like tobacco.

HERBS TO DISCOURAGE THE TOBACCO HABIT

Many people claim that herbal smoking mixtures have helped them to give up the use of tobacco. *Herbs for smoking are nonhabit-forming.* The smokers switched to a pipe and reduced the amount of tobacco by adding more and more herbs to the blend. They state that in this way they were able to wean themselves from the use of the commercial tobacco product and to finally quit smoking completely. As an additional measure toward achieving the goal, some people chew a tiny piece of *gentian root* at intervals throughout the day, claiming that it helps lessen the craving for tobacco.

(*Additional References:* Joseph E. Meyer, *The Herbalist,* Hammond, Ind.: Indiana Botanic Gardens, 1960. Clarence Meyer, *The Herbalist Almanac.* Hammond, Ind.: Indiana Botanic Gardens, 1965.)

17

ROUNDUP OF MISCELLANEOUS HERBS

In order to cover as many herbs as possible, the following section is comprised of an alphabetically arranged list in which each plant's usage and benefits is described briefly.

BURDOCK

SYNONYMS: Clotburr, Bardana.
PARTS USED: Root, seeds, leaves.

Burdock (*Arctium lappa*) is a coarse biennial which ranges from two to three feet in height and bears purple flowers. The burrs hitch a ride on every switching tail, hairy dog, woolly sheep, skirt, or trouser leg. Although a native of Europe it follows man wherever he goes and is now quite at home in almost every section of the world, flourishing in fields, ditches, roadsides and cultivated grounds. The stamina of this lowly plant is remarkable; persecution with the plow or scythe may retard but never halt its victorious march.

Burdock has been employed as a medicine for a very long time. In his work published in 1640 Parkinson wrote: "The juice of the leaves given to drink with old wine doth wonderfully help the biting of any serpents. . . ." The U.S. Dispensatory of 1888 cited its use in a number of disorders, especially for chronic skin diseases such as eczema and psoriasis, with the following directions:

To prove effectual, its administration must be long continued. A pint may be given daily of the decoction,

168

made by boiling two ounces of the root in three pints of water down to two pints. The fluid extract and syrup have also been prepared. The fresh leaves have been employed both externally and internally in cutaneous eruptions [skin breakouts] and ulcerations.

Guibourt found that burdock contains *inulin*. Further analysis by other scientists has shown that it also produces a bitter crystalline glucoside, fixed and volatile oils, *vitamin C, iron, niacin,* mucilage, sugar, a little resin and some tannic acid. In Europe the root is used in herbal blood purifying mixtures and pills. The Japanese boil the roots in salted water and eat them with sauce or butter like salsify. Those living in the rural regions of Russia claim that a broth prepared from burdock roots, when taken daily, stops the hair from falling out and stimulates its growth. As an accessory measure they wash the hair with alkali water in which three tablespoonfuls of the roots have been boiled.

We find the following information in the *Encyclopedia of Health and Home:*

An infusion of the seeds or of the roots of burdock, drank freely, is an excellent remedy for boils, styes and felons. . . . A pint of the infusion may be drank in the course of 24 hours.

The seeds are a very valuable blood purifier, either when used alone or combined with sarsaparilla, in equal parts. Dose of the tincture, from 30 to 60 drops, four times a day.

For the prevention of styes the same book gives this advice: "Make a strong tea of burdock seeds or ground century plant and take a tablespoonful three or four times a day."

CAMOMILE

There are two varieties of camomile which are employed for remedial purposes. They are given as follows:

Camomile (*Anthemis nobilis*)

SYNONYMS: Roman Camomile, Double Camomile.
PARTS USED: Flowers, herb.

This is a European plant which grows wild in temperate

regions and has been naturalized in the United States. The botanical name is from *anthemon*, "a flower," in reference to the great number of flowers the herb produces. It was given the common name of Roman camomile by Joachim Camerarius in 1598.

The medicinal use of Roman camomile dates from antiquity. The Egyptians consecrated it to their gods because of the high esteem in which it was held as a remedial agent. In Rome, a tea was prepared from the flowers and used as a bitter tonic and blood purifier. The French drank it after a meal to aid digestion, and boiled the herb as a compress for piles. Women drank camomile tea for menstrual cramps and suppressed menstruation. The tea was also believed *to clear the complexion*. Consumptives were advised to sit close to a bed of camomile and breathe deeply of its fragrance which allegedly had a purifying effect on the lungs. The herb was believed to ease pain and remove fatigue when used in the bath. An infusion prepared with the flowers is still used today as a rinse to bring out the golden highlights of blond hair.

As a "Plant Physician"

Camomile enriches the soil, according to this excerpt from an old herbal:

It is remarkable that each camomile is a plant physician, since nothing contributes so much to the health of a garden as a number of camomile herbs dispersed about it. Singularly enough, if another plant is drooping and dying, in nine cases out of ten it will recover if you place a camomile plant near it.

Constituents and Modern Uses

Roman camomile contains a volatile oil, tannic acid, anthemic acid, and a glucoside.

Old-fashioned camomile tea is still a favorite today. Medical herbalists recommend it as a remedy for the hysterical and nervous conditions of women. Two cups of the tea taken daily after childbirth is said to clean and strengthen the uterus. Europeans consider camomile one of the finest agreeable bitters for "nervous stomach." For this purpose the tea is drunk cold rather than hot, three times a day. It is also used in many countries in the form of a wine bitters which is made by steeping one-half ounce of the flowers in one quart of Port or Madeira wine.

Medical herbalists sometimes prescribe camomile tea for the condition of *gallstones*. Certain dietary restrictions are also followed during this course of treatment. Claudia V. James refers to the use of the plant for this disorder when she writes: "Taken as a tea it [camomile] dissolves gallstones . . . I can vouch for this myself."[1]

Reported Uses in Retention of Urine

Dr. Vogel says that elderly men who find it difficult to urinate at times can obtain relief by the use of a herbal steam bath. He gives the following directions:[2]

Some herbal infusion, such as camomile, is poured into a suitable container together with boiling water. A narrow board laid across the vessel will enable you to sit over the hot, rising steam which can be retained by covering yourself with blankets. Your body will thus be thoroughly heated up, urinary spasms will be released and the water will once more begin to flow.

Chamomile (*Matricaria Chamomilla*)

SYNONYMS: German Chamomile, Single Chamomile.
PARTS USED: Flowers

The flower heads of German chamomile are much smaller than those of the Roman variety. This European plant has also been naturalized in the United States. The flower is said to be dedicated to St. Anne, the Mother of the Virgin, seemingly because of the herb's botanical name, *Matricaria*, which is derived from *mater* and *cara*, meaning "beloved mother."

Constituents and Uses

German chamomile has been used as a carminative (relief for flatulence), tonic, and general sedative. It contains a bitter extractive, a volative oil, mineral salts and tannic acid. The tea is a popular beverage in European countries where

---

[1] *Herbs and the Fountain of Youth* (Edmonton: Amrita Books).
[2] *Nature Doctor.*

it is served before retiring to *assure a good night's sleep*. It is also used in many countries for stomach disorders, and for pains in the throat or neck when due to swollen glands. Some types of earache and ringing noises in the ears are said to have been successfully treated with German chamomile.

This plant has been reported to be a valuable *children's remedy* especially for the treatment of *nightmare and restless sleep*. An old English physician, Dr. Schall, claimed that the tea was not only an effective remedy for nightmare but was also an excellent preventative of this complaint. In Russia one to two teaspoonfuls of chamomile tea is given to infants for constipation. It is also employed in many countries for flatulent colic, and ailments due to teething.

The following item appeared as a reprint in the *Herbalist Almanac*:

> Six or eight chamomile flowers to a teacup filled with boiling water makes a drink at once soothing to a patient who is irritable, unreasonable and nervous because of flatulence and simple colic. Two teaspoonfuls of such an infusion will quickly quiet the howling child with gas pains. . . . With this useful carminative, simple gas disappears from little ones as if by magic.

CELERY

PARTS USED: Seeds, stems.

In ancient times celery (*Apium graveolens*) was used as a medicine rather than a food. Hippocrates prescribed it as a diuretic and it is still employed for the same purpose today. Records show that in the 17th century the plant was a rare item in England and apparently was not used as a common vegetable until almost 200 years later.

Celery provides an *abundance of calcium, potassium, phosphorus, sodium*, and *iron*. It also contains *vitamins A, B*, and *C*, in addition to *potash, sulphur, silicon, magnesium, apiol*, and an *insulin* ingredient. Its therapeutic action is said to be carminative, diuretic, tonic, stimulant, emmenagogue, and nervine.

Celery is best known for its beneficial effect in conditions of arthritis, rheumatism, lumbago and nervousness. Dr. Leclerc, however, reports that he has often employed it with successful results in chronic cases of Bright's disease.

Rheumatism

An item carried in an Australian newspaper stated that celery cooked in milk and eaten freely *neutralizes uric acid* and other excess acids in the body and, therefore, is an excellent remedy for rheumatism. A health book written around the turn of the century recommended this remedy for the same disorder:

> Take of garden-celery, cut it into small pieces, and boil in water until soft. Of this liquid let the patient drink freely, three or four times a day. It is recommended at the same time, to use it as an article of diet, prepared as follows: Put new milk, with a little flour and nutmeg, into a saucepan with the boiled celery, serve it warm with pieces of toast, and the painful ailment will soon yield. Such is the declaration of a physician who has time and time again tried the experiment and with uniform success.

The seeds used in the form of an extract, decoction, or powder are also considered effective for the treatment of rheumatism.

Variety of Uses

Dr. Kirschner gives these facts relating to the therapeutic value of celery:[3]

> Japanese physicians prescribed celery for rheumatism. For one month the patient was placed on a diet of celery in all forms. When the patient got better, people attributed it to the healing power of celery. Since we Americans know of *celery's alkaline reaction* in the body, and of the valuable minerals (particularly sodium) which it contains in abundance, it is not to be wondered at that great benefit was derived from following such a diet.
>
> That most Americans over-indulge in concentrated, acid-forming starches, is generally conceded. This results in deposits of insoluble inorganic calcium. Food chemists have demonstrated that the organic sodium in celery helps keep the inorganic calcium in solution until at least some of it can be eliminated. Thus celery

[3] *Nature's Healing Grasses.*

helps in both the treatment and prevention of *arthritis*.

Every juice bar in every health food store in the country serves celery juice. Raw celery juice is the answer for persons finding it difficult to eat celery in its whole state, due to its fibrous content. If you have a liquefier or juicer, it is easily prepared at home. Should you find the taste of celery juice too strong, try blending it with carrot or other mild vegetable juices. It is also good with pineapple or apple juice.

Instead of the many patented preparations on the market, it is much wiser to use celery juice for the occasional acid stomach. The sodium in celery is a great neutralizer. And because of the sobering effects of raw celery juice, health food stores often serve it to drinkers as an antidote for alcoholism. . . .

Young, tender leaves, taken from the heart of the celery plant, also can be used to make a delicious therapeutic drink called "Lemon-Celery Delight." Here is the recipe:

> one large, or two small lemons
> one cup chopped celery leaves
> one pint cold water

Place in liquefier and triturate. Add more water and sweeten to taste with honey or brown sugar.

In spite of a sulphur acid in the leaves, their residue is strongly alkaline. They contain vitamins A, B, and C; also potassium, sodium and an insulin ingredient. Diabetes, acid condition, gout and other ills are helped by them.

CORN SILK

PART USED: Flower pistils of maize.

Corn Silk (*Zea mays* or *Stigmata maidis*) is the fine, yellowish or greenish threads commonly called "silk of the ear" of ordinary Indian corn (maize). In the old days a tea made from corn silk was a popular folk remedy for complaints of the bladder. Physicians soon began employing it in their practice as a diuretic and for conditions of cystitis. The *Medical News*, 1881, recommended the use of corn silk for these purposes. In the same year an article written by Professor L. W. Benson appeared in the *Therapeutic Gazette* in which he reported that he found the remedy both gentle and effective. Dr. John Davis, a physician of Cincinnati stated that a decoction of corn silk, when combined with dried pods of beans was the most active and effective of all the diuretics he had ever employed.

Corn silk gradually came to the notice of the medical profession in Europe, and various writings on this newly introduced remedy began appearing in foreign scientific journals. A number of impressive articles rapidly followed which resulted in an increased demand on American manufacturing pharmacists. The 17th edition of the U.S. Dispensatory listed its uses as follows:

> Zea (corn silk) has been highly recommended by various surgeons as a mild stimulant diuretic, useful in acute and chronic cystitis, and in the bladder irritation of uric acid and phosphatic gravel. It has also been employed in gonorrhea, and has been affirmed by M. Landreux to be a useful diuretic and even cardiac stimulant in the dropsy of heart disease. It has been commonly used in the form of infusion, two ounces to the pint of boiling water, taken almost *ad libitum* [as much as one wishes]; but the fluid extract, dose one to two fluid drachms every two or three hours, is an excellent preparation.

Pharmaceutical Constituents of Corn Silk

Fischer and Rademaker determined the presence of *maizenic* acid in dried corn silk; however, it had been described before that by Dr. Vautier. In addition to the acid, Fischer and Rademaker found that it contains a fixed oil, chlorophyll, gum, sugar, resin, albuminoids, phlobaphene, cellulose, salt, and water.

Dr. Neiderkorn of Lloyds cited the following uses of corn silk:

> *Stigmata maidis* is indicated in cystic irritation, due to phosphatic and uric acid concretions. In these cases the urine is usually scant and of a strong odor. The remedy not only relieves the bladder and urethral irritation, but tends also to prevent the formation of gravel and calculi. It is an important and favorite remedy in the treatment of urinal disorders of the aged, especially where the urine is strong and scant, and throws a heavy sediment. *Sigmata* should always be thought of in inflammatory conditions of the urethra, bladder, and kidneys, where it is evident that the in-

flammatory trouble is due to the presence of urinary concretions.

Dr. Clymer says:[4]

Where there is a tendency to the formation of gravel, or where it is known to exist, give:

Tincture *Stigmata maidis* one oz.
Tincture Triticum [Couch grass] one-half oz.
Dose 10 to 60 drops in hot water as required.

Dose of *Stigmata maidis* in other conditions, 10 to 60 drops.

DAMIANA

SYNONYM: Mexican Damiana
PARTS USED: The leaves and tops.

Damiana (*Turnera diffusa*) is indigenous to Lower California, Texas, and Mexico. The chemical constituents of this plant are only partly known. A resin and volatile oil are present and it is said to contain phosphorus. Damiana is cited as aphrodisiac, tonic, and diuretic. Its powers as a tonic for nervous or sexual debility are believed to be increased when the herb is combined with palmetto berries. The Indians of Northern Mexico have used this plant since time immemorial for nervous and muscular weakness by drinking a tea prepared from the mashed leaves.

Early in the century, W. H. Meyers, M.D., of Philadelphia, wrote:

I have given it [damiana] quite an extensive trial in my practice and as a result, I find that in cases of partial impotence or other sexual debility, its success is universal. I pronounce it the most effective and only remedy that in my hands produces a successful result in all cases.

The use of damiana as a remedy for impotence was also cited in other medical writings which appeared around the same time. The dose recommended by two American physicians was: "Of the fluid extract, from 15 drops to a tea-

4 *Nature's Healing Agents.*

spoonful; of the solid extract three to six grains; of the sugar-coated pills, one or two."[5]

Reported Modern Uses

Damiana has been scientifically accepted in Mexico as a healing agent in disease resulting from debility of the nervous system. In that country it is regarded as a reliable remedy for exhaustion, catarrhal inflammation of the bladder, and in cases of sexual impotence especially when caused by excesses. It is also used for orchitis resulting in atrophy of the testicles, and for spermatorrhea (involuntary emissions). The plant is reputed to exert a favorable influence on the spinal column and some Mexican physicians employ it as a brain tonic. It is also prescribed in nephritis (kidney inflammation).

We find the following statements in Potter's new *Cyclopaedia of Botanical Drugs and Preparations*:[6] "Damiana is very largely prescribed on account of its aphrodisiac qualities, and there is no doubt that it has a very great general and beneficial action on the reproductive organs. It also acts as a tonic to the nervous system."

Yemm[7] recommends a mixture of one ounce each of the fluid extracts of damiana, kola, and saw palmetto for "nervous and sexual debility." He suggests a small teaspoonful in a wineglass of water three times a day before meals, and adds that a herbal laxative should also be used if constipation is present. In addition he advises that the diet be light and easily digestible.

FIG

PART USED: Fruit.

It is believed that figs (*Ficus carica*) were first cultivated in Egypt and Arabia. They were known and highly valued in Crete in 1500 B.C. and a short time later in Greece. The Greeks fully realized that some fruit trees required pollination but they did not understand why. In the fourth century B.C. Aristotle wrote that the young fruits of the fig tree had

---

[5] *Encyclopedia of Health and Home.*

[6] R. C. Wren, F.L.S., (8th Edition; London: Health Science Press, 1968).

[7] *The Medical Herbalist.*

to be visited by insects otherwise they would drop off without maturing.

Figs were introduced into America by the Spaniards, and by the end of the 16th century many varieties had been established. In 1629 Captain John Smith reported that he had observed the harvesting of almost "a hundred bushels of excellent figges" in a settlement of Jamestown, Virginia.

Figs as Food and Medicine

The famous laxative properties of figs have been appreciated for centuries. When the fresh fruit is not available about five or six unsulphured figs are soaked in a jar of cold water for 24 hours. In the morning the softened figs are eaten. Some people also drink the water in which the figs have been soaked.

In the first century A.D., Pliny wrote:

> Figs are restorative and the best food that can be taken by those who are brought low by long sickness, and are on the way to recovery. They increase the strength of young people, preserve the elderly in better health, and make them look younger, and with fewer wrinkles. They are so nutritious as to cause corpulency and strength; for this cause, professed wrestlers and champions were in times past fed with figs.

Written in the 11th century, the *Regimen of the School of Salerne* stated that a cataplasm (medicated poultice) of figs would heal "scrofula, tumour, glands, [and] kernels. . . ."

Boils

The use of the fig as an external application for boils dates from antiquity. The Bible relates the story of King Hezekiah who was dying from a diseased condition of the body which terminated in a boil. His life was saved when the Lord answered his prayers through the prophet Isaiah. *And Isaiah said, Take a lump of figs. And they took and laid it on the boil, and he recovered.—2 Kings 20:7.*

In reference to this Biblical account, Dr. Mead, a renowned medical man of the last century, wrote:

> It seems to me extremely probable that this king's disease was a fever which terminated in an abscess;

for in cases of this kind those things are always proper which promote suppuration, especially digestive and resolving cataplasms; and dried figs are excellent for this intention. Thus, the Omnipotent, who could remove the distemper by His word alone, chose to do it by the effect of natural remedies. And here we have a useful lesson given us in our adversities; not to neglect the use of those things which the bountiful Creator has bestowed upon us, and at the same time to add our fervent prayers that he would be graciously pleased to prosper our endeavors.

The fig is still used today as a folk remedy for the same purpose. In Bavaria it is roasted, split, and applied to a boil, while figs cooked in milk are used for sores and ulcerated gums. Records show that Aaron Burr once applied a fig poultice to a swollen jaw and by the next day the swelling had gone.

Miscellaneous Fig Remedies Reported

Culpeper cited the use of the fig tree for a number of disorders including chilblains, coughs, shortness of breath, bruises, and so on. He stated that, "The milk that issues from the leaves or branches when they are broken off, being dropped upon warts takes them away." Many people still use this method at the present time, claiming that if the wart is touched with the fresh juice several times a day for two or three days it will turn black and drop off leaving the skin clear. Culpeper also advised a decoction of the leaves to be used as a wash for ulcers and running sores. For toothache and ear noises he said: "The juice being put into a hollow-tooth eases pain, also pain and noise in the ears being dropped into them. . . ."

Figs were used for many purposes in the early monasteries. The monks prepared a cough syrup by boiling the green leaves with honey. An ointment was made by burning the wood of the tree and mixing the ashes with hog's lard. This was applied to sores, swollen glands, bruises, and chilblains. For sore throat a few chopped, dried figs were soaked, then later boiled in a pint of water until they became pulpy. The decoction was carefully strained and the fig water used as a gargle.

In some lands, figs are boiled in barley water and the beverage used for pulmonary complaints. The natives of

South America use the sap of the fig tree as a remedy for internal parasites. The parasites are digested by the active principle contained in the sap which is a proteolytic enzyme. It is said to be harmless to the intestines unless ulceration is present, in which case it should not be used.

Properties Contained in Figs

Two important food qualities are found to an unusual degree in the fig; a marked laxative effect and a high excess alkalinity of ash. The bulk of the seeds and fibre in combination with some special solvent in the juice is believed to be the reason for its laxative effect. Figs also contain a protein digesting enzyme called *ficin*. The fruit is rich in calcium, the mineral so necessary for the health of the bones and teeth. A rich amount of iron and copper is found in dried figs, both important blood-building elements, and scientists tell us that figs are of considerable value in the prevention or treatment of nutritional anemia. The fruit is also said to be of benefit in conditions of low blood pressure. Fresh figs are a good source of vitamin C but the dried fruit retains very little. In addition they provide some of the B vitamins, vitamin A, sodium, phosphorus and potassium.

Anti-Cancer Factor in Figs?

Reports have shown that cancer is seldom found in areas where figs are freely eaten. According to a news item, a French scientist believes that the fruit possesses an anti-cancer factor which can prevent pre-cancerous conditions from forming. Infinitesimal radioactive bodies were reported to be present in figs. In the opinion of Dr. L. F. Bordas, the anti-cancer factor appears to be related to these radioactive bodies.

As a Constipation Remedy

In writing on natural methods for the relief of constipation, Dr. Vogel says:[8]

A further remedy for constipation is the drinking of a glass of hot water first thing in the morning; if this

8 *The Nature Doctor.*

by itself is insufficient, eat some fig-paste which you can make yourself in the following manner: Take three oz. of figs, three oz. of raisins, one-third oz. powdered senna pods, one—two-oz. ground linseed. Mix all the ingredients, put through a mincer, shape into rolls and store them in a cool place where they keep quite well.

FRINGE TREE

SYNONYMS: Old-Man's Beard, Snowdrop Tree.
PART USED: Rootbark.

Fringe tree (*Chionanthus virginica*) is a native to the United States. It is an ornamental shrub, easily cultivated and especially adapted to lawns because of its beautiful flowers and deep green, glossy foliage. The botanical name is from *chion*, "snow," and *anthos*, "a flower," in reference to its long racemes of pure white flowers.

Remedial Use of Fringe Tree

Fringe tree contains *chionanthin* and saponin. Medical herbalists employ it as a remedy for acute jaundice, migraine, bilious sick headache, enlarged spleen, and weakness of the liver.

This interesting account was written during the last century by Professor I. J. M. Goss:

Some 32 years ago, I had been very badly salivated in an attack of simple bilious or intermittent fever, by my preceptor, and it resulted in an attack of jaundice, for which I was again salivated several times, with the result of an increase of the jaundice. I now gave up to die, for I had tried six or eight of the best physicians in Georgia. . . . About this time I was introduced by a fellow student to try the "old woman's remedy," *Chionanthus* (Old Man's Grey Beard as they called it), which grew plentifully upon the sandy land near Augusta, Georgia.

I procured a small quantity, and made a tincture in gin, and took a tablespoonful before each meal. In a few days my appetite began to improve, and my skin very rapidly cleared, and in some ten days my jaundice was gone; my skin was clear of bilious hue, and I felt like another man. I subsequently met with many cases of jaundice, and found the remedy so prompt to remove it, that I published my experience in the *Eclectic Medical Journal* of Philadelphia, since which time I have used it in a great many cases with success. I now use a saturated tincture, made by adding eight ounces to one pint of alcohol (96 percent). Dose, one drachm, three times a day.

Dr. Felter of Lloyd's reported the following information on fringe tree:

Chionanthus exerts a special influence upon the liver, and to a slight extent upon all the organs engaged in digestion. . . . The indications for its exhibition are: Yellowness of the skin and eyes; slight or fully-developed jaundice, with a sense of uneasiness and general pains simulating colic. It is one of the most certain remedies employed, whether the case is of jaundice, formation and passage of gallstone, bilious colic (indicated by yellowness of skin), acute dyspepsia, acute or chronic inflammation of the liver, or the irritable liver of the hard drinker.

Chionanthus is also indicated by a sallow skin, with expressionless eyes and hepatic tenderness; the passage of light grayish stools and scant urine which stains the clothing yellow. The liver-pain . . . may range from a slight uneasiness, with a feeling of weight and fullness, to an intense pain converging from the gall-bladder to the umbilicus, and attended with nausea, vomiting, and marked prostration.

In reference to this account given by Felter, Dr. Clymer[9] says, "The dose of the tincture is from five to ten drops in water." He adds:

In bilious colic it is best to first cleanse the stomach by giving an emetic . . . and this accomplished, follow with:

Tincture *Chionanthus* one-half oz.
Tincture *Hydrastis* [Golden seal] one oz.
Dose ten to 20 drops in water every three hours and, in addition, with each dose, three grains of *capsicum*.

In all conditions where the urine is scant, give five

[9] *Nature's Healing Agents.*

to ten drops tincture *Chionanthus* in an infusion of motherwort tea.

In all cases of acute indigestion where it is clearly indicated that undigested food remains in the stomach, cause emesis . . . and this accomplished, follow up the treatment by giving:

> Tincture *Chionanthus* one-half oz.
> Tincture Gentian one-half oz.
> Dose five to 15 drops before each meal.

Gallstone Conditions

Dr. Jon Evans of England writes on the value of different herbs for the treatment of gallstones and biliary colic.[10] He explains that constipation, sedentary habits, starchy and excess fatty foods are probably the predisposing causes of gallstones. He advises that the diet should consist of fresh fruit, fresh green vegetables, and lean meat if the patient is not a vegetarian. Low fat cottage cheese can be included. Starches, sweets, and chocolate are to be avoided and definitely nothing fried, and no eggs or fats. He recommends dandelion coffee in place of pure coffee.

Evans places the herb Greater Celandine (*Chelidonium*) at the top of his list and says, "I have used this superlative plant for the treatment of countless gall bladder conditions with highly satisfactory results." When treating gallstones and biliary colic, he says he has found that the plant produces the most favorable results when used in the form of a fluid extract:

> Ten to 12 drops fluid extract *Chelidonium*
> Three times a day after meals in a little water.

The second remedy which he highly recommends as an aid in expelling gallstones, and which he says also prevents their formation is fringe tree. Evans points out that its use is effective in jaundice and liver derangements as well. After first citing the celandine remedy, Evans says, "Fringe tree (fluid extract) can also be taken quite safely, 12 drops in a little water three times daily." He adds that the two remedies may be combined, "equal proportions of both herbal extracts. Dose: One teaspoonful three times a day in water."

[10] *Health From Herbs*, September–October 1967, p. 12.

GENTIAN

PART USED: Root.

There are a great many varieties of gentian, although not all are employed as medicines. One species which is widely used as a therapeutic agent is the yellow-flowered gentian known botanically as *Gentiana lutea*. It grows in Central and Southern Europe, especially on the Pyrenees and Alps. The root, which is imported, has an intensely bitter taste and is the only part of the plant that contains medicinal properties.

Gential was named after Gentius, king of Illyria, who was also a botany student. He is reputed to have been the first to discover the medicinal value of the plant which bears his name. Over a dozen remedies were credited to it at that time. It was used for debility, fatigue, derangement of the stomach, liver disorders, and as an antidote for poison. A wine in which the root had been steeped was considered excellent for chills due to exposure. Many of the complex preparations handed down from the Arabians and Greeks contain gentian as one of their ingredients.

A story which dates from the 11th century credits the use of the plant with checking the plague which had devastated Hungary during the reign of Ladislaus. The king humbly prayed that when he shot an arrow into the air it would be guided to some plant that could be used to halt the terrible pestilence. He discharged his arrow and found that it had pierced a gentian root. The remedy was tried at once and the results were said to be remarkably successful.

Gentian Bitters

Bitters is the popular name for a liquor in which a bitter herb, root, or leaf has been macerated. They are used as tonics or stimulants to increase the appetite and to improve digestion. Bitters are generally classified as follows: *Aromatic bitters* contain aromatic oils but little tannin; *astringent bitters* contain tannin but little aromatic oil; *simple bitters* are practically free from tannin and aromatic oil. Gentian root is employed as a simple bitter. It contains gentisic acid, gentiopicrin, gentianose, gum, pectin, starch, ash, and a faint trace of volatile oil; no tannin.

The use of bitters is as "old as the hills." The ancient

Romans, notorious for their food orgies, were convinced that bitters were important for digestion. In the last century, Dr. J. Paris of the Royal College of Physicians wrote that, "It may be laid down as a truth, that bitters stimulate the stomach."

Gentian enters largely into the composition of many different formulas for bitters, and is very popular in the mountainous regions of Germany and Switzerland where it is known as *Enzien*. The Swiss mix it with wine to relieve fatigue and in making beer and liquor. It is also employed for the relief of aches and pains in the bones due to chilliness and cold. Coriander seeds are often added to overcome the bitter flavor, or a piece of licorice root may be chewed immediately after to neutralize the strong taste left in the mouth.

Gentian Bitters as a Remedy

Bitters can be made either with a single botanical or as a special combination of herbs depending upon the flavor and action desired. Taken before meals they stimulate the appetite and impart a beneficial influence to the stomach. They are especially valued by people inclined to a sedentary mode of life.

Father Kneipp, of European fame, strongly advocated the use of gentian bitters. He writes:

Before all, I advise you to prepare extract of gentian. The gentian roots are for this purpose well dried, cut small, and then put into bottles with brandy or spirit. [Steep for one week, then strain.]

This extract is one of the best stomachics. Put six to eight tablespoonfuls of water into a glass, and pour in 20 to 30 drops of extract; take this mixture daily for some time. The good digestion will soon be indicated by a no less good appetite. If the food is felt to lie heavy in the stomach, and is troublesome, a little cordial made with a teaspoonful of extract in half a glass of water, will soon stop the disorder.

Gentian is likewise very good for cramp in the stomach. When after a long journey during which for days together eating fares badly and drinking still worse, people arrive at their destination dead tired and almost ill, a tiny bottle of gentian tincture taken by drops on sugar, will render excellent services.

Nausea and attacks of faintness are removed by taking a teaspoonful of tincture in water; it warms, enlivens, and brings body and mind to peace again.

Dr. Swinburn Clymer gives his medical opinion of gentian bitters as follows:[11]

> An active, safe stomach bitters of great value. Gentian is always indicated when the activity of the digestive organism is enfeebled, and when there is nausea and faint feeling due to indigestion. It is best combined with other agents such as *Hydrastis* [Golden seal]. In slow digestion it is always indicated as it will speed up the digestive powers and aid digestion of food. It will irritate in large doses, but in small doses reduces irritation of the mucous membranes. In mental weariness, and depression over the solar plexus it is the first agent indicated. Dose (of the tincture) three to 20 drops.

As a bitters combination, Clymer suggests the following:

> Tinctures *Berberis* one-quarter oz.; *Gentian* one-half oz.; and *Chelone* one-quarter oz. Mix thoroughly. The dosage is five to 15 drops. This combination is exceptionally valuable to restore the digestive organism, correct the bile and create a normal appetite.

Dr. Skelton lists this recipe for gentian wine tonic:[12]

> Gentian root (crushed)......two ounces
> Dilute (Proof) Spirit
>   of Wine..............................one and a half pints
> Macerate 14 days, shake up daily, express and filter.
> Dose: from 30 to 60 drops. Excellent tonic, useful in cases of debility, loss of appetite, etc.

Note: Prepared herbal tinctures and extracts may be obtained from various herb companies.

HIGH CRANBERRY

SYNONYMS: Cramp Bark, Guelder Rose, Squaw Bush, Snowball Tree.

PART USED: The bark.

[11] *Nature's Healing Agents.*
[12] *Science and Practice of Herbal Medicine.*

This deciduous shrub, *Viburnum opulus*, grows in the rich soils of the northern part of the United States, Canada, Europe and Asia. When the plant is cultivated, its snow-white flower heads become compact which justifies its common name of snowball tree. In its wild state it produces bright red berries resembling ordinary cranberries (low cranberry); however, they are too bitter to be considered palatable.

Rafinesque said that pills, and also medical plasters, were made from high cranberry and that some of the western Indian tribes smoked the bark as a substitute for tobacco. John Lighthall wrote, "It is usually called cramp-bark from the fact that it is such a powerful antispasmodic, and is noted for subduing cramps so readily." He claimed that he had employed it in hundreds of cases with "happy results" and added that he would have been at a loss in his practice without it. In his opinion it was particularly effective in relieving menstrual cramps for which condition he principally prescribed it. He lists the following directions for its use.

Dose of the tincture, from ten to 30 drops three or four times a day. The hot tea is best for severe cramps. Dose: a big swallow every three or four hours.

Pharmaceutical Constituents of High Cranberry

High cranberry contains valeric acid, tannin, salts, resin, and a glucoside known as *viburnin*. Medical herbalists employ it for cramps, spasms, and hysterics. Its use is reputed to bring rapid relief from cramping of the extremities. For cramps in the legs, Drs. Wood and Ruddock early in the century, recommended the following: "Make a strong tea of the high cranberry bush bark, and drink one-third of a teacupful, and it will stop the cramp in 20 minutes." They add that persons who have been repeatedly troubled with cramping of the extremities should drink the tea night and morning for one or two weeks and "their trouble will seldom return."

HOPS

PART USED: Flowers (strobiles)

The hop plant (*Humulus lupulus*) is native to North

America and Europe. It is largely cultivated in many countries for its cones or strobiles, which are used medicinally and in the manufacture of beer and ale. The word hop is taken from the Anglo-Saxon *hoppan* meaning "to climb" as this twining perennial plant attaches itself to neighboring objects and climbs to a great height. The botanical name *Humulus* is derived from *humus*, "moist earth," the type of soil in which the hop thrives best.

In *The British Medica Flora*, 1837, we read:

> The first mention of hops occurs in a letter of donation by King Pepin (King of the Franks, d. 768) which speaks of *humulariae*, meaning probably Hop-gardens. Beckman does not find the word *lupulus* to occur earlier than the 11th century. About the beginning of the following century, hops were introduced into the breweries of the Netherlands. They seem to have been unknown in England—for brewing purposes—til brought from Artois about the year 1524.

Use of Hop Pillows in Nervous Ailments

Centuries ago, hop pickers claimed that the strong aroma of the plant exerted a soothing influence on the nerves. Pillows stuffed with hops were soon used in place of ordinary pillows to insure a good night's sleep. They became so popular for this purpose that they were used by royalty. It is recorded that the use of a hop pillow was prescribed for George III in 1787 with excellent effect. Records also show that it was employed with very good results during an illness suffered by the Prince of Wales in 1879.

The soporific value of the hop pillow was mentioned in the 17th edition of the U.S. Dispensatory: "A pillow of hops has proved useful in allaying restlessness and producing sleep in nervous disorders. They should be moistened with water containing a trace of glycerine previously to being placed under the head of the patient in order to prevent rustling."

Hop pillows have maintained their popularity to this day. Some people sprinkle them with a little alcohol, claiming that it helps to bring out their soporific properties.

Reported Medicinal Uses of Hops

The active principle in hops is a glandular yellowish powder called *lupulin* which is obtained from the dried strobiles. The peculiar fragrant odor is due to a volatile oil. The taste is slightly astringent and extremely bitter.

Hops are prescribed for sleeplessness, hysteria, and nervous irritation. Also employed in atonic dyspepsia, debility, and indigestion. A tea made with hops to which a small amount of red pepper is added is said to ease the craving for alcohol and to settle the stomach. Many years ago Professor Sandburn of Montreal stated that he had found hops to be an excellent remedy for patients suffering from nervous sick headache. It was to be used as follows: "Make a tea, and of that take a small teacupful every three hours. During a severe attack, every two hours. Drink it hot." Another doctor is quoted to have said that a wineglassful of a decoction of hops taken twice a day for several weeks was used with good effect in some cases of Bright's disease.

Findings of Scientific Studies of Hops

Scientific research has been conducted with the hop plant. Staven-Gröberg reported that hops had a depressant effect on the central nervous system of frogs. Sikorski and Rusiecki found that certain bitter substances in hops produced a sedative action in birds and mice.

In 1934, Leclerc reported the findings of a study he had made. He said that hops contain appetizing and tonic properties and also act as a nervine in overcoming insomnia. This sedative action was also found to exert its calming influence on the genital organs. The active principle of hops (lupulin) has been used with good effect in war psychosis. Leclerc also stated that it acts as a stimulant to the glands and muscles of the stomach and at the same time calms the hyperexcitability of the gastric nerves.

Herbal Tonics in General

The herbal kingdom gives us the finest tonics it is possible to get. People do not realize that all herbs with bitter principles are a tonic in some form or another.

This formula is a good general tonic, excellent for convalescents, men and women over 40 and particularly those women troubled with the change of life.

one-half oz. Hops

one-half oz. Bogbean
one-half oz. Centaury
one-half oz. Holy Thistle
one-half oz. Agrimony
one-half oz. Wormwood
Add Senna [a laxative] if required.

Directions—Mix well and place in two pints of water, bring to the boil and simmer for 15 minutes. Strain. Dose—half a teacupful three times a day before meals. —from "A Practitioner's Case Book," H. Darwent.[13]

HYDRANGEA

SYNONYMS: Seven Barks, Wild Hydrangea.

PART USED: Root.

Hydrangea (*H. arborescens*) is known by the common name of *seven barks* because the bark peels off in separate layers of different colors. The botanical name is from *hydor* —water, and *angeion*—a vessel, in reference to the cup-like form of the capsule or seed vessel. However, some say that this name was given due to the fact that hydrangea is a marsh plant and requires lots of water.

Case of Terminal Illness Reported Healed with Hydrangea

Many years ago a woman, the mother of 12 children, was seriously ill, passing blood. The doctor told the family that she only had a few days to live. A neighbor happened to drop by and when he told the stricken family that seven barks would heal the mother, the father replied that he had not the slightest idea where he might find the plant. The neighbor quickly informed him that his farm was full of it. Small amounts of the decoction made by boiling one ounce of the root in one pint of boiling water were carefully dripped into the mouth of the semi-conscious woman, who was gently nudged so that she could manage to swallow it. In a few days, much to the astonishment of the doctor and the family, the woman was well. She wrote of her experience which was published in the forum of a newspaper and before long she received over 400 letters inquiring about seven barks. For 15 years the family dug and mailed hundreds of packages of the root until they finally sold the farm.

Cherokee Seven-Barks Remedy

Seven barks was an old Cherokee Indian remedy used for disorders of the urinary system. It was first brought to the attention of the medical profession in *The New Jersey Medical Reporter*, 1850, by Dr. S. W. Butler. His father, a physician and missionary had lived among the Cherokee and used the root of this plant with considerable advantage in treating calculi complaints. Later its value in these conditions was confirmed by Drs. Atlee D. Horsley and John C. S. Mankur. Dr. Butler employed it either as a regular decoction or as a syrup by mixing honey or sugar with the decoction.

Early in the twentieth century, physicians who wrote books on home remedies invariably cited *seven barks* as a valuable healing agent. For example, the following is a typical write-up of the remedy from those times.

> *Hydrangea*, Seven Barks.
> Part Used: The root.

> It is an admirable remedy for gravel, and relieves that excruciating pain experienced when the gravelly formations pass through the ureters from the kidneys to the bladder. Its curative qualities for inflammation of the kidney as well as other affections of the urinary organs are now generally recognized. . . . Dose of the decoction, one teaspoonful several times a day.

Chemical analysis has determined that *seven barks* contains starch, resin, gum, albumen, phosphoric acid, ferrous and other salts. In modern Europe, medical herbalists prescribe small doses of the decoction of the root for removal of gravel or stone in the bladder. It is also valued abroad for its power of preventing gravelly deposits from forming.

LADY'S SLIPPER

SYNONYMS: Nerve Root, Yellow Moccasin Flower, American Valerian.
PART USED: The root.

This species of wild orchid (*Cypripedium pubescens*) is

distributed from the lower part of Canada through our northern states to Mexico, South America, the Pacific islands and India. It was given the name of lady's slipper because of the shape of its flowers.

Chemical analysis has shown that it contains a volatile oil, sugar, starch, ash, fixed oil, tannin, and resin. The root of this plant is the part used in medicine. It is said to exert a beneficial action on the nervous system and is considered one of the most excellent and safest nervines in the plant kingdom. Medical herbalists employ it for nervous irritability, hysteria, sleeplessness, nerve depression, and during the period known as *change of life* (menopause). They often combine lady's slipper with equal parts of scullcap (*Scutellaria laterifolia*) for greater effectiveness in treating these disorders; for nervous sick headache it is combined with balm (*Melissa officinalis*).

Old-time family physicians often recommended the use of this herb. For example, the following is a typical prescription of those times:

> *Lady's Slipper*
> Part Used: The root.
>
> This plant should be used in the form of the fluid extract in doses of 15 to 25 drops. . . .
> This medicine is an excellent nervine, and acts as a tonic to the exhausted nervous system. Hence it is adapted to cases of nervous irritability and sleeplessness, and gives rest and refreshing sleep, and for this purpose is one of the best among domestic remedies. . . . It may be used alone or combined with scullcap, in the various nervous afflictions such as hysteria, headache, or in other diseases. Whenever a mild and safe nervine is needed lady's slipper root is very generally used in the form of infusion, made by steeping about one ounce of the root in boiling water. Dose, from a half to a teacupful every hour or two, or oftener according to symptoms.

A doctor in the last century was reported to have employed the root as a remedy for neuralgia, hypochondriasis, and morbid sensitivity of the nervous system in general. He administered it in powdered form, 15 grains three times a day.

MARSHMALLOW

SYNONYMS: Wymote, Sweet Weed, Althea.
PARTS USED: Leaves, root, flowers.

Marshmallow (*Althea officinalis*) is a perennial herb from two to four feet in height with pale purplish flowers. It is naturalized from Europe and grows on the borders of salt marshes from the Massachusetts coast to New York.

Marshmallow has been used as a remedy from the very earliest periods. Records show that Charlemagne, 742–814 A.D., demanded that it be cultivated in his domain. Dioscorides described the plant under the Greek name signifying "to heal." Its domestic use finally introduced the herb to professional medication.

Pharmaceutical Constituents and Uses

M. Bacon discovered a principle in the root which is identical with *asparagin*. Marshmallow also contains pectin, bassorin, tannin and phosphates. Its therapeutic action is classified as demulcent, mucilaginous and emollient.

A decoction of marshmallow root is extensively employed in Europe as a remedy in irritation and inflammation of the mucous membranes. In France the powdered root is used in the preparation of electuaries and pills. Because of its soothing properties, medical herbalists generally employ marshmallow in combination with other herbs for bronchitis and coughs. To remove obstinate inflammation and to prevent mortification, the powdered or fresh pulped roots are applied as poultices. In European countries its value in this direction is considered so great that it has been called "mortification root." It is frequently combined with equal parts of slippery elm when used in the form of a poultice.

The uses of this herb were set forth as follows:

The leaves, flowers, and root—chiefly the latter—are the parts used, and in the form of a decoction, making a thin mucilage. It is highly valuable in affections of the lungs, bowels, and urinary organs, especially in inflammations of the kidneys, bladder, and urethra. . . . The leaves make an excellent fomentation herb, and the powdered roots an excellent poultice for inflammatory swellings, bruises and burns.

Colitis (Inflammation of the Bowels)

Darwent covers the condition of colitis in his medical writings.[14] He expresses astonishment at the number of people that suffer from this disorder and says that the cause is generally improper diet, or a number of things such as sudden chilling of the body when heated, impure water, using strong purgatives, drinking ice water, or that worms may sometimes account for the condition. He adds that women of a nervous type are susceptible to colitis. Darwent lists the symptoms and treatment as follows:

Symptoms

Mucus Colitis.—If the large intestine is affected there is usually dyspepsia, constipation and the passing of mucus, skin, or a jelly-like substance from the bowel.

Ulcerative Colitis.—Diarrhea, sometimes constipation, greenish or yellowish motions, pain of a griping nature, there may be blood, shred or mucus passed in the motions.

The main symptom in both cases is this passing of mucus or skin in the motions and a feeling of distress and soreness in the abdomen which is aggravated on slight pressure.

The hands and feet are cold, abdomen hot, sometimes also feverishness and thirst. In severe cases there is loss of weight with signs of collapse and prostration.

Treatment

Never give strong purgatives for constipation in this trouble; use licorice powder or compound syrup of rhubarb in small doses, frequently if necessary. Give milk only or Slippery Elm Food til the trouble is well in hand, and revert to solid foods with caution. I have found this formula most successful:

one oz. Marshmallow Root
one-half oz. Lady's Slipper or Valerian Root
one-quarter oz. Slippery Elm

Mix well and boil half in two pints of water for 15 minutes. Strain while warm and the dose is half a teacupful warm, every two hours during the day.

[14] "A Practitioner's Case Book," *Health From Herbs,* September–October, 1967.

Darwent points out that quick results cannot be expected, adding that it will take steady perseverance. However, he assures us that he has known this remedy to help restore people to health who have had colitis for many years.

Relieving Duodenal Ulcers

The herbal formula for duodenal ulcers, developed by Capt. Frank Roberts, M.N.I.M.H., of Bristol, England, was reprinted in a health publication. Records show that thousands of people suffering from this painful condition have responded to the effectiveness of this herbal remedy when used in combination with a few simple dietary rules. It is presented here as follows:[15]

Fluid extract	Goldenseal	....	three and a half oz.
"	"	Echinacea	.... three and a half oz.
"	"	Cranesbill	.... three and a half oz.
"	"	Poke root	.... three and a half oz.
"	"	Marshmallow	.... three and a half oz.

The 17½ ounces constitute the entire treatment, and will last from three to four months of continuous medication.

The ingredients are mixed to make one bottle of medicine. Dose: 30 drops, in a wineglassful of water, three times daily between meals; about two hours after breakfast, lunch, and tea.

First and second weeks. Dietetic restrictions are necessary during the first 14 days. During this period it is advised that meat and fish should not be taken. All other foods are permissible. During the first fortnight [two weeks] small frequent meals or "snacks" are recommended by Capt. Roberts. These should take the place of large, hearty meals.

Alcohol in any form should be avoided. Smokers should reduce tobacco to a minimum.

Third and fourth weeks. It is recommended that during these weeks there should be a gradual increase in variety and quantity, with a consequent reduction in the number of "snacks."

Fifth week. Normal meals at usual meal times. Great

[15] *Health From Herbs,* February 1954.

care should be taken at this time not to overeat. By this time most sufferers are free from pain, and the appetite is vigorous.

Healing of the ulcers usually takes place during the second month. Sometimes there is a return of pseudo-symptoms at this time owing to the astringent action of the cranesbill root, which sometimes develops tension on the duodenal membrane. At this stage a cloud of acute disappointment may descend upon the patient, he believing the old trouble to be still there after all.

This is the signal to discontinue taking the medicine for 48 hours to allow easing of the tension. It can then be resumed at half doses three times daily, and continued until complete supply of medicine has been taken.

MOTHERWORT

SYNONYMS: Lion's Ear, Lion's Tail.
PART USED: Herb.

This perennial plant (*Leonurus cardiaca*) has been naturalized from Europe and Asia. It ranges from two to five feet in height and is found growing in fields, pastures, banks, and roadsides. It is said that the herb was originally imported because of its reputation as a healing agent.

Motherwort Known as the "Herb of Life"

Motherwort is an exotic botanical. It is considered by some to be a longevity plant and is traditionally known as the "herb of life." A quaint old proverb states: "Drink motherwort [tea] and live to be a source of continuous astonishment and grief to waiting heirs!" This herb is so highly esteemed among the Japanese that they dedicate one of their four great festivals to it. A special drink is prepared from the plant in commemoration of one of their emperors who was not expected to reach the age of 15, but who lived to be 70 after drinking a daily beverage made from the flowers of motherwort.

Culpeper wrote: "There is no better herb to take melancholy vapours from the heart, to strengthen it, and make [a] merry, cheerful, blithe soul than this herb."

Reported Remedial Use

Herbalists have valued the plant as a heart tonic for centuries, and it is for this reason that motherwort was given the botanical name of *cardiaca*. This is remarkable in view of the fact that the ancients could not possibly have known that the herb contains an abundance of calcium chloride. Scientists have found that this mineral compound is necessary for the health of the muscles. Since the heart is also a muscle, it requires calcium for strength, and to regulate the rhythm of the heartbeat. Laboratory solutions in which hearts are kept "alive" outside the body are largely composed of calcium.

Motherwort is used as a tonic, nervine, antispasmodic, and emmenagogue. It it still employed today as a remedy for weakness of the heart, heart palpitations, and poor circulation. It is also considered valuable for female disorders and is reputed to have a very good effect on the womb. F. Newman Turner, N.D., F.N.I.M.H., M.B.N.O.A., cites the following use of the herb:[16]

> *Leonurus cardiaca* Motherwort is an old remedy for simple heart conditions, providing a mild tonic and an effective preventative of heart disease.
>
> It is a gentle antispasmodic, beneficial in patients who become nervously aware of the heart and concerned about their heart, possibly through nervous reflex.
>
> It is especially useful in heart conditions, the menopause and menstrual abnormalities.
>
> Up to one-half or even one dram of fluid extract of *Leonurus* may be taken.
>
> This is the main ingredient of a famous old heart pill still sold by leading herbal wholesalers.

The following information on the healing value of the plant appeared in *The Medical Herbalist:*[17]

> *Medicinal Properties.* The chief influence is directed towards the uterine organs, giving tone and adding strength to the relaxed tissues. Mildly relaxing to the heart, giving to the nerves tone, and strengthening the heart considerably. The whole nervous system is gradually brought under the power of *Leonurus*. Among other uses to which this herb may be applied are in-

---

[16] *Fitness and Health From Herbs*, January 1963, p. 27.
[17] Yemm, p. 56.

flammation of the uterus, kidneys, uterine tension, uterine irritation, thoroughly toning and strengthening the pelvic viscera. Indeed, its reinvigorating qualities properly qualify it for the office of restoring all the conditions of nervous diseases peculiarly feminine.

Preparations and Uses. The simple infusion is made thus: Motherwort, one ounce; boiling water, one pint. Stand covered half-hour. Dose: One wineglassful four times daily.

Uterine Inflammation

Make and use the following in uterine inflammation:

Motherwort *(Leonurus cardiaca)* ....one oz.
Scullcap *(Scutellaria officinalis)* ....one oz.
Water betony *(Scrofularia aquatica)* ....one oz.
Water dock *(Rumex hydropathum)* ....one oz.
Black horehound *(Ballota nigra)* ....one oz.

Boil in five pints of water for half an hour; towards the end, add half a teaspoonful of ginger. Strain. Dose: one wineglassful four times daily, before meals.

Inflammation of the Kidneys

In cases of inflammation of the kidneys, make the following:

Motherwort *(Leonurus cardiaca)* ....one oz.
Water dock *(Rumex hydropathum)* ....one oz.
Valerian *(Valeriana officinalis)* ....one oz.
Wood betony *(Betonica officinalis)* ....one oz.
Plantain *(Plantago major)* ....one oz.
Mugwort *(Artemisia vulgaris)* ....one oz.

Boil in six pints of water half-hour; towards the end add half teaspoonful powdered ginger. Strain. Dose: One wineglassful four times daily, before meals.

Acute Ovaritis

Make and use the following in cases of ovarian tension:

Motherwort *(Leonurus cardiaca)* ....one oz.
Wormwood *(Artemisia absinthium)* ....one-half oz.

Water dock *(Rumex hydropathum)* ....one oz.
Black horehound *(Ballota nigra)* ....one oz.
Sunflower *(Helianthus anuus)* ....one oz.

Boil in five pints of water for a half-hour; sieve.
Dose: One wineglassful four times daily. This will
be found to be of excellent service in acute ovaritis.
The medicine is well qualified to meet such cases,
being anti-inflammation, relaxing; also tones and imparts strength.

PLANTAIN

SYNONYMS: Broad-leaved Plantain, White Man's Foot, Common Plantain.
PARTS USED: Leaves, root.

Plantain *(Plantago major)* is distributed throughout the
United States and Europe. It is a common flowering plant
which grows in fields, pastures and roadsides. The generic
name is derived from *planta*, the sole of a foot, in allusion
to the shape of the leaves as they lay on the ground. It was
called "white man's foot" in New Zealand and Australia and
also by the North American Indians because it arrived from
Europe with the settlers and sprang up wherever they went.
The ancient Romans called the herb Waybread.

Remedial Background of Plantain

Plantain has been used as a healing agent for hundreds
of years. Dioscorides of Greek antiquity recommended it for
the treatment of stubborn leg ulcers which refuse to heal,
and medical herbalists at the present time frequently employ
the juice of the plant for the same purpose. Pliny said that
an entire book was written about the medicinal virtues of
plantain by a famous physician named Themison. The Saxons
bound the crushed leaves around the forehead with wool to
relieve headache. The herb was widely used in epidemics
which occurred during famine or among the soldiers in the
field. It was considered a natural cleanser for infectious diseases caused by contaminated water or unsanitary conditions.
At one time it was a standby remedy for bacillary or amoebic
dysentery. For these disorders, three handfuls of the root and
leaves were boiled in a pint of water and the patient given a

teacupful as often as he desired. It was also taken daily as a remedy for catarrh in the head.

Plantain as Used by the Indians

The Iroquois pounded the fresh leaves of plantain and used them as poultices for wounds, coughs, colds, and bronchitis. A tea prepared from the roots was employed by the Meskwaki Indians as a remedy for intermittent fever. Many tribes valued the plant as a poultice for rattlesnake bite, insect stings, sores, painful rheumatism, burns, and swellings. In her writings, Densmore refers to the use of the herb by the Chippewa. Here is one example:

System or part affected .... Wound.
Symptoms .... Bites of poisonous reptiles.
Part of plant used .... Leaves and root.
How prepared .... Fresh, chopped fine and applied to bite. This was sometimes spread on a fresh leaf of the plant.

Remarks: An incident of the use of this plant was related. Mrs. Razer had a relative who was bitten by a poisonous snake while picking berries. Her husband put a tight bandage around the arm above the bite; then searched for the plant. Before he could find it, the woman's arm was badly swollen. He cut little gashes in the arm, moistened the root, applied it, and the woman's life was saved.

Constituents of Plantain

Plantain contains various salts, such as potash and potassium; wax, pectin, resin, citric and oxalic acids. Potash salts are essential to recovery after injury as they promote healing of the tissues. Potassium is present to some degree in all green herbs but the quantity provided by plantain is said to be considerable. This mineral is very important to the health of the body. A lack of potassium may cause such conditions as liver trouble, weak heart, dropsy, enlarged glands, female trouble, upset stomach, or swollen testicles. A British surgeon specializing in cancer believes that adequate amounts of potassium may be an important factor in the prevention of this dreaded disease.

As Used by Many Nations

Plantain is widely employed as a medicinal agent in Arabia where the herb is called "lamb's tongue." The people of Bavaria use it for the treatment of earache. In Ireland a poultice of the leaves is applied to wounds, cuts and inflammations. A boiled, strained solution is prepared from the plant for use as an eyewash in Jamaica. It is given in China for a variety of disorders and is said to promote fertility. In Greece the juice of the leaves is administered for infections of the mouth and gums, and the root chewed for toothache. A poultice of plantain is still one of the most widely used folk remedies for bee stings.

Reported Relief of Neuralgia

In their medical writings, Wood and Ruddock stated: "Plantain is a superior remedy for neuralgia. Take two to five drops of the tincture every 20 minutes. Usually a few doses will give relief."

Reported Uses for Ear Trouble

Dr. Alfred Vogel advises: "Anyone with a tendency to ear trouble should take the fresh plant extract from the broad-leaved plantain *(Plantago major)* for a few months, so as to eradicate it. This is one of the best remedies for the ears and will also sharpen the hearing."[18]

Ribwort

Father Kneipp writes on the value and uses of another variety of plantain known botanically as *Plantago lanceolata,* which is commonly called *ribwort.* He tells us that in his day when country people suffered a wound, they quickly searched for the plant and squeezed the leaves until they could manage to obtain a few drops of the sap. This was either placed directly on the fresh wound or a cloth was moistened with it and applied. If the leaf did not yield the sap but only became soft and moist from squeezing, then the mashed leaf itself was bound on the wound. Kneipp says that healing progressed rapidly and explains that, "The

[18] *The Nature Doctor,* p. 110.

plant sews the gaping wound together as with a golden thread, and as rust never gathers on gold, so all putridness and proud flesh flies from the ribfort."

He also considered the herb a valuable remedy for internal use, stating:

> The effects of this plant on interior parts are not less advantageous. Would that hundreds of people would gather these medicinal leaves in spring or summer, crush them, press the sap out of them, and drink it! Numberless interior complaints, which shoot up like poisonous mushrooms out of the impure blood and the impure juices, would not arise. Those are wounds which, truly, do not bleed, but which are in many ways more dangerous than bloody ones.

> The dried leaves of ribwort yield likewise a splendid tea against interior phlegm-obstructions.... With the dried leaves of ribwort, lungwort (Pulmonaria officinalis) can be well used in equal quantities.

SHEPHERD'S PURSE

SYNONYMS: Shepherd's Heart, Pickpurse, Casewort.
PART USED: Herb.

Shepherd's purse (Capsella bursa-pastoris) is a small common evergreen plant which grows in every part of the world. It adapts itself as easily to the extreme climates of tropical and Arctic regions as it does to those of temperate zones. The herb bears a few arrow-shaped leaves at its base and clusters of small white flowers which form above these at the top. The common name was given to the plant because the seed vessels or pods somewhat resemble a small purse.

With reference to the medicinal use of shepherd's purse, Culpeper said: "The juice being dropped into the ears, heals the pains, noise and mutterings thereof. A good ointment may be made of it for all wounds, especially wounds in the head." Dr. Fernie tells us that shepherd's purse was said to be the chief remedy of the *seven marvelous medicines* prepared by the Count Mattei of Bologna. The Count's followers believed that these herbal medicines were effective in diseases otherwise intractable. The six other plants were water betony, knotgrass, cabbage, stonecrop, watercress, and fever-few.

Constituents and Uses

Shepherd's purse contains the valuable blood clotting vita-min K, so essential in preventing abnormal bleeding. A vola-tile oil is obtained by distillation. A tannate, fixed oil, soft resin, various salts, and an alkaloid known as *bursine* are also present. The plant is cited as hemostatic, anti-scorbutic, diuretic, stimulant and tonic. The 17th edition of the U.S. Dispensatory listed its value and use as follows:

It has been used as an anti-scorbutic, also in haema turia and other hemorrhages, and in amenorrhea and dropsy. Two to four fluid ounces of the fresh expressed juice may be given at a dose; or a quarter to a half fluidrachm of the fluid extract of the dried plant.

In his writings, Dr. Yemm includes an extensive coverage of the medicinal use of shepherd's purse:

Its influence is directed towards the renal and vesical organs, soothing irritation, relieves hematuria. Gives positive relief in excessive menstruation. In ulcerated condition, catarrh, and abscess of the ureters and blad-der it has proved effective; with *couch grass* it is a rare combination as a stimulating diuretic. It is gently stimulating and mildly relaxing to the renal and urinary tract. The flow of urine is relieved and increased. Its results are positive in lumbago. In urethral irritation, in cases of scalding urine, its benefit is soon felt. It alleviates catarrhal conditions of the renal organs and irritable spermatorrhea. Indeed the whole pelvic viscera is charged with new vigour, either directly or indirectly, it is evidently one of the best agents to be used as stated. . . . Bleedings and floodings are said to come under its arresting influence; also dropsy. Puerperal hemorrhage has been known to promptly cease a few minutes after a cupful of the infusion has been taken, and has often been similarly and successfully employed in many forms of hemorrhages. Make as follows: Shep-herd's purse, two ounces; water, three half-pints; boil down to one pint. Dose: One wineglassful four times daily.

Remedy for Bed Wetting

For bed wetting, use the following:

Shepherd's purse
    (Capsella bursa-pastoris) ....one-half oz.
Agrimony *(Agrimonia eupatoria)* ....one-half oz.
Lady's slipper
    (Cypripedium pubescens) ....one-half oz.
Corn silk *(Stigmata maidis)* ....one-half oz.
Oak bark *(Quercus robor)* ....one-half oz.
Licorice root (crushed)
    (Glycyrrhiza glabra) ....one oz.

Steep a few hours in two pints of boiling water; strain; add two ounces glycerin. Dose: One teaspoonful before each meal and at bedtime.

Gravel in Urine

In case of gritty or gravelly deposit in the urine, make the following:

Shepherd's purse
    (Capsella bursa-pastoris) ....one-half oz.
Peach leaves *(Prunus persica)* ....one-half oz.
Marshmallow *(Althea officinalis)* ....one-half oz.
Red sage *(Salvia officinalis)* ....one-half oz.

Steep in two pints boiling water 30 minutes; strain. Dose from one teaspoonful to a wineglassful as required.

Incontinence of Urine

The following is quite as useful in incontinence of urine:

Shepherd's purse
    (Capsella bursa-pastoris) ....one-half oz.
Yarrow *(Achillia millefolium)* ....one-half oz.
Agrimony *(Agrimonia eupatoria)* ....one-half oz.
Prepare as above.

TWIN LEAF

SYNONYMS: Rheumatism Root, Ground Squirrel Pea.
PART USED: The root.

This is a small perennial plant which is found growing in

woods and near rivers from New York to Wisconsin, and southward. It was officially named *Jeffersonia diphylla* in honor of Thomas Jefferson.

Twin leaf contains gum, tannic acid, pectin, starch, a bitter principle similar to polygalic acid, a fatty resin, iron, lime and silica. The root is said to be tonic, antispasmodic, and expectorant when used in small doses, but in large doses acts as emetic. It is reputed to be an effective remedy for neuralgia. Early in the century, a Judge Crane of Cincinnati gave the following account which was printed in a health book:

> For what it has done for my wife and daughter I would not take thousands of dollars. At times the pain [of neuralgia] was so terrible as to throw them into convulsions. The prescriptions of the best physicians were used in vain. They found no relief until they tried twin leaf which acted almost like a charm. . . .
> I recommended it to a friend who had been suffering with neuralgia for three days and nights without sleep or rest. One side of her face was completely blistered from the effects of her physician's prescription. One dose gave her immediate relief, followed by ten hours' sleep.

The medical authors of the book in which these experiences were recorded stated that the root may be prepared and used in any one of the following ways: As a decoction, "The dose is one to two wineglassfuls three times a day. Of the tincture, use two to four teaspoonfuls. It has been used with great success by pulverizing the root and taking a dose about the size of a pea every hour or so till the pain subsides."

VALERIAN

SYNONYMS: English Valerian, Great Wild Valerian, Setwall.
PART USED: Root.

Valerian *(Valeriana officinalis)* is a large herbaceous perennial found throughout Europe, Northern Asia and China. This herb is not to be confused with lady's slipper which is often called American valerian, although both plants are said to possess similar therapeutic action.

The odor of valerian is generally considered disagreeable,

yet it was used as a perfume during the 16th century and is still employed for that purpose in the Orient today. The *wild nard* described by Pliny and Dioscorides is believed to be a species of this plant. Valerian was listed among the home remedies in the domestic books of the 11th century. Gerard mentions that the poorer classes of England added the herb to their broths, pottages and meats. Valerian has been used for hundreds of years as a remedy for nervous disorders.

Constituents

This plant contains valeric, formic, and acetic acids, in addition to starch, resin, a glucoside, and two alkaloids. Valerian is reputed to act as a sedative to the entire nervous system. The distressing symptoms of noises in the ears are said to be greatly relieved by drinking a decoction made with this herb, provided the remedy is persevered with. Dr. William Fox gives the following directions for the medicinal uses of valerian:

It is very similar in its properties to the American valerian [lady's slipper] and may be used instead of it. It is especially useful in cases of nervous derangement, especially nervous females, in hysterical, restless and irritable conditions. Dose—of an infusion of the root, one to two wineglassfuls; of the tincture, 20 to 30 drops in sweetened water three or four times a day.

WOOD BETONY

SYNONYMS: Betony, Bishopswort.
PART USED: The herb.

Wood betony (*Betonica officinalis*) is a European plant. It bears purple-red flowers arranged in whorls at the top of the stem. The name is from the Celtic *ben*, "the head," and *ton*, "good," in reference to its alleged virtues as a remedy for head complaints. Pliny says that it was first named Vettonica in honor of the Vetonnes, a people of Spain. In former times the plant was considered so valuable as a healing agent that proverbs such as "Sell your coat and buy betony," and "You are more virtuous than betony," were originated.

Records show that Antonius Musa, physician to Augustus Caesar, valued the plant as an effective remedy in no less than 47 diseases and Culpeper tells us that, "It was not the practice of Caesar to keep fools about him." Musa wrote a book devoted entirely to the medicinal uses of betony, stating for example that, "It preserves the liver and bodies of men from the dangers of epidemic diseases ... it helps those who loath and cannot digest their meat, those that have weak stomachs and sour belchings." Apparently Culpeper also found the herb to be of considerable value for he said: "It is a very precious herb, that is certain, and most fitting to be kept in a man's house." Parkinson wrote: ". . . it is said also to hinder drunkenness being taken beforehand and quickly to expel it afterwards."

Recorded Uses of Wood Betony

Dr. F. Herring, in writing of the herb in *New Preparations*, said:

I know of no other single remedy in the materia medica that produces such marked results in the treatment of chronic liver affections as this. The usual dose of the fluid extract is from 15 to 30 drops three or four times daily. The tincture is equally useful. It has proved very successful in chronic lung affections, when there is a slimy mucous expectoration, accompanied by a tight cough. It is almost a specific for chronic inflammation of the bladder and kidneys. . . .

Nervous Tension—Head Pains

Dr. Evans refers to the medicinal value of wood betony as follows:[19]

In medical practice I have found many patients suffering from nervous tension who get irritable and excited and complain of head pains of a purely functional nature. They also sleep badly, sometimes complaining of dreams. For this symptomatic picture I strongly recommend wood betony. A simple infusion can be made with one oz. of the herb to one pint of boiling water, a wineglassful to be taken frequently. I have found it highly successful and can be used in domestic medicine.

[19] *Health From Herbs*, March–April 1967, p. 74.

Dr. O. Phelps Brown covers the remedial use of wood betony in his writings. He says that the bruised green herb or an ointment made from it will draw out splinters, thorns, or other foreign objects from the flesh, and that it is also a valuable application for sores, ulcers and wounds. He recommends the herb in powdered form mixed with honey for colds, coughs, wheezing, pains in the side and back, griping pains in the bowels, and for gas pains. He says that an infusion taken as a tea is strengthening to the womb, and beneficial for inflammation of the kidneys and bladder. In addition, he tells us that it is good for liver complaint, headache and an "excellent remedy for dyspepsia or indigestion."

Alleviating Hay Fever

Wood betony is included in a herbal combination recommended for use in the condition of hay fever. In reference to this disorder, Louise Morley, M.N.I.M.H., of England, writes:[20]

> We now come to the perennial question of hay fever. We blame all kinds of things for this condition, from dry dust-raising winds and airborne pollen, to hay-cutting. No doubt these aggravate nasal congestion and allergic rhinitis. Local irritation can be considerably reduced by internal treatment. Catarrh is sometimes an accompanying condition. For these insufferable burdens simple infusions of Yarrow, Euphrasia or Eyebright can work wonders.
> Try the following:
> Wood Betony four drachm Fluid Extract; Yarrow eight drachm Fluid Extract; Euphrasia six drachm Fluid Extract; Tincture Capsicum ten drops.
> Aqua [water] to eight oz. Dose: Three teaspoonfuls in a wineglass of water.

WORMWOOD

SYNONYMS: Absinth, Ajenjo, Old Woman.
PARTS USED: The leaves and tops.

There are many varieties of wormwood. The one we are considering here is known botanically as *Artemisia absin-*

thium. It is a small perennial plant native to Europe but has been naturalized in many regions of North America and other parts of the world.

Wormwood is extremely bitter and was regarded by the ancients as a tonic and stomachic especially useful in gastric debility. A species of this plant is mentioned in several occasions in the Bible where its bitterness is compared with sin. Pliny says that no herbal beverage was more ancient in origin than a decoction of wormwood. Roman victors of chariot races were given a draught of the herb for good health and long life. Among the Egyptians it was regarded as a sacred plant and carried in religious processions. Pliny tells us that the Latin name of the plant was derived from the goddess Artemis who knew all its virtues and imparted this knowledge to mankind. According to tradition, however, it was Artemisia, Queen of Caria, who gave her name to the plant in appreciation for the great benefits she had obtained from it.

Properties and Uses

Wormwood contains tannin, succinic acid, volatile oil, resin, absinthin, malates and nitrates of potassium and ash. During the Middle Ages this herb was used in great quantities by wool cloth manufacturers as a moth repellent. A book printed in 1802 states: "The smoke arising from lighted bundles of Wormwood, expels bees from their hives, when honey is to be collected, without destroying these useful insects." Wormwood was the principal ingredient of the famous *Portland Powder* which was employed at one time as a remedy for gout. Joseph Miller wrote that a "cataplasm of the green leaves was commended to Mr. Ray by Dr. Hulse as a good external remedy against the swellings of the Tonsils and Quinzy." Pliny and Dioscorides considered the herb as anthelmintic and tonic. In reference to its use Thomas Greene said:

It is an excellent tonic with strong stimulant properties, useful in weak digestion, flatulency, dyspepsia and other complaints arising from a debilitated condition of the stomach and digestive organs. It must always be given in small doses as it is apt to give rise to vertigo. It is sometimes good for offensive breath arising from the stomach. Steeped in vinegar (two tablespoons to one pint of vinegar) it is excellent to use for sprains to reduce swelling and to take away strain. Woolen cloths dipped in it and applied to a sprain removes discoloration and pain. It keeps moths away from clothes. Take one teaspoonful of the herb to one cup of boiling water—steep—use as other herbs.

As Used for Fallen Arches

Village healers in some parts of the world treat fallen arches with a liniment made of wormwood steeped in rum. One man reported that he was unable to work for over three months due to this fallen arch disability. He consulted a number of medical doctors who tried special shoes, massage, and other treatment, but their efforts failed to correct his condition. In desperation the patient sent for the village healer. He was told to prepare a liniment by placing one ounce of powdered wormwood in a pint of rum and to let it steep for one week, shaking the bottle thoroughly every night. At the end of the week the clear liquid was to be strained off, placed in a clean bottle and capped tightly. He was advised to rub this herbal liniment on his feet day and night and, in between times, keep the feet bound with gauze. These instructions were carefully followed and within three weeks the patient was able to return to work. He stated that there had been no recurrence of the disability since using the liniment over 20 years ago.

Reported Uses for Liver Complaint and Indigestion

In the opinion of Fr. Kneipp wormwood ranks among the best of the herbal stomachics. He says it assists digestion, stimulates the appetite and relieves gas, when taken as a tea or powder. For an offensive breath which is caused by a disordered condition of the stomach, "wormwood is of excellent effect." He adds:

Whoever is suffering from liver complaint, let him take the little box of wormwood powder instead of his snuff-box, and put a pinch of its contents into his first spoonful of soup or sprinkle it like pepper on his food once or twice a day. The decreasing yellowness of the skin will soon show the improvement of the gall, and the patient, whose breath has been, as it were, laced up by the foul air and often still more foul juices, will breathe more freely again.

Wormwood can also be used as a tincture, which may be preserved for a long time. As a single little corn of incense glimmering on the charcoal will fill a whole room with perfume, so a little leaf of wormwood is sufficient to give a bitter taste to the contents of a whole spirit-bottle—a sign of the virtue of the tincture and its effects.

Travelers who are much troubled with indigestion and nausea, should never forget to take with them as a faithful companion their little bottle of wormwood-tincture.

Wormwood tea, used as eye-water, has often rendered the best services in eye complaints.

A Serious Battle Wound Healed

The following incident occurred in the year 1527 during a terrible siege of Rome. Benvenuto Cellini, a famous artist of that period, was wounded on the battlement of the fortress of St. Angelo while fighting in the service of Pope Clement VII. Cellini's autobiography states:

> A cannon shot reached me, which hit the angle of a battlement, and carried off enough of it to be the cause why I sustained no injury. The whole mass struck me in the chest and took my breath away. I lay stretched upon the ground like a dead man, and could hear what the bystanders were saying. Among them all, Messer Antonio Santacroce lamented greatly exclaiming: "Alas! alas! We have lost the best defender that we had!" Attracted by the uproar, one of my comrades ran up; he was called Gianfresco, and was a bandsman, but was far more naturally given to medicine than to music. On the spot he flew off, crying for a stoop of the very best Greek wine. Then he made a tile red hot, and cast upon it a good handful of Wormwood; after which he sprinkled the Greek wine, and when the Wormwood was well soaked, he laid it upon my breast, just where the bruise was visible to all. Such was the virtue of the Wormwood that I immediately regained my scattered faculties.

EPILOGUE

If we really stopped to compare the herbal with the chemical, the natural with the synthetic, we would realize that Nature is the Great Alchemist. Plants extract inorganic chemicals from the soil which are remarkably converted into organic material for absorption into the plant's own living structure. Iron supplied by the vegetables we eat or the herb teas we drink, rarely if ever disagrees with the human system, but inorganic iron which comes from other sources tends to bind and constipate. This is only one of many similar examples.

Far too long has man strayed from the natural mode of living. But there are signs that we are beginning to re-learn some of the lessons Nature so patiently tries to teach us. Pharmacologists don't laugh about home remedies anymore. Letters submitted to them regarding folk medicine are answered and the claims thoroughly investigated. Research teams are in dear earnest as they carefully examine age-old remedies such as onion poultices to counteract pneumonia, honey and vinegar to clear the blood and sinuses, and herbal cataplasms to reduce swelling or infection.

Whatever your illness may be, do not despair. Remember that good health is a part of Nature and it is unlikely that within her vast storehouse she has not provided the material that can bring about your return to health. As we have seen, plant research is not new, but up until now, it has never received such concentrated scientific support. Perhaps in the not too distant future the so-called incurable diseases of today will be rolled up like a scroll and numbered among the things that once used to be.

GLOSSARY OF TERMS

Alterative: A vague term to indiacte a substance which alters a condition by producing a gradual change toward the restoration to health.

Anodyne: Eases pain.

Anthelmintic: Expels or destroys intestinal worms.

Antidote: Agents which counteract or destroy the effects of poison or other medicines.

Antiemetic: Lessens nausea and vomiting.

Antiperiodic: Agents which modify or prevent recurrence of certain periodic febrile diseases.

Antiscorbutic: Counteracts scurvy.

Antiseptic: Destroys or inhibits bacteria.

Antispasmodic: Prevents or allays spasms or cramps.

Aperient: Causes a natural bowel movement.

Aphrodisiac: Stimulates the sex organs.

Appetizer: Stimulates the appetite.

Aromatic: Agents which emit a fragrant smell and produce a pungent taste. Used chiefly to make other medicines more palatable.

Astringent: Causes contraction of tissues.

Bactericidal: Pertains to something which destroys germs.

Balsamic: A healing or soothing agent.

Bitter Tonic: Bitter tasting properties which stimulate the flow of saliva and gastric juice. Used to increase the appetite and aid the process of digestion.

Cardiac: Agents which have an effect on the heart.

Carminative: Expels gas from the stomach.

Cataplasm: Poultice.

Cathartic: Causes evacuation from the bowels. There are different types of cathartics. Aperients or laxatives are mild and gentle in their actions. Purgatives are powerful and produce copious evacuations and are used only by adults afflicted with stubborn conditions.

Cholagogue: Increases the flow of bile and promotes its ejection.

Cordial: Invigorating and stimulating.

Corroborant: Invigorating; tonic.

Counterirritant: Agents applied to the skin to produce an irritation for the purpose of counteracting a deep inflammation.

Demulcent: Soothing, bland. Used to relieve internal inflammations. Provides a protective coating and allays irritation of the membranes.

Depurative: A purifying agent.

Detergent: Cleansing.

Diaphoretic: An agent which produces perspiration.

Digestive: Aids digestion.

Diuretic: Increases the flow of urine. (Because of their soothing qualities, demulcents are frequently combined with diuretics when irritation is present.)

Drachm: A unit of measure. In domestic medicine one drachm equals approximately one teaspoonful.

Emetic: Causes vomiting.

Emollient: Emollients are used externally only. They are employed for their softening and soothing effect.

Escharotic: Caustic.

Expectorant: Induces expulsion or loosens phlegm of the mucous membranes of the nasal and bronchial passages.

Febrifuge: Reduces fever.

Fungicide: Any substance that destroys fungi.

Hemostatic: Drugs employed to control bleeding.

Homeopathic: According to the principles of homeopathy.

Homeopathy: Briefly stated, the theory and its practice that disease is cured by remedies which produce in a healthy person effects similar to the symptoms of disease in a sick person —*Similia Similibus Curentur*, "like cures like." For example, peeling or eating a raw onion produces a watery discharge from the eyes and nose, therefore the onion is the homeopathic remedy for the type of cold characterized by these symptoms. Homeopathic substances are drawn only from natural sources. Remedies generally come in very tiny tablets or pellets. Potencies are microscopic. Homeopathic physicians consider the patient as a whole—his emotional and mental states as well as his physical condition.

This system was founded by the famous Dr. Samuel Hahnemann. It has been in use for over 200 years.

Laxative: Causes the bowels to act.

Lithotriptic: Used for dissolving stone in the kidneys or bladder.

Mucilaginous: Emits a soothing quality to inflamed parts.

Nervine: An agent which acts on the nervous system to temporarily relax nervous tension or excitement.

Nutrient or Nutritive: Nourishing.

Pectoral: Relieves affections of the chest and lungs.

Purgative: Causes copious evacuations from the bowels. Purgatives are more drastic than laxatives or aperients, and are generally combined with other agents to control or modify their actions. Used only by adults.

Refrigerant: Relieves thirst and produces a sensation of coolness.

Resolvent: A substance which is applied to reduce swelling.

Sedative: Calms the nerves.

Spasmolytic: Lessens spasms.

Specific: An agent or remedy that has a specific effect on a particular disease.

Stimulant: Increases or quickens various functional actions of the system.

Stomachic: Substances which give strength and tone to the stomach. Also used to stimulate the appetite.

Sudorific: Produces copious perspiration.

Tonic: Invigorating and strengthening to the system.

Vermifuge: Expels or destroys worms.

Vulnerary: Employed for healing wounds.

Explanation of Terms Relating to Various Methods of Herbal Preparations

Decoctions: Decoctions are certain preparations made by boiling herbal substances in water for a considerable period of time. Hard materials such as roots, barks, and seeds, are usually prepared in this way as they require longer subjection to heat in order to extract their active principles. Generally one ounce of the botanical substance is placed in one pint of cold water. The container is then covered and the solution allowed to boil for one-half hour, after which it is then strained, cooled and ready for use. However, since some of the water boils away, many herbalists prefer to use one and one-half pints of water so that when the boiling period has ended the decoction measures approximately one pint.

Directions cited for various herbal remedies sometimes call for shorter or longer boiling periods, or differences in the amount of the herb which is to be used in making the preparation. In these instances the specific directions given are followed rather than the general rules, and this also applies to the preparation of infusions and tinctures.

Extracts: Extracts are made in a variety of ways, depending on the best method by which the plant's properties may be obtained, such as high pressure, evaporation by heat, and the like. Extracts are generally supplied by the various herb companies.

Fomentations: Local applications of cloths wrung out in hot water, with or without the addition of medicinal agents.

Infusions: Infusions are frequently called teas, and are generally prepared in the amount of one ounce of the plant substance to one pint of water. However, in some instances where the plant contains very active principles, less is sufficient. Usually the softer substances of the herb such as the blossoms and leaves are prepared as infusions. A pint of boiling water is poured over the herb, the container covered, and the solution allowed to steep (stand) for 15 minutes (occasionally stirring). When the steeping period has ended, the infusion is strained and used. Infusions are also frequently prepared by placing a teaspoonful of the plant substance in a cup and pouring boiling water over it. It is then covered with a saucer and allowed to steep for 15 minutes, after which it is strained and used. Sometimes a little honey is added to make the infusion more palatable. Infusions are never allowed to boil.

Poultices: Poultices are used to apply moist heat to draw or soothe. The fresh leaves are generally used, if available, and are crushed and steeped in boiling water for a short period of time. The leaves are then spread between two pieces of cloth and applied as hot as can be comfortably borne to the affected part, then covered with a dry cloth to retain the heat. A second poultice is prepared and used the moment the first one begins to noticeably lose the heat. The powdered herb is often used as a substitute for the fresh leaves. Enough of the powdered herb for several poultices is placed in a double boiler. Hot water is stirred into the powder until it attains the consistency of a paste. The paste is then spread between two pieces of cloth, applied and renewed several times.

Tinctures: Tinctures are spirituous preparations made with pure or diluted alcohol (not rubbing alcohol) or brandy, vodka, or gin. Tinctures are employed because some herbs will not yield their properties to water alone, or may be rendered useless by applications of heat. In other instances, a herb will more readily impart its active principles when prepared as a tincture. Generally, four ounces of water and 12 ounces of spirits are mixed with one ounce of the powdered herb. The mixture is allowed to steep (stand) for two weeks, the bottle shaken thoroughly every night. After the steeping period has elapsed the clear liquid is strained off and the sediment discarded. The tincture is then bottled for use.

HERB DEALERS AND HOMEOPATHIC PHARMACIES

If your doctor has no objections, and you wish to try the various herbal or homeopathic remedies described in this book, you will want to know where you can obtain the herbs or homeopathic formulas. The list of distributors submitted here is given solely for the convenience of the reader. These companies are not connected in any way with the author or publishers of this book. You may send for their catalogs or price lists since they deal in mail orders as well as over-the-counter sales. Catalogs or price lists are free on request, except where otherwise stated.

Where You May Purchase Your Herbs

Calumet Herb Company
P.O. Box 248
South Holland, Illinois 60473

Franklin Chemists
764 Franklin Avenue Pharmacy, Inc.
764 Franklin Avenue
Brooklyn, New York

Harvest Health, Inc.
1944 Eastern Ave., S.E.
Grand Rapids, Michigan 49507

Haussmann's Pharmacy, Inc.
534—536 Girard Ave.
Philadelphia, Pennsylvania 19123

Herb Products Company
11012 Magnolia Boulevard
North Hollywood, California 91601

Indiana Botanic Gardens
P.O. Box 5
Hammond, Indiana 46325
(Herbalist Almanac, 25¢)

Kiehl Pharmacy, Inc.
109 Third Avenue
New York, New York 10003

Nature's Herb Company
281 Ellis Street
San Francisco, Calif. 94102
(Catalog 10¢)

Penn Herb Company
603 North 2nd Street
Philadelphia, Pennsylvania 19123

Canada

Dominion Herb Distributors, Inc.
61 St. Catherine St. W.
Montreal 18, Quebec, Canada

Nu-Life Nutrition Ltd.
871 Beatty Street
Vancouver 3, B.C.

Homeopathic Pharmacies

Hahn & Hahn
Homeopathic Pharmacy
324 W. Saratoga Street
Baltimore, Md. 21201

Luyties Pharmacal Company
4200 Laclede Avenue
Saint Louis, Mo. 63108

D. L. Thompson Company
844 Yonge Street
Toronto, Ont., Canada

Walker Pharmacal Company
4200 Laclede Avenue
Saint Louis, Mo. 63108

Wise's K.C. Homeopathic Pharmacy
4200 Laclede Avenue
St. Louis, Mo. 63108

The Dr. Bach Flower Remedies

Obtainable from:

The Dr. Edward Bach Healing Centre
Mount Vernon
Sotwell, Wallingford, Berkshire, England.

INDEX

A Practitioner's Case Book, 190, 194n

Abrasions, remedy for in olive oil, 24

Acne, sassafras as remedy for, 104

Acronycine as possible anti-cancer principle, 111

Agrimony as one of Dr. Bach's flower remedies, 149

Ague, treatment of with nettle tea, 32

Albert Einstein College of Medicine, 116

Algae from the sea, 52

Alkaline reaction of celery, 173-174

Allen, William Gordon, 89n

Alvarez, Dr. Walter, 107

American Journal of Clinical Nutrition, 21

American mandrake as possible anti-cancer agent, 116

American Medical Association, 109

American Medicinal Plants, 165

American valerian, lady's slipper known as, 205

Anderson, Dr. Dorothy H., 93

Anemia, nettles for treatment of, 31-32

Anemia, nutritional, figs as useful remedy for, 180

Anemia, possible cause of by over eating onions, 49-50

Angelica as herbal smoking mixture, 157-158

Anise, Indian use of, 66
modern usage of, 69

Anti-cancer agents, search for in algae, 62

Anti-cancer factor of figs, 180

Anti-hemorrhagic properties of mistletoe, 85

Antibacterial power of pipsissewa, 70

Antibodies, formation of by principle of immunity, 115

Antispasmodic, eucalyptus as, 161

Aphrodisiac, damiana as, 176-177

Apocannoside as anti-cancer principle, 110

Apple cider vinegar for relief of athlete's foot, 138

Arabian Nights, 133

Arabian physicians first aware of dandelion's medicinal properties, 11

Arches, fallen, wormwood liniment as remedy for, 210

Armour and Company, 114

Aromatic bitters, 184

Arterial cleansing agent, kelp as, 57

Arteries, benefits for from olive oil, 20-21

Arteries, hardening of, less prevalent among Mediterranean peoples, 21
mistletoe as remedy for, 87

Arteries, weak, strengthened by use of dandelion, 16

Arteriosclerosis, zinc deficiency seemingly one cause of, 61

Arthritis, celery as remedy for, 172-173
sassafras as remedy for, 104-105

Arvanis, Dr. Christo, 20-21

Asakusa Nori, 53

Asthma, elder bark as treatment for, 6
elecampane as remedy for, 78
eucalyptus for relief of, 161

221

nettle leaves folk remedy for, 28

Astringent bitters, 184

Astringent root, Indian use of, 66-67

Athens University, 20

Athlete's foot, herbal foot bath for, 138

Attar of roses, discovery of, 134

Australian scrub ash as possible anti-cancer agent, 111

Ayurvedic system of medicine in India and Pakistan, 32-33, 48

Bach, Dr. Edward, 147-156

Bach Foundation carrying on founder's work, 155-156

Bacon, M., 193

Baldness, possible remedy for in olive oil, 23

Bamboo grass as possible anti-cancer agent, 111

Bamfolin, 111

Bancroft's Compendium of 1883, 40

Bard, Dr., 40

Barometer of nature, dandelion as, 11

Bartram, T. H., 7n, 15-16, 31-32, 38, 86-87

"Bath of life," rosemary known as, 122

Bathing, correct, important for good health, 130-131
   temperature important, 132

Bathing benefits from herbs, 128-142
      (see also under specific benefit)

Bearberry as herbal smoking mixture, 158

Beauty benefits, using herbs for, 128-142
      (see also under specific benefit)

Beauty cream from elder flow-ers, 3

Bedwetting, shepherd's purse remedy for, 203-204

Bee stings, plantain as widely used folk remedy for, 201

Beech as herbal smoking mixture, 159

Beer brewing, buckbean substitute for hops in, 159

Beets as possible anti-cancer agent, 111-113

Beets in jelly of carrageen, recipe for, 60

Benson, Professor L. W., 174

Benzoin as herbal beauty aid, 141

Betony, 206-207

Beverage from carrageen, recipe for, 60

Bile secretion stimulated by olive oil, 22-23

Birth control plant, Indian, scientific research on, 79-80

Bishop, C. J., 70, 70n

Bitters, 184-186

Bittersweet as possible anti-cancer agent, 110

Bladder problems, use of corn silk as remedy for, 174
   elder as remedy for, 8-9
   parsley as remedy in, 91-93, 94

Bladderwrack, 54-56
   goitre, prevention of, 54
   iodine, source of, 53-54
   nutritionalist's views, 54-55
   obesity control, iodine for, 55-56
   using, ways of, 56-57

Blancmange, recipe for, 59

Bleeding, arresting of by use of nettles, 29

Bleeding gums, sage as remedy for, 38

Blemishes on skin, herbal aids for, 142-143

Blood clotting, shepherd's purse important in, 203

Blood disorders, nettles for treatment of, 31-32

Blood root and sage in gargle, 39

Blue, Dr. J. A., 80

Blue flag as Indian remedy, 73
  modern usage, 77

Blyth, Winifred, 15n

Boils, external application of figs as cure for, 178-179
  sassafras as remedy for, 104

Bone and joint pains, rosemary as remedy for, 123-124

Boorhave, 5

Borax crystals often added to herbs in bath, 132

Bordas, Dr. L. F., 180

Boston Evening Post, 158

Botanical Catalog, 59n, 143

Bowels, inflammation of, use of marshmallow as remedy for, 194-195

Bragg, Paul C., 40, 41

Brain, action of parsley on, 95

Brain cortex, action of sage upon, 37

Brain tonic, damiana as, 176-177

Breasts, neuralgia of, remedy for in olive oil, 25

Breneman, Dr. William, 80

Brewer's yeast as possible anti-cancer agent, 113-114

Brieskorn, 37

Bright's disease, use of celery as remedy for, 172
  hops as remedy for, 189

British Medica Flora, The, 188

Brockbank, Dr. E. M., 23

Bronchitis, Gypsy use of colts-foot and yarrow as cures for, 1
  marshmallow in treatment of, 193
  onion as remedy for, 45

Brown, Dr. O. Phelps, 208

Buckbean as herbal smoking mixture, 159

Buckland, Frank, 45

Bunions, herbal foot baths for, 138

Burdock, 168-169

Burnett, Dr., 29

Burr, Aaron, 179

Butler, Dr. S. W., 191

Butternut, Indian use of as remedy, 74-75
  modern usage, 77

Cajal Institute in Madrid, 21

Cajuput, oil of, used to relieve muscular aches, 135

Calaguala as possible anti-cancer agent, 114

Calamus for herbal bath, 136

Calluses, herbal foot baths for, 138

Calotropin as anti-cancer principle, 110

Calvacin as anti-tumor agent, 114

Camerarius, Joachim, 170

Camomile, 169-172

Campbell the poet, 27

Camphorated oil used for muscular aches and pains, 135

Camptothecin as anti-leukemia principle, 114

Canadian Journal of Botany, 70n

Cancer, "green hope" in fight against, 107-119
  (see also "Green hope" against cancer)

Cancer, mistletoe as treatment for, 89-90

Cancer, skin, Gypsy use of violet plant as cure for, 2

Caraway seeds as effective diuretic, 69

Cardiac cases, modern European use of elder bark as

diuretic for, 6
Carmack, Dr. Marvin, 80
Carrageen, 57-61
   in diet, 58-59
   recipes, 59-61
   ulcers, peptic, 58
   uses, 58
Castellanos, Professor Adolfo, 21
Cataracts, eye, successful herbal remedy of Indians for, 80-81
Catarrh, sage as remedy for, 38
Celery, 172-174
Cellini, Benvenuto, 211
Cerebrospinal irritation, sage as relaxing agent in, 37
Chambers, Kenton L., 82
Chamomile, 171
Change of life, lady's slipper used for, 192
Chapped hands, herbal aids for, 138
Chase, Dr. A. W., 78, 163
Chemotherapy greatest hope for some cancer patients, 109
Chia seeds, health value of, 39-40
Chicory as one of Dr. Bach's flower remedies, 149
Chilblains, herbal aids for, 138-139
Chimaphilin found in pipsissewa, 70
Chinese Book of Poetry, 52
Chionanthin in fringe tree, 181
Cholesterol conditions, protection of olive oil against, 21
Cholin in dandelions essential to liver function, 12
Christian traditions associated with rosemary, 121
Cincinnati Eclectic Medical Institute, 116
Circulation, healthy, promoted

by use of dandelions, 16
Circulation stimulated by warm bath, 136
Circulatory disorders, mistletoe as remedy for, 84
Classification of mental states by Dr. Bach, 148-149
Cleanser, natural, plantain as, 199
Clematis vitalba one of Dr. Bach's flower remedies, 149
Clinical Review Espagnol, 21-22
Clymer, Dr. Swinburne, 13, 125, 176, 182, 186
Colbatch, Sir John, 84
Colds, popular use of elderberry wine for, 7
Coles, 11
Colic, chamomile tea as remedy for, 172
Colitis, use of marshmallow in treatment of, 194-195
Collip, 47
Colt's tail used in Indian remedy for diarrhea, 80
Coltsfoot as herbal smoking mixture, 159-160
   bronchitis, Gypsy use for, 1
Columbia University, 92
Comstock, Dr. A., 37
Concentration, abilities of, strengthened by use of sage, 37
Confectionery, angelica as flavoring for, 158
Constipation, chronic, use of dandelion as remedy for, 16
   figs, 180-181
   nettles, 31
   olive oil as remedy for, 22
Conti's hair shampoo, 23
Convulsions, mistletoe as ancient remedy for, 84
Corn silk, 174-176

as herbal smoking mixture, 160

in combination with dandelion for remedy of urinary disturbances, 13-14

Corns, herbal foot baths, for, 138

Cortanso, 40

Cosmetic cream from carrageen, 61

"Cramp-bark," 186-187

Croup, onion as French remedy for, 46

Cubeb berries as herbal smoking mixture, 160-161

Cucumber skins as skin beauty aid, 142-143

Culpepper, 5, 84, 121-122, 142, 164, 179, 196, 202, 207

Cyclopedia of Botanical Drugs and Preparations, 96, 96n, 103, 177

Cymarin as anti-cancer principle, 110

Cystitis, corn silk as remedy for, 175

parsley piert as remedy for, 96-97

Czetsch-Lindenwald, 36

Damiana, 176-177

Dandelion as healing wonder, 10-17

"Dandelion coffee," 12, 16

Darwent, H., 88, 190, 194-195

Davis, Adelle, 54

Davis, Dr. John, 174-175

De la Vente, 63

de Rovira, Dr. German J., 85

Deafness, olive oil as remedy for, 24-25

Deer's tongue as herbal smoking mixture, 161

Densmore, Frances, 80-81, 81n, 135, 200

Deutsch, Patricia and Ron, 156n

Diabetes, parsley recommended

for, 93-94

symptoms of sometimes due to sudden shock, 144

Diabetics, use of dandelion for, 17

Diarrhea, effective Indian herbal remedy for, 80

uses of the elder against, 6

Digestive system, wormwood as remedy for problems of, 210

Digitalis for heart conditions derived from foxglove plant of Gypsies, 1

Dioscorides, 69, 193, 199, 206, 209

Discouraging smoking habit, herbs for, 167

Dispensatory of the United States of America, 25, 28, 36n, 58, 161, 168, 175, 188, 203

Dittany - American as herbal smoking mixture, 161

Diuretic, potent, corn silk as, 175

Diuretic properties of dandelion, 12

Dog wood, use of by Indians, 67

Dogbane, possible anti-cancer agent in, 110

Domestic Dictionary & Housekeeper's Manual, The, 60-61

Domestic Practice, 130

Dring, J. L., 8n

Druids, mistletoe as herb of, 83

Dry skin, remedy for in olive oil, 24

elder as remedy for, 8

Du Pratz, 64

Duodenal ulcers, use of marshmallow as remedy for, 195-196

Dysentery, treatment of with nettles, 29

Dyspepsia, dandelion formula

excellent remedy for, 15, 16

Ear trouble, plantain as remedy for, 201
  rosemary as remedy for, 124
Eczema, burdock in treatment of, 168-169
  sassafras as remedy for, 104
Elder as favorite remedy of all time, 2-9
  Father Kneipp, remedies of, 6
  folk remedy, 2-3
  modern uses, 6-9
Elderberry ointment, Gypsy recipe for, 3
Elderberry wine, popular use of for colds, 7
Eldrin constituent of elderberry, 6
Elecampane, Indian use of as remedy, 74
  modern usage, 78
Elephantus elatus as possible anti-cancer agent, 110
Emetine possible anti-cancer principle, 115-116
Emotions, effect of herbs on, 144-156
Encyclopedia of Health and Home, 22n, 24n, 28n, 46n, 169, 177n
Enigma Fantastique, 89n
Enteritis, successful treatment of with nettles, 29
Enzien, 184-186
Epilepsy, mistletoe as ancient remedy for, 84
  modern European use of elder bark as treatment for, 6
Epstein, Dr., 8
Eucalyptus as herbal smoking mixture, 161
  relief of muscular soreness, 135
Evans, Dr. Jon, 88, 183, 207
Evelyn, John, 5

Excretion of wastes function of skin, 129-130
Eye cataracts, successful treatment of with Indian herbal remedy, 80-81
Eye first-aid, olive oil as, 24
Eyelashes, benefits of olive oil for, 25
Eyes, sore, elder as cure for, 2
  wormwood as remedy for, 211
Family physician, belief of in medicinal properties of onion, 45-46
Fatty acids, absorption of increased by olive oil, 23
Felter, Dr., 182
Feminine difficulties, motherwort as remedy for, 198-199
Fennel seeds as effective diuretic, 69
Ferenczi, Dr., 111-112
Fernie, Dr., 26, 28, 42-43, 45-46, 78, 202
Fever, thirst in, elder as cure for, 2
Ficin enzyme in figs, 180
Fig, 177-181
  anti-cancer factor, 180
  boils, 178-179
  constipation remedy, 180-181
  food and medicine, 178
  properties of, 180
Fingernails, benefits of olive oil for, 25
Fireweed used in Indian remedy for diarrhea, 80
Fitness and Health from Herbs, 26n, 47n, 197n
Fleabane, Canada, used in Indian remedy for diarrhea, 80
Flower remedies of Dr. Bach, 148-150
  case histories, 150-154
  dissemination, 155-156
  medical opinion, 156

mentally-induced illnesses, remedies for, 149-150

Rescue remedy, 154

sun method of extraction, 149-150

Flu, modern use of elder flowers in treatment of, 6-7

Folk remedies using onions, 44-46

Food and Life Yearbook of Agriculture, 54

Food medicine, onion as, 44-46

Food value of olive oil, 19

Fox, Dr. J. Dewitt, 20, 22, 32

Fox, Dr. William, 36-37, 105, 206

Foxglove plant for heart conditions used by Gypsies, 1

Fragrance in baths, 133-134

Freckles, herbal aids for, 142-143

French, Dr. David, 79

Fringe tree, 181-183

Fujiwara, Motonori, 114-115

Fuller, H. C., 98-99

Galen, 110, 130

Gall bladder tonic, use of olive oil as, 22-23

Gallstones, camomile tea as cure for, 171

fringe tree, 183

Greater Celandine, 183

Gall stones often prevented by dandelion coffee, 16

Gargle, use of sage as, 38-39

Garlic as possible anti-cancer agent, 114-115

Gastric balance restored by use of dandelions, 16

Gaultier, Rene, 84-85, 86

Gentian, 184-186

bitters, 184-185

Gypsy use of as tonic, 1

Gentian root, chewing of, aid to giving up smoking habit, 167

Gentian wild, Indian use of, 67

Gerard, 28, 35, 96, 206

Ginseng as herbal smoking mixture, 162

Glucokinin discovered in onion, 47

Gnat bites, herbal aid for, 140

Goitre and "goitre belts," 54

Golden seal, combination of with gentian bitters to relieve digestive distress, 186

in combination with dandelion for remedy of urinary disturbances, 13-14

Goss, Professor I. J. M., 181-182

Gout, treatment of with nettles, 29

Granata, Dr. E., 23

Gravel, seven-barks as remedy for, 191

nettle tea, treatment with, 32

shepherd's purse remedy for, 204

Greater Celandine used to remove warts, 139

for treatment of gallstones, 183

"Green Drink" popular method of using kelp, 56

"Green hope" against cancer, 107-119

causes, 108

herbs, search for curative possibilities in, 108-119

(see also "Herbs, search for cancer cure in")

metastasizing, 107-108

research accelerated, 108-109

Russian research, 118-119

Green Men, 13

Greene, Thomas, 209

Grief important factor in physical ailments of elderly, 145

Grollman, Dr. Arthur P., 116

Gromwell as Indian birth con-

trol plant, 79-80
Guibourt, 169
Gum benzoin as beauty aid, 141
Gums, benefits to from olive
    oil, 23
Gums, bleeding, sage as rem-
    edy for, 38
Gurwitch, Professor, 49
Gypsy beauty cream, 3
Gypsy knowledge of herbal
    remedies, 1-2

Hair and gums, benefits to from
    olive oil, 23
Hair health, rosemary used for,
    126
Hair tonic, sage as, 39
Hamdard Digest, 20
Hands, chapped, herbal aids
    for, 138-139
Hartwell, Dr. Jonathan L., 118
Hay fever, alleviation of with
    wood betony, 208
Hay-flower foot bath, 137
Headaches, use of hops as rem-
    edy for, 189
  mistletoe as remedy, 87
  rosemary as remedy, 121-126
  wood betony as remedy, 207-
    208
Health Bulletin, 62*n,* 119*n,* 145
Health properties of dandelion,
    11-12
Health Research, 5*n*
Health value of olive oil, 19-26
Heart and arteries, benefits for
    from olive oil, 20-21
Heart and stomach remedy,
    rosemary as, 122-123
Heart muscles, strengthening by
    using rosemary, 125
Heart tonic, motherwort as, 197
"Heaven grass," Japanese ref-
    erence to seaweed as,
    52-53
Helenin in elecampane as pow-
    erful bactericide, 78

Hemingway, Jane C., 116
Hemophilia, arresting one case
    of by using nettles, 29
Hemoptysis, mistletoe as rem-
    edy for, 85
Hemorrhages, congestive, use of
    mistletoe in, 86
Hemorrhages, uterine, arresting
    of by use of nettles, 29
Hemorrhaging, shepherd's purse
    valuable in arresting, 203
"Herb of life," motherwort
    known as, 196
Herbal Simples, 45-46
Herbalist, The, 61*n,* 167*n*
Herbalist Almanac, The, 167*n,*
    172
Herbs, search for cancer cure
    possibilities among, 109-
    118
  American mandrake, 116-117
  Australian scrub ash, 111
  bamboo grass, 111
  beets, 111-113
  bittersweet, 110
  brewer's yeast, 113-114
  calaguala, 114
  calvatia giganteum, 114
  Camptotheca acuminata, 114
  dogbane, 110
  elephantus elatus, 110
  garlic, 114-115
  Indian hemp, 110
  ipecac, 115-116
  juniper, 116
  Meadow rue, 110
  milkweed, 110
  periwinkle, 117
  tylophora, genus of, 117
  violet, 118
  woody nightshade, 110
*Herbs and the Fountain of
    Youth,* 171*n*
Herbs for Daily Use, 2, 2*n*
Hernia, condition of contributed
    to by vitamin A defi-
    ciency, 93

Herpes zoster, sassafras as remedy for, 104
Herring, Dr. F., 207
High blood pressure, nettles for treatment of, 31-32
High cranberry, 186-187
Hill's Family Herbal, 71
Hippocrates, 4, 9, 34, 84, 98, 130, 172
Historical Dictionary, 165
Hives, dandelion herbal formula as remedy for, 14
nettles in treatment of, 28, 32
Homeopathic World, 149, 155
Hops, 187-190
pillows for soothed sleep, 188
Horseweed used in Indian remedy for diarrhea, 80
Horsley, Dr. Atlee D., 191
Huckleberry as possible treatment for diabetes, study of, 79
Hunter, John D., 65-69, 101, 158, 165
Hyde, Arthur C., 97-98
Hydrangea, 190-191
Hydrastis, 14
Hypersensitivity, sage as relaxing agent for, 37
Hypothalamus connection to pituitary important in study of psychophysiological illness, 146
Hyssop as beauty aid, 140

Ibanez, Professor Julian Sanz, 21
Immunity, principle of in fighting cancer, 115
Impatiens royaleii as one of Dr. Bach's flower remedies, 149
Impatiens to treat poison oak and ivy, 139
Impetigo, use of sassafras as remedy for, 104
Impotence, damiana as remedy for, 176-177
Incontinence of urine, shepherd's purse remedy for, 204
India, nettles therapy in, 32-33
onion therapies in, 48
Indian hemp as possible anticancer agent, 110
Indian Household Medicine Guide, The, 72-76, 101
Indiana University, 79
Indians, American, herbal health secrets of, 63-82
Indigestion, wormwood as remedy for, 210-211
Influenza, modern use of elder flowers in treatment of, 6-7
Insect bites, herbal aids for, 140
Insensible perspiration, 129
Institut d'Hygiene, 21
International remedy in plantain, 201
Intestinal worms successfully treated with seaweed, 62
Inulin, elecampane rich source of, 78
found in burdock, 169
nutritive element in dandelions, 16
Iodine source in kelp, 53-54
Ipecac as possible anti-cancer agent, 115-116
Irish moss, 57-61
in diet, 58-59
recipes, 59-61
ulcers, peptic, 58
uses, 58
Irish moss jelly, 59
Iron, organic, more easily absorbed by system, 212
Irradiation, protection against by use of olive oil, 21-22
Iscadore in treatment of cancer, 90
Itchiness of skin relieved by warm bath, 136

James, Claudia V., 171
James, Dr., 122
Jaundice, treatment of with net-
    tle tea, 32
Jefferson, Thomas, 205
Jewel weed, use of to treat
    poison oak and ivy, 139
Johnson, Dr., 130
Joint pains, rosemary as rem-
    edy for, 123-124
Jokel, Dr., 8
Jordan, Dr., 10
Journal of Allergy, 80
*Journal of Pharmaceutical Sci-
    ences,* 116
Juniper as possible anti-cancer
    agent, 116

Kelp, 53-57
    goitre, prevention of, 54
    iodine, source of, 53-54
    nutritionalist's views, 54-55
    obesity control, iodine for,
        55-56
    using, ways of, 56-57
Keys, Dr. Ancel, 20-21
Khus-khus roots for fragrant
    bath, 133-134
Kidney ailments, dandelion as
    remedy for, 16
    motherwort as remedy for,
        198
    parsley as remedy for, 93, 95
King, Dr. John, 116
Kirschner, Dr. H. E., 55-56,
    93n, 173
Kneipp, Father Sebastian, 5-6,
    28, 35, 122-123, 137,
    185-186, 201-202, 210-
    211
Knowledge of Plants, 11
Knox, John R., 116
Köcher, 37
Kryukova, Lidiya, 118
Külz, 47
Kupchan, Dr. S. Morris, 110,
    116

Kuts-Chereaux, Dr., 78
Kuzin, Alexander, 118
Kyoto University, 115

La Vie Claire, 21
Lady's slipper, 191-192
Lakhovsky, Professor, 49
"Lamb's tongue," Arabian name
    for plantain, 201
Lancet, 145-146
Laryngitis, sage as remedy for,
    38
Lavender for fragrant baths,
    134
Lavoisier, 129
Laxative, butternut as, 75
    dandelions, 16
    figs, 178
    olive oil, 22
Le Clerc, Dr., 11, 29, 172, 189
Lee Foundation, 65n
Legendary powers of elder tree,
    4
Leigh, Dr. Denis, 145
"Lemon-Celery Delight," recipe
    for, 174
Leroi, Dr. A., 89
Let's Get Well, 54, 54n
Leukemia, possible hope for ar-
    resting in *Camptotheca
    acuminata,* 114
LeVaillent, 35-36
Lexicon, 19
Licorice as herbal smoking mix-
    ture, 162
Life everlasting as herbal smok-
    ing combination, 162
Lighthall, John, 72-78, 101, 187
Lilly Research Laboratories, In-
    dianapolis, 111
Liqueurs, angelica as flavoring
    for, 158
Liver, cancer of, brewer's yeast
    as preventive of, 113-114
Liver ailments, dandelions as
    remedy for, 10, 11
    fringe tree for treatment of,

181-182
rosemary as remedy for, 125
Liver infections, wood betony as remedy for, 207
Liver difficulties, wormwood as remedy for, 210-211
Lorincz, Dr. Albert B., 108-109
Lovage for fragrant baths, 134
Low blood pressure, figs as remedy for, 180
Lumbago, celery as remedy for, 172
Lung bleeding, arresting by use of nettles, 29
Lupulin in hops, 188-189
Lyle, Dr. T. J., 55

M-rays, mysterious, found in onions, 49
MacDonald, R. E., 70, 70n
Maitrinke, sweet woodruff used in flavoring of, 166
Maizenic acid in corn silk, 175
Mandrake, American, as possible anti-cancer agent, 116-117
Mankur, Dr. John C. S., 191
Marigold flowers for wounds, Gypsy use of, 1
Marjoram as herbal smoking substitute, 162-163
Marshmallow 193-196
Master-of-the-Woods as herbal smoking mixture, 166-167
Masterwort as herbal smoking mixture, 157-158
May Wine liqueurs, sweet woodruff used in flavoring of, 166-167
Mead, Dr., 178-179
Meadow rue as possible anti-cancer agent, 110
Medical Flora: or Manual of Medical Botany of the United States of North America, 101
Medical Herbalist, The, 3, 3n,
14, 14n, 177n, 197-198
Memoirs of a Captivity Among the Indians of North America, 65
Memory improved by use of rosemary, 123
Menière's disease, 124
Menopause, lady's slipper as remedy for, 192
  mistletoe to reduce discomforts in, 85-86
Menstrual cramps, high cranberry as remedy for, 187
Menstruation, excessive, treated with nettle tea, 32
Menstruation, painful, parsley recommended for, 93
Mental exhaustion, remedy for in sage, 37
Mental states, classification of by Dr. Bach, 148-149
Mentally-induced illnesses, remedies of Dr. Bach for, 149-150
Metastasizing of cancer cells, 107-108
Meyer, Clarence, 167n
Meyer, Joseph E., 167n
Meyers, Dr. W. H., 176
Michelet, 131
Michigan State University, 114
Migraine, use of mistletoe as remedy for, 86-87
  nettles, 31
  rosemary as remedy for, 124-125
Milkweed as possible anti-cancer agent, 110
Miller, Joseph, 209
Millet as Indian birth control plant, 79-80
Millspaugh, Dr. Charles F., 165
Mimulus luteus one of Dr. Bach's flower remedies, 149
Mind-cancer link, 145-147
Minerva Dietologica, 23

Mints well-known remedy for flatulence, 126
Mistletoe, mystic herb, 83-90
  ancient remedy, 84-85
  cancer, treatment for, 89-90
  constituents, 85
  modern uses, 85-88
  nervous illness, Gypsy use for, 1
  tranquilizer, natural, 88-89
  varieties, two, 84
"Mitogenetic" radiation from onions, 49
Monardes, Nicholaus, 100
Morley, Louise, 208
"Mortification root," 193
Motherwort, 196-199
  heart tonic, 197
  "herb of life," 196
  kidney inflammations, 198
  uterine difficulties, use for, 197-198
  womb, effect on, 197
Mountain birch, use of by Indians, 67
Mousse from carrageen, recipe for, 60
Mucous membranes, marshmallow as remedy for, 193
Mullein as herbal smoking mixture, 163-164
Mure, Dr. James E., 74
Musa, Antonius, 206-207
Muscular aches and pains, herbal baths to relieve, 135
My Water Cure, 5-6, 137n

Natata, Toshikazu, 114
Natchez Indian herbalists, renown of, 63-64
National Cancer Institute, 2, 62, 79, 107, 117
National Institutes of Health, 107, 117
Nature Doctor, The, 30n, 47, 87, 125, 171n, 201n
Nature's Healing Agents, 13, 125, 173, 182, 186
Nature's Healing Grasses, 55, 93, 173
Naturopath, The, 41, 81-82, 119
Neff, Dr., 72
Neiderkorn, Dr., 175
Nephritis, damiana as remedy for, 177
  mistletoe as remedy in, 86
Nervine, excellent, in lady's slipper, 192
Nervousness, celery as remedy for, 172
  damiana as remedy for, 176
  lady's slipper as remedy for, 192
  mistletoe as remedy for, 1, 84
  olive oil, remedy for, 26
  rosemary as remedy for, 123
  valerian used as remedy for, 206
Nervousness, relieving by herbal bath, 135-136
Nettle as versatile healer, 27-33
Nettle rash, dandelion herbal formula as remedy for, 14
Nettles for skin ailments, Gypsies' use of, 2
Neuralgia, elder treatment for, 8
  plantain as remedy for, 201
  twin leaf as remedy for, 205
Neuralgia of breasts, remedy for in olive oil, 25
Neurasthenia, sage as remedy for, 37
Neuritis, elder as remedy for, 8
  mistletoe as remedy for, 87-88
New Jersey Medical Reporter, The, 191
New Medical Guide, The, 141
New Preparations, 207
New York Academy of Sciences, 145
Night sweats, sage as remedy for, 37
Nightmares, chamomile tea ex-

cellent remedy for, 172

Ninon de Lenclos, 142

Norske Magfa Laege Videns-kaben, 8n

Nosebleeding, arresting by use of nettles, 29

Nutrition in dandelions, 12

Oat straw foot bath, 137

Oatmeal bath still popular for relief of itchy skin, 137

Oil of St. John's Wort as remedy for sores and abrasions, 24

Olive oil as healer, 18-26

Onion as source of natural medicinals, 42-50

Onychorrhexis, remedy for in olive oil, 25

Orchitis, damiana as remedy for, 176

Oregon State University, 79, 82

Orr, William G., 26

Oudar, Dr., 29

Ovarian cysts, dandelion herbal formula as remedy for, 15

Ovaritis, motherwort as remedy for, 199

Pakistan, nettles therapy in, 32-33

Palarea, Dr. Edgar R., 80

Palsy, sage as remedy for, 34

Pancreas, onion stimulating to, 47

Paris, Dr. J., 185

Park, Philip R., 57

Parkhurst, 19

Parkinson, 168, 207

Parsley, 91-99

Parsons, M. E., 40

Pattern of Health, The, 156

Peace, olive tree as emblem of, 19

Peacock, 70

Pearson, Dr. A. J., 43

Pensky, Jack, 115

Peppermint herb tea and elder flowers, benefits from combination of, 7

Peptic ulcers, carrageen as remedy for, 58

Perfumes, rosemary used in manufacture of, 123

Periwinkle and dandelion combination, uses of, 17

Periwinkle as possible anti-cancer agent, 117

Personal Beauty, 141

Pfizer Pharmaceutical Company, 117

Pflanzliche Arzneizubersitungen, 36

Pharyngitis, sage as remedy for, 38

Photographic plates, use of carrageen for, 58

Physical complaints, herbal baths to relieve, 134-136

Physio - Medical Therapeutics, Materia Medica and Pharmacy, 55n

Pillows of hops for good night's sleep, 188

Pilocarpine effects counteracted by sage, 37

Pine oil bath to relieve tension, 136

Pipe Tree another name for elder, 4

Pipsissewa, Indian use of, 67

modern usage, 70

Pituitary gland, connection of to hypothalamus important in study of psychophysiological illness, 130-131

Pityriasis, sassafras as remedy for, 92, 104, 146

"Plant physician," camomile tea as, 153, 170

Plantain, 177-179, 199-202

Pleurisy, treatment of by Indians, 59, 66

Pliny, 4-5, 34, 42, 69, 135, 163, 178, 199, 206, 209

Podophyllin an active resin in American mandrake, 116

Podophyllotoxin as anti-cancer principle, 117

Poison oak and ivy; herbal aids for 139-140

Poison oak remedy, Indian, 81-82

Polyphenols, 80

Poore, Dr. Gerald A., 111

Pope, Dr. R. D., 93

Poplar as valuable Indian remedy, 72-73

Poplar tree best host for mistletoe plant, 85

Pores of skin essential for waste excretion, 129

Pories, Dr. Walter J., 61-62

"Portland Powder" as remedy for gout, wormwood as constituent of, 209

Potassium essential to health of body, 178, 200

Potter's New Cyclopedia of Botanical Drugs and Preparations, 85, 85n, 96, 96n, 103-104, 177

Powell, Dr. Eric, 26, 47-48, 55, 77, 123,

Prevention magazine, 20, 26, 119n

Pring, Martin, 102

Properties of dandelion for giving health, 11-12

Properties of elder, healthful, 6

Prostate problems, parsley recommended for, 93-94

Psoriasis, burdock as remedy for, 168-169

Psychological aspects of physical illness, 144-145

Psychophysiological phases of cancer, 145-146

Public Health Service, 62, 79, 80, 108

Pythagoras, 52

Quinsy, sage as remedy for, 35-36, 37

Quelch, Mary Thorne, 2, 2n

Rafinesque, C. S., 101-102, 165, 187

Rao, Dr. Koppaka V., 117

Recipes from carrageen, 59-61

Red clover, Indian use of as remedy, 75

Red clover blossoms for relief of athlete's foot, 138

Red raspberry as herbal smoking mixture, 164

Reed College, Oregon, 79

Reeded nails, remedy for in olive oil, 25

Regimen of the School of Salerne, 178

Remedial uses of nettle, 27-29

Remedies, dandelion, 12-14
   medical doctor's opinion, 13
   urinary disturbance, use in, 13-14

Renal dropsies, modern European use of elder bark as diuretic for, 6

Rescue remedy of Dr. Bach, 154

Research in cancer field accelerated in past fifteen years, 108-109

Research Triangle Institute, 101, 114

Rheumatism, celery as remedy for, 173
   dandelion in treatment of, 17
   nettles, treatment with, 28
   parsley recommended for, 93-94
   rosemary as remedy in, 123
   sassafras as remedy for, 104-105

Ribwort, 201-202

Richards, Dr. Guyon, 56-57

Roberts, Capt. Frank, 195

Rock Water as one remedy of

Dr. Bach, 148

Rodale, J. I., 20, 23

Roman baths, 131

Rosemary, 120-127
as herbal smoking mixture, 164

Roses for fragrant baths, 134

Ruddock, Dr., 28-29, 46, 187, 201

Rush, Dr., 78

Russian cancer research, 118-119

Safe Treatment for Nervous Stress and Anxiety Tension, 88-89

Saffiotti, Dr., 109

Sage as herbal smoking mixture, 164-165
for good health, 34-41

Saliva, use of sage to inhibit flow of, 37-38

Sambunigrin contained in elder, 6

Sandalwood for fragrant baths, 134

Sandburn, Professor, 189

Sap pine, Indian use of, 68

Sarsaparilla, Indian use of as remedy, 75-76

Sassafras as herbal smoking mixture, 165
as medicinal agent, 100-106
modern use, 103-106
arthritis and rheumatism, 104-105
skin disease, 104
tips, 105
research findings, 103
use by Indians, 100-102
"wonder drug," early, 102-103

Schall, Dr., 172

Scheller, Professor Fritz, 111

Schmidt, Dr. Siegmund, 111-112

Schreier, Dr. Emil, 117

Sciatica, elder as remedy for, 8
mistletoe as remedy for, 87

Science and Practice of Herbal Medicine, 15, 15n, 38, 38n, 95, 95n, 186n

Science and study of Indian herbs, 79

Science News Letter, 79n

Scott, Cyril, 93-95

Sea, plants from, 51-62
algae, 52-55
carrageen, 57-61
kelp, 53-57
values of algae, other, 61-62

Seaweeds as rich source of minerals and vitamins, 52-54

Secretion-inhibitory action of sage, 37

Sedative action of hops, 189

Seguin, 116, 129

Seven barks remedy, 191

"Seven marvelous medicines" of Count Mattei of Bologna, 202-203

Sexual debility, damiana as remedy for, 177

Shepherd's Purse, 202-204

Sherman, Dr. Henry, 92

Shimkin, Dr. William B., 108, 109

Shock, sudden, results of upon system, 144-145

Sikorski, 189

Simple bitters, 185

Skelton, Dr. John, 15, 38, 95, 186

Skin, dry, remedy for in olive oil, 24

Skin, essential function of, 129-130

Skin cancer, Gypsy use of violet plant as cure for, 2

Skin diseases, burdock in treatment of, 168-169
dandelion herbal formula as remedy for, 15
elder as remedy for, 8
modern use of sassafras for, 104

Skovronskii, V. A., 69

Sleep problems with children, chamomile excellent remedy for, 172

Slippery elm, Indian use of, 68
  modern usage, 70-71

Sloan - Kettering Institute for Cancer Research, 113, 114

Smoking mixtures, herbal, 157-167
  angelica, 157-158
  bearberry, 158
  beech, 159
  buckbean, 159
  coltsfoot, 159-160
  corn silk, 160
  cubeb berries, 160-161
  deer's tongue, 161
  dittany-American, 161
  eucalyptus, 161
  ginseng, 162
  licorice, 162
  life everlasting, 162
  marjoram, 162-163
  mullein, 163-164
  red raspberry, 164
  rosemary, 164
  sage, 164-165
  sassafras, 165
  sumach, 165-166
  sweet clover, 166
  sweet gale, 166
  sweet woodruff, 166-167
  yerba santa, 167

Snowball tree, 186-187

Snuff of powdered dry nettles to check nose bleeding, 32-33

Soporific properties of hop pillows, 188

Sores, remedy for in olive oil, 24

Sparks, Dr., 10

Spermatorrhea, damiana as remedy for, 177

Spikenard, Indian use of, 69

elecampane, added to, 74, 78

Spleen, mistletoe as ancient remedy for disorders of, 84
  dandelion in treatment of, 17
  sage as remedy for, 35

Stanley, Dean, 18

Staven-Grönberg, 189

Stigmata maidis, 14

Stomach powder, dandelion herbal formula for, 14-15

Stomach remedy, rosemary as, 122-123
  wormwood as remedy for, 209-211

Stone seed as Indian birth control plant, 79-80

Strangury, 48

Suguira, Dr. Kanematsu, 113

Sumach as herbal smoking mixture, 165

Sun method of extracting specific herbal properties, 149-150

Sunburn lotion, olive oil as, 24

Supernatural background of elder, reported, 4

Superstition surrounding elder tree, 4

Suski, 53

Svoboda, Dr. G. H., 111

Sweet clover as herbal smoking mixture, 166

Sweet flag for herbal bath, 136

Sweet gale as herbal smoking mixture, 166

Sweet woodruff as herbal smoking mixture, 166-167

Synede, 12

Taraxacin an alkaloid isolated from dandelion root, 11, 16

Taylor, Dr. Alfred, 119

Temperature of bath important, 132-133

Temperature of body, regulation of by skin, 129

Tension, relieving by herbal bath, 135-136

Tension, wood betony as remedy for, 207

Therapeutic Gazette, 174

Therapeutic Uses of Viscum album, 85n

Therapie der Gengenwart, 112-113

Thrush, sage as remedy for, 38

Thyroid gland, malfunction of due to sudden shock, 144-145

Thyroid normalizer, blue flag as, 77

Thyroxin, proper amount of iodine essential for secretion of, 53-54

Tibbi system of medicine in India and Pakistan, 32

Tobacco, herbal smoking substitutes for, 157-167

  discouraging smoking habit, herbs for, 167

  mixtures, 157-167

    (see also "Smoking mixtures, herbal")

Tonic, Gypsy use of gentian as, 1

Tonsillitis, sage as remedy for, 38

Toxemia, remedy in kelp, 57

Tranquilizer, natural, in mistletoe, 86, 88-89

Traveler's Joy one of Dr. Bach's flower remedies, 149

Trub, Dr., 112-113

Tuberculosis, help of sage in treatment of, 35

Tuberculosis, nettles valuable aid in treating, 30

Tumors, Gypsy use of violet plant as cure for, 2

Turner, F. Newman, 197

Twin leaf, 204-205

Tylophora, vine from genus of possible anti-cancer agent, 117

Ulceration of mouth and throat, use of sage as remedy for, 37

Ulcers, olive oil as remedy for, 20

Ulcers, duodenal, use of marshmallow as remedy for, 195-196

Ulcers, peptic, use of carrageen as remedy for, 58

Unani system of medicine in India and Pakistan, 32, 48

University of Chicago, 108

University of Honduras, 114

University of Minnesota, 21

University of Texas, 119

University of Wisconsin, 110

Uremia, use of shepherd's purse to combat, 17

Urinary difficulties, corn silk as remedy for, 175-176

  dandelion, use of, 13-14

  elder as remedy for, 8-9

  onion in remedy of, 48

  parsley as remedy for, 92, 93, 95

  seven-barks as remedy for, 191

Urinary retention helped by camomile steam bath, 171

Ursolic acid discovered in sage, 36

"Urtication" to treat rheumatism in Germany and Russia, 28

U.S. Dispensatory. See *Dispensatory of the U.S.A.*

U.S. Public Health Service, 62, 79, 80, 108

Uses of Plants by the Chippewa Indians, 81, 135

Uterine difficulties, motherwort as remedy for, 197-198

Uterine hemorrhages, arresting of by use of nettles, 28, 29

Uterus, strengthening of by use of camomile tea, 170

Valerian, 205-206
noted for soothing effect on nerves, 135

Vanilla leaf as herbal smoking mixture, 161

Vapor bath favorite of North American Indians, 130

Vervain and mistletoe tranquilizing combination, 89

Vervain as one of Dr. Bach's flower remedies, 149

Viburnic acid contained in elder, 6

Vinblastine anti-cancer drug from periwinkle, 117

Violet as possible anti-cancer agent, 118

"Visca-drops" of mistletoe extract, 87

Vogel, Dr. H. C. A., 30-31, 30n, 48, 87, 125, 171, 180-181, 201

Von Czarnowski, Dr., 8-9

von Wartburg, Dr. Albert, 117

Wall, Dr. Monroe E., 114

Warning about overeating of onions, 49-50

Warts, figs as cure for, 179
herbal aids for, 139
removal of by local application of dandelion juice, 16, 139

Waste excretion function of skin, 129-130

Weeks, Nora, 149, 156n

Weinberger, Austin S., 115

Wesley, John, 34

Western Reserve University, 115

Westlake, Dr. Aubrey T., 156

Wheat germ oil to remove warts, 139

"White Indians," learning of Indian herbal secrets from, 64-69

"White man's foot," 199-202

Wild Flowers of California, The, 40

Wild vanilla as herbal smoking mixture, 161

Wilson, Dr., 10, 130

Wilstatter, Professor, 112

Womb, effect of motherwort on, 197

Women's Health Queries, 15, 15n

"Wonder drug," early, sassafras as, 102-103

Wood, Dr., 28-29, 46, 187, 201

Wood betony, 206-208

Woody nightshade as possible anti-cancer agent, 110

Worms, butternut as remedy for, 77

Worms, intestinal, successfully treated with seaweed, 62

Wormwood, 208-211

Wounds, Gypsy use of marigold for, 1
remedy for in olive oil, 24

Wren, R. C., 96n, 103n, 177n

X-rays, protection against by use of olive oil, 21-22

Yarrow for bronchitis, Gypsy use of, 1

Yemm, John R., 3n, 14, 177, 197n, 203-204

Yerba santa as herbal smoking mixture, 167

Yeshiva University, 116

Zinc, algae as source of, 61-62